THE GAME
TO SHOW
THE GAMES

Inside the multibillion dollar battle
for sports on television

Morgan Wick

Azzurri Publishing

Table of Contents

1

Rags to Riches

SITUATED ON US 6 ABOUT 20 miles southwest of Hartford, the town of Bristol, Connecticut, was one of the early New England industrial towns. Incorporated in 1785, a few years after the end of the American Revolution, its economy took off as it became known as a clock-making town, eventually becoming home to the American Clock and Watch Museum. Later, it became known as the "Bell City" for its role as a center of doorbell production. As you approach the town from New York along quaint two-lane Route 6, the 19th-century style of architecture New England is so famous for gives way to forests and then a large reservoir, until you cross a railroad track and begin seeing rows of strip malls and small houses on your left, nothing to distract you too much from the Connecticut foliage and fields. Approaching in the other direction, from Hartford, the four-lane highway slows down and shrinks to two, then as soon as you hit the line you're slammed with gas stations and car dealerships as the road widens again through modern suburbia. Approaching from Providence and other southeastern points (or even Hartford) on Route 72, the expressway seemingly isolated from all civilization comes to an end just short of the town line, but the road continues as a four-lane divided parkway, avoiding the Forestville area and continuing not to engage with the surrounding, though visible, community until after it passes Malones Pond, beyond which it speeds past apartment buildings and incongruous houses.

Approaching from New Haven, which is almost due south of Bristol, Google Maps recommends taking Interstate 91 to Meriden, then turning onto I-691. As I-691 approaches its west end, a single lane splits off to form an on-ramp to eastbound I-84, leaving the other two lanes to continue west. The long ramp passes over multiple other roads and a sign welcomes you to Bristol's neighbor Southington before the ramp even reaches I-84. The freeway remains fairly straight but abruptly turns left as you hit Exit 30, then swings right and remains relatively straight again, but prepares to curve to the right as you take Exit 31 to route 229. As the off-ramp rises to meet the road, a collection of signs on the left informs you what awaits in Bristol if you turn that way, none of them mentioning the most salient feature of this road into Bristol. After the initial spurt of gas stations and a turn-off to a Target near the I-84 interchange, Route 229 settles down past some relatively nondescript houses and other businesses; though initially a four-lane highway, the southbound side soon shrinks to a single lane as the highway becomes lined mostly with trees. For about the next mile and ¾, the general character of the road is of green trees and grass fields sprinkled with more houses and a few churches, punctuated with occasional spurts of businesses.

And then, before you even get to the town line, you see it. At first, all you see is just a mass of brick buildings, only different in height from any other office park, stretching off into the distance. Then the trees end as more buildings appear to your right, just as the road turns left, widens back to four lanes, and hits a stoplight at the entrance to this massive complex spanning 123 acres – until recently a simple, two-lane, dead-end road passing a massive parking lot en route to a single large building of brick and glass, but now a four-lane entrance of its own leading to a large, landscaped traffic circle and from there to a sleek, modern arch covering the entrance gates equipped with LED screens and protecting over a million square feet of working space in 18 buildings.[1] If you look beyond the traffic circle from the highway, you see a huge array of satellite dishes pointing to the sky, and as you turn back to the road you see facing you, in a mostly red area where the landscaping is still in the beginning stages of poking through, four large bold red letters informing you just what you are looking at: "ESPN".

Those four letters are the name of the single most powerful brand in American media, once a plucky underdog in the American sports landscape, now a seemingly unstoppable multi-billion dollar juggernaut that has become the profit engine of the Walt Disney Company, far more important to the House of Magic than Mickey Mouse, Spider-Man, or

Chewbacca, and probably a major reason why the latter two are part of the Disney family.[2] Here, in a random town in the middle of Connecticut, is the capital of the American sports universe, a place that now finds itself at the epicenter of an increasingly heated debate over the increasingly important role of sports to the cable TV industry, the many millions of dollars flowing into Bristol from the pockets of cable TV consumers and from there to leagues and conferences across America and the world, and even the future of the television business itself.

* * *

No one could have imagined any of this when a man named Bill Rasmussen bought a single acre of land sight unseen on the site of a former dump to be the home of what was then called the "ESP Network" from the city of Bristol in 1978.[3] Rasmussen had recently been fired by the Hartford Whalers (the hockey team that would later become the Carolina Hurricanes) and wanted to create a monthly cable show about Connecticut sports which turned into an idea for a national 24/7 cable sports network.[4]

Until just a few years before, cable television, then known as community antenna television or CATV, was little more than a way to deliver television signals to mountainous and other areas that couldn't receive them. As strange as this may sound now, the notion of "pay TV" was considered absolute poison at the time, and several attempts to create pay TV services had come and gone by the wayside.[5] But cable had a big advantage over broadcast: it could simply accommodate more channels. 82 channels had been allocated for terrestrial television broadcasting, but less than half of them could be used in any given area because there had to be at least one channel's buffer between one station and the next, and channels above 69 were rarely used for anything other than translators of larger stations and would eventually be reallocated for other services in 1983, meaning no area had more than 16 stations and most had substantially fewer.[6]

Most of those stations were UHF stations that were still, for the most part, second-class citizens to the old-standard VHF stations;

reception of UHF stations was often troublesome and the audiences miniscule. The FCC had only opened up the UHF band in 1952 after lifting the freeze on new stations, but didn't actually require set manufacturers to include UHF tuners until a decade later.[7] There were only 12 of the prime VHF channels, so no market could have more than seven – 2, 4, 5 or 6, 7, 9, 11, 13 – and only New York and Los Angeles had that, though Seattle would come close, only lacking channel 2 because it was used by Vancouver, BC's CBC affiliate.[8] (4 and 5 are separated by about a channel's length, and 6 and 7 are separated by the entire FM band and a few other uses; in fact, those with FM radios could pick up the audio from a station on channel 6 by tuning to 87.7.)[9] Most areas had no more than three or four VHF stations – affiliates of the Big Three television networks, CBS, NBC, and ABC, plus a public television station.[10] The remaining UHF stations were home to an eclectic hodge-podge of programming; most grabbed whatever cheap programming they could get their hands on, but there were quite a number of eclectic operations taking up space in the band.[11]

Cable had the use of the entire television spectrum at its disposal[12], and in the late 50s they attempted to import distant signals from outlying markets into their coverage area, but broadcasters protested at the increased competition and the FCC put the kibosh on the importation of distant signals.[13] In 1972, however, they began to lift the restriction[14], which allowed Ted Turner, four years later, to turn his station in Atlanta, then called WTCG, into America's first "superstation" by exporting it to cable companies across the South, with Atlanta Braves games as the star attraction.[15] Cable attracted an even more eclectic and diverse mix of people looking to get their shows on the free channels cable had available, from hippies to Nazis, even if the audiences were even more miniscule.[16]

But something far bigger was about to transform cable and television in general: satellite transmission, which could allow anyone to beam a signal to a satellite above the earth and deliver it to anyone in the country.[17] In 1975 Time-Life began beaming HBO, which had been launched in a few systems in Pennsylvania and New York in 1972, across the country on satellite, starting with the famed "Thrilla in Manila" between Muhammad Ali and Joe Frazier.[18] HBO charged a fee to subscribers but then provided them with movies and sports commercial-free.[19] Besides Ted Turner, televangelist Pat Robertson soon joined the fray with his Christian Broadcasting Network, as did what was then called the Madison Square Garden network, eventually renamed to USA Network.[20]

Most of these channels had schedules similar to the broadcast networks, with all different types of programming airing throughout the day, from movies to sports to sitcoms to dramas. ESPN was the first "narrowcast" channel, airing nothing but sports all day long. Most people said it would never work, that no one would want to watch a single type of programming all day.[21] But Rasmussen felt he had a killer app: live coverage of the earlier rounds of the NCAA tournament for the first time, on the heels of the historic 1979 national championship game between Larry Bird's Indiana State and Earvin "Magic" Johnson's Michigan State.[22] Rasmussen convinced Stuart Evey, a vice president at Getty Oil, to use his considerable clout to get the board to fund his idea; Evey's influence and commitment to the network was probably the only reason it survived years of massive losses under Getty.[23] Evey brought in Chet Simmons, who once helped build ABC Sports and was running NBC Sports at the time, as the new network's president, bringing it instant credibility.[24] Simmons, for his part, came up with another piece of signature programming: live coverage of the NFL Draft for the first time, to the utter disbelief of Commissioner Pete Rozelle, to whom the concept sounded like reading names from the phone book.[25] Evey and Simmons would end up forcing Rasmussen out of his own creation a little over a year after ESPN went on the air.[26]

In those days, most of ESPN's schedule consisted of taped sporting events, with the occasional forays into whatever live events they could get the rights to to put on the air, including the immortal Australian Rules Football. The NCAA Tournament, and the other college basketball that went along with it, was their crown (and only) jewel, and ESPN essentially built March Madness into what it is today with their idea to whip around the country to wherever the action was taking place.[27] Evey convinced ABC to buy a minority stake in the network in 1982, even though the network was still losing mountains of money, and the two of them teamed up to score the rights to the fledgling USFL, while Simmons, whose relationship with Evey was becoming increasingly heated, accepted an offer to become the new league's commissioner.[28] In 1984, after Getty was bought by Texaco, ABC bought 80% of the network with the remaining 20% stake going to RJR Nabisco in order to get Don Ohlmeyer, whose consulting firm was funded by RJR Nabisco's head, to consult for them.[29]

Another landmark in ESPN history occurred in 1984. For years, the biggest colleges had been chafing under the NCAA's strict control of television contracts that restricted how many games could be shown and shared the wealth with smaller colleges. They banded together as the College Football Association and took the NCAA to court. The case made it all the way to the Supreme Court, which ruled 7-2 that the NCAA's control over televised college football violated the Sherman Anti-Trust Act. The colleges were now free to sell their games however they wished – and ESPN would be able to televise live college football games for the first time. *NCAA v. Board of Regents of the University of Oklahoma* would mark a major turning point in the history of college football, and ESPN would play a big role in it.[30] But the moment when ESPN finally "arrived" came when it wrangled a package of nine games from the National Football League in 1987. With the kingpin of American sports in its back pocket, ESPN could finally begin turning a profit.[31]

But ESPN kept growing and growing, even when one might have thought they had reached their peak. Major League Baseball put together a package of enough games to build an instant competitor to ESPN in 1989, forcing ESPN to pay more than the bean counters were comfortable with, but once they had it in the bag they could forestall any competitor, especially after the 1993 launch of ESPN2.[32] On the heels of the NFL deal, the company hired a former magazine editor named John Walsh and tasked him to build a legitimate news operation within their walls and turn *SportsCenter* into a top-notch destination for sports news; it paid off when Keith Olbermann and Dan Patrick turned the late-night *SportsCenter* into appointment viewing from 1992 until Olbermann's acrimonious departure in 1997, with a four-month hiatus while Olbermann helped launch ESPN2.[33] ESPN became a hip destination in and of itself during the 90s with Olbermann and Patrick's run on

SportsCenter and the slick "This is SportsCenter" commercials that built a mythology around ESPN's Bristol headquarters.[34]

And ESPN kept on acquiring rights and staving off potential competitors; it brought "extreme" sports into the mainstream, and greatly shaped them, with the 1995 advent of the X Games[35], and when Time Warner started making plans for its own sports news network, CNN/SI, in 1996, ESPN rushed ESPNEWS to the air.[36] ESPN picked up a full season of NFL rights in 1998[37], and with the acquisition of NBA rights in 2002, ESPN would become the first entity to hold all four major professional sports simultaneously.[38] And when ABC lost *Monday Night Football* in 2005, ESPN paid over a billion dollars, more than any other NFL rightsholder, to move from Sunday to Monday nights and began setting cable viewership records left and right, while ABC's remaining sports properties were rebranded "ESPN on ABC". ABC Sports was no more; the little network ABC had bought a minority stake in more than twenty years earlier had now consumed their entire sports operation.[39]

And yet, ESPN still wasn't done. In 2008, college football's Bowl Championship Series was midway through a four-year deal with Fox, a network whose only other college football was the Cotton Bowl, and who had, by that point, been utterly stymied in any attempt to acquire any other college football rights, resulting in a minor disaster on-air as announcing teams with no regular-season experience called important college bowl games and producers obsessed over marching bands.[40] ESPN, meanwhile, was smarting over the fact ABC had lost the BCS rights four years earlier. So it presented the BCS with an offer for $125 million, more than enough to beat Fox's $100 million offer, for four years to televise all five BCS games on ESPN. In a move that would have been unthinkable in 1979, college football's national championship, the most popular sporting event of each year outside of the NFL or Olympics, would air on the cable channel ESPN, not on any of the four broadcast networks, as would "the granddaddy of them all", the Rose Bowl.[41] ESPN was no longer the plucky underdog run out of a ramshackle building in Bristol, Connecticut. It was truly "the worldwide leader in sports", and it seemed nothing, not even the Super Bowl or World Series, was beyond its reach.

* * *

Acquiring the rights to all four major professional sports, and numerous other widely popular events besides, is one thing, but when ESPN is taking over the venerable *Monday Night Football* franchise, even if one considers the changes the NFL made to its scheduling that makes it not quite comparable, and airing the single most popular sporting event of the year outside the NFL or Olympics, the culmination of the entire college football season, as well as such venerable events as the Rose Bowl, the Open Championship in golf, and Wimbledon in tennis in their entirety, we should pause and dig deeper into exactly how ESPN arrived at this position of dominance. How on Earth was ESPN willing and able to pay more than any of the broadcast networks for an event as popular as the BCS National Championship Game? Why did ESPN want to put the game on ESPN, not ABC, to begin with, and why did they want to move the Rose Bowl from ABC, which they had a separate contract with, to ESPN?[42] The answer lies in a combination of the increased popularity of cable television, which put ESPN in 86% of American TV households by 2008,[43] and the business model adopted by most cable networks that ESPN had played a critical role in pioneering.

In 1982, ESPN, still bleeding money like crazy, began going around to cable operators asking for a carriage fee of a few cents per subscriber. Cable operators were outraged. Cablevision's contract was expiring and ESPN CEO Bill Grimes and COO Roger Werner flew to Long Island in March of 1983 to get them to accept a carriage fee. Talks were extremely contentious, and Grimes and Werner got to the point of threatening to pull the plug on the whole thing, but eventually, Cablevision's directors caved. They would pay ESPN ten cents a subscriber.[44]

It was a watershed moment in the history of the cable business. Henceforth, rather than collect all their money from advertising as the broadcast networks did, cable networks would operate dual revenue streams, collecting money from both advertising and from subscriber fees from cable companies, and it soon became the norm in the industry. But no one has ever done it better than ESPN. Today, thanks in part to the negotiation of yearly 20% increases in its fees to pay for the full-season NFL deal in 1998,[45] ESPN charges $6.61 a subscriber – money it collects from every single customer who receives ESPN on their cable system, no matter how much, or how little, of it they watch – and that $6.61 pays only for the main channel, not for ESPN's numerous auxiliary networks. The next-most expensive national non-premium cable channel is TNT at $1.65.[46] Even broadcast stations, taking advantage of "retransmission-consent" rules allowing them to collect their own money from cable operators, can collect upwards of $1.50.[47]

Bill Rasmussen had stumbled onto the absolute best field for him to build a cable network around given the future course of the television business. Thanks to the Internet and the general fracturing of the media audience, young people, especially those in the 18-49 money demo and *especially* especially men in that demo, are getting harder and harder to reach, and sports are the one place guaranteed to attract eyeballs in that money demo. Sports are also one of the few types of programming that are DVR-proof, that you can't just record and watch later or watch online; you have to watch live sports as it happens.[48] That makes sports rights some of the most valuable programming on television, programming everyone running a television outfit is falling over themselves to get as much of as possible. ESPN collected a projected $8.2 billion in revenue in 2012, more than all but the biggest media conglomerates, accounting for nearly half the operating profit of the Walt Disney Company and in turn making Disney the most profitable company in American media,[49] even though Disney only owns 80% of the Worldwide Leader in Sports, with Hearst owning the 20% that ABC sold to RJR Nabisco in 1984.[50] ESPN's heft is so mighty that even other multi-billion dollar media conglomerates find themselves jealous of Disney's ESPN-fueled profits.

This book is about everything that has resulted from this perfect storm that has made live sports the most valuable programming on television, ESPN its biggest beneficiary, and cable television's dual revenue streams the best way to take advantage of it. It is about how other big media conglomerates have gone all-out for their own piece of the lucrative sports pie, and how their efforts have made it the most lucrative time in history to be a sports league or other entity that can give them that piece, the biggest of which have aimed to keep some of it for themselves. It is about how this dynamic has made its presence felt in seemingly every area of sports as networks, making up an increasing part of sports leagues' bottom line, increasingly call the shots, especially in college sports where ESPN has become the de facto governing body – how, in the words of *The Atlantic's* Derek Thompson, "television economics are sports economics, and sports economics are television economics."[51] And it is about the possibility, as more and more sports networks hit the airwaves, as the rights fees networks pay to leagues skyrocket, as the carriage fees networks charge cable operators follow in kind, as cable operators pass those increased costs on to consumers, and as new technology becomes a more and more viable alternative to cable, that this dynamic is not sustainable, that it is inflating a bubble in sports rights that's bound to pop once consumers who couldn't care less about sports decide they're mad as hell and they're not going to take it anymore.

2

Follow the Leader

FOR GEARHEADS, AUGUST 17, 2013, may well go down as Black Saturday. The first signs of it had come the previous day, when many of the personalities heading up Speed Channel's coverage of NASCAR practice and qualifying started talking about the end of an era, and the network's Trackside talk show held its final edition ever. Then, when they woke up the following morning, Speed had been replaced with something called Fox Sports 1. For much of the day, Fox Sports 1 carried much of the same NASCAR coverage that had been on Speed, but that night it aired a bunch of fights from the glorified cagefighting promotion known as the UFC, followed by a couple of snarky Canadians yukking it up alongside a bunch of ex-jocks talking about nearly every sport except their beloved cars. The succeeding days would see Speed's lineup of car-oriented shows completely gone by the wayside, replaced by a bunch more shows talking about nothing but stick-and-ball sports. Just like that, the only network gearheads had that was totally dedicated to cars was gone.

Speed fans were not happy, and quickly took to the Internet to voice their displeasure, flooding the comments of just about any article having anything to do with the new network. Here are just some of the comments they posted, all reprinted with spelling, grammatical, and other errors intact:

> what idiot decided we needed another stick and ball sport station? mma? boxing? you people are totally out of touch. speed was a car channel, the only car channel...hopefully this channel will fail miserably and maybe we'll get a car channel back. we don't need more retired jocks and announcer wannabes telling us the same retread crap that we get fed on 100 other channels.

did you really need anther stick and ball channel? I thought cutting wind tunnel to 30 min. was bad enough but then to cancel it!!...I have an idea, change the classic espn channels format. I can't believe anyone whatches that channel...car guys spend a lot more money on motorsports than most stick and ball sports fans. I can only hope you will change your minds, but I will not know because I will not be watching any espn channels![1]

who in the world decided to take speed off the air my god another sports program channel really no speed channel come on this sucks now what I can watch chopped but nothing about cars which is a large industry you have gear heads every where that watched speed n all the shows including Barret - Jackson action . also gearz and all the other shows like pinks and motorcycle racing this sucks

we did not need another all live sports channel, not everyone watches sports, we want all the car shows back from speed and everything else it had on it, now what, where did all those shows go? this is crazy that corporations keep messing with everyones lives on what we have to watch and we still have to pay the price for it.

All of my car shows, car repair shows, collector car shows are gone. Not on the air anymore. No more Stacy doing donuts in a Year One Bandit Trans Am, or climbing mountain trails in some crazy 4X4 that he just welded together. NO, Just another ESPN Wannabee Channel sadly similar to how Comcast destroyed Versus with my fishing and hunting shows. Now both of those lame ass channels are playing European Soccer games instead. Seriously. Fox and Comcast can both go screw themselves.[2]

the reason America is a great country is because of change. What makes it the best country on the planet is admitting our mistakes. FX1 is an obvious mistake. Im sure this channel was created to further better the lives of Fox share holders. SPEED was what built America, cars. trucks. racing. DIY! shows. buying selling/auctions. Ive been patiently awaiting some good from FX1, its just not there. a huge mistake! please, bring back SPEED, u can even keep your crappy FX1 channel, just put channel 607 back on my receiver so Americans can feel like Americans again. am i the only one that feels like moving to Canada? ha, i hear SPEED still aires there. Fix this mistake FX1, i refuse to watch your programming, at least ESPN is original. l.o.l.[3]

While Discovery's Velocity network remained and remains focused on cars, and several old Speed programs found their way to the fledgling MavTV network, neither is anywhere near as prominent or widely-distributed as Speed was. Speed fans had been swept up by a force far bigger than their own corner of the world, one no demographic could be rich enough to avoid. That the new Fox Sports 1 format was a carbon copy of ESPN, and so many other networks, was precisely the point: ESPN was making over $8 billion a year, over half a billion from subscriber fees alone, and a business model that's making that kind of money is one any businessman would be falling over themselves to emulate.

Fox had spread out many of their sports contracts across several different networks - besides Speed, there was FX, Fox Soccer, and Fuel - but by consolidating them all onto a single network Fox hoped to charge cable companies higher subscriber fees and lure away some of the massive ESPN audience. Speed, in fact, was a victim of its own success: its presence in nearly 90 million households was far more than Fox Soccer, which had barely 50 million, and Fuel had even less, so it was, from the perspective of the Fox corporate bean-counters, a logical choice to convert to a knockoff of, and hopeful competitor to, ESPN.[4]

It didn't work out the way Fox had hoped - several cable operators balked at paying the increased rights fees Fox demanded, insisting on paying the same rate they had been paying for Speed, and Fox only gave in a couple days before the launch[5] - and the ratings proved rather miniscule, especially by comparison to ESPN, but with rights to major college football and basketball and big-time European soccer on top of the UFC, and Major League Baseball, the NASCAR Sprint Cup Series, and the World Cup and US Open golf tournament coming down the pike,

Fox likely felt that, in the long-term, they could take a bigger bite out of ESPN's pie than anyone else. What were a few pissed-off gearheads to them when those were the stakes?

* * *

One of the more underrated developments in television history was the rise of digital cable in the late 90s and early 2000s. Doubtless anyone who subscribed to cable at the time may have heard their cable company trying to sell them on "digital cable", and knew that upgrading to digital meant access to more channels than what they had otherwise, but probably didn't know what it meant beyond that. Digital cable, though, was more than a corporate buzzword and way to get customers to pay the cable companies more money. It was a development that may have had as much impact on the history of television as the rise of cable television itself.

Before the advent of digital cable, cable television may have offered more channels than over-the-air broadcasting, but it was still very limited by the same technical constraints broadcasters faced. Cable operators could only offer more channels because they didn't have to space channels apart as much as broadcasters did, but their channels still took up the same amount of space, and cable had its own constraints on the amount of space it could use. As a result, very few cable operators had more than a hundred channels, with most having 75 at most, and as much as a third of that was taken up by local broadcast stations.[6]

The result was a Darwinian competition for what few spots were available, with cable operators trying to offer customers the most choice in the space available. At the time, most "narrowcast" channels staked their ground to their own turf with no one else stepping on it, so ESPN was able to stake its ground as the "sports channel". The most popular channels, however, were general-entertainment channels not much different from what was available on broadcast. Putting sports on FX made sense for Fox in this environment, when ESPN's biggest challengers dating back to the 80s were the Turner networks and USA, general-entertainment networks all. In this context, in fact, Turner arguably held the upper hand when it came to sports with the NBA, half the NFL season, TBS' long-standing Atlanta Braves coverage, and more.[7] The continued presence of NBA games on TNT and baseball games on TBS today is very much an anachronism, a relic of those pre-digital days.

The growth of digital cable, as well as the direct-broadcast satellite services that developed during the 90s (such as DirecTV, which boomed in popularity on the back of its exclusive carriage of the NFL's out-of-market games), changed all that by allowing an explosion of channels of all types. People had been talking about the possibility of television growing to a thousand channels; now half that number was very much a reality, even as HD increasingly chewed up that capacity as the latter decade progressed.[8] Brand-new channels sprung up that were even more niche, looking to fill out all the new space the cable operators had, while existing channels expanded their brand onto more specialized channels (including CNNSI and ESPNEWS) and previously niche channels found their corner increasingly crowded out and broadened their appeal in response. In the short term, it was a vindication for ESPN's all-sports strategy; digital cable ended the first war over sports on cable with ESPN scoring a resounding victory, while setting the stage for a second war, allowing numerous other contenders to stake their own claims on ESPN's turf. Why did Fox need to put sports on FX when they could spread FX itself to several other networks (including Fox Soccer's rebrand to FXX) and still have enough room for two all-sports networks?

* * *

One of the new channels digital cable made possible was the 1999 launch of NBA.com TV, which launched with highlights, live look-ins, and other NBA-produced programming; although it started as almost a glorified barker channel for the League Pass out-of-market package, some saw it as a bulwark for the league in case they needed to take their games in-house in the post-Jordan era, as well as a hedge on this Internet thing whose role in sports going forward no one was quite sure of yet.[9]

The NBA has long been at the forefront of new revenue streams and innovation, especially during David Stern's leadership. The standard was that sports leagues had a network partner and a cable partner, and each only aired your product one or two days a week, but as it entered a new round of negotiations with NBC and Turner in 2002, Stern was open to a brand new scheme hatched up by ESPN, which wanted to get into the NBA without having to compete with Turner. ESPN and Turner would share cable coverage of the NBA, with ESPN having games on Wednesdays and Fridays and TNT holding on to a Thursday doubleheader that would be the only games of the night. ABC would take over the broadcast package, but wouldn't show any games until Christmas and only show 15 games total (less than half of what NBC was showing); TNT would show the All-Star Game, and the playoffs would air mostly on ESPN and TNT until the Finals.[10]

Placing its product so heavily on cable was a big risk for the NBA, but the end result was that the league saw a 25% increase in its rights fees despite a recession and ratings tanking in the post-Jordan era, as well as games all throughout the week.[11] The new deal also put games on the renamed NBATV, and began a long relationship between that network and Turner, almost by accident: the league originally wanted to partner with Turner on a new basic-cable general sports network, but cable operators balked.[12]

The NBA blazed a trail that other leagues would eventually follow; the NHL Network launched in Canada in 2001 and the United States in 2007, while Major League Baseball, though late to the network party, eventually launched one in 2009. The NFL launched the NFL Network, its time filled mostly with programming from the NFL Films library and some basic studio shows, the year after the NBA's landmark 2002 deal, and it would end up becoming the focal point of the controversy over sports on cable for the latter half of the decade.

* * *

The NFL's 2005 rights negotiations turned out to be a landmark for multiple reasons. ESPN was looking to renew its Sunday night package while ABC looked to continue a relationship dating back over 35 years airing *Monday Night Football*. But Disney was in disarray as Michael Eisner was on his way out as its head, having recently fought off a takeover bid by

Comcast, and both Eisner and the NFL were concerned about the dwindling ratings for *MNF*. The league wanted to move the NFL's main primetime package to Sunday, where people would already be home and where flexible scheduling could allow the league to ensure quality matchups throughout the season, but ABC was loath to interfere with the ratings hits they had found on Sunday night.[13]

Bob Iger, Eisner's heir apparent, was convinced NBC had no interest in the NFL, and so was willing to wait for the dust to settle over his own ascension, but the league's executive vice president of media, former ESPN head Steve Bornstein, slowly brought Dick Ebersol around and inked a $600 million/year deal to take over NBC's Sunday nights. It's possible Disney could have kept both packages for much less than they ultimately paid had they jumped in sooner; instead, Iger was left with no choice but to accept a $1.1 billion deal to put Monday night games on ESPN. (Under the old arrangement, ESPN and ABC had paid $1.15 billion combined.) Just like that, ABC's Monday night tradition was over.[14]

NBC benefitted from the new flex-scheduling arrangement, but ESPN began setting cable ratings records left and right. By the time ESPN's first season of Monday night games was over, it already accounted for the nine most-watched programs in ESPN history – in other words, more than half the Monday night games in just the first season had beaten every single Sunday night game on ESPN – including one game that became the most-watched program in cable television history, beating a 1993 CNN debate between Al Gore and Ross Perot, a record ESPN would set again each of the next three seasons and then hold until the BCS deal came along.[15]

Monday Night Football still had cachet, was still a destination program, even if the NFL considered it to be on par with ESPN's old Sunday night package and lower in the pecking order than what NBC had; it was the one game that had people's undivided attention all day, and ESPN was able to build up to it all day and make it a true event. NFL games may have put ESPN on the map, but the move to Monday night established ESPN's NFL games – and thus ESPN itself, and cable as a

whole – as destination, must-have television. On the flip side, the end of
Monday Night Football marked the end of ABC Sports itself; by the time
the 2006 season, the first under the new deal, started, all sports
programming on ABC had been rebranded as "ESPN on ABC", complete
with ESPN graphics. Soon, the sports that were airing on ABC began to
inexorably dwindle.[16]

But the NFL also opened a package of eight games on Thursday and
Saturday nights up for bid. While Comcast on behalf of its Versus
network, NBC Universal on behalf of USA, and Turner all expressed
interest, the league ultimately opted to put the games on its own network,
foregoing a rights fee in exchange for getting better distribution for its
network whose profits the owners would all share in. It didn't work as
planned; for the rest of the decade the league constantly fought cable
providers for carriage. Comcast initially offered the network to its digital
cable subscribers the first year but moved it to a sports package the next,
while Time Warner Cable and Cablevision, among others, held out
entirely, many refusing to carry the network unless the league made the
Sunday Ticket out-of-market package available to them. By 2008, the
network was in only 35 million homes, and by 2009, the only two cable
operators in the top nine to carry the network at all were Comcast and
Cox, with Comcast's deal coming up for renewal in April of that year.[17]

The league was able to get broad distribution for the network on
Comcast again and break several other holdouts by offering a modified
version of the Red Zone channel DirecTV had been offering Sunday
Ticket subscribers as a premium service, but it couldn't get Time Warner
Cable and Cablevision on board until it increased NFL Network's
schedule to a full season in 2012.[18] It was the first high-profile carriage
dispute arising from quality sports programming being placed on a
marginally-distributed network that cable providers were loath to carry at
the prices they were being charged, but it would be far from the last.

* * *

ESPN has had near-monopoly status over the sports landscape for a long
time – and by the mid-2000s, it had reached the point that the Justice

Department began looking into it. At issue was the notion of "warehousing" inventory with college conferences: ESPN was signing deals left and right with just about every collegiate conference, taking in way more inventory than they had space to air on ESPN and ESPN2, yet they refused to sell their excess to anyone else. Many smaller conferences accused ESPN of hoarding inventory to keep it away from potential competitors and limit conferences' exposure.[19]

The issue was brought to a head by a fledgling network named College Sports Television, or CSTV, which had launched in 2002. CSTV, the first network dedicated entirely to college sports, was too small to compete for any rights from the major conferences, but it hoped to pick up some rights from the better mid-majors – only to find that ESPN had all the rights they were looking for and weren't giving them up, and threatened any conferences that looked to do business with CSTV.[20]

In 2004, CSTV took their case to the Justice Department. Though then-President George Bodenheimer dismissed the importance of the investigation in 2013, ESPN's lawyers took it seriously and cautioned executives to tread lightly. ESPN was in the midst of negotiations with the Western Athletic Conference at the time, whose commissioner wanted to make a deal with CSTV that would yield more money and TV appearances, while the school presidents wanted a deal with ESPN that could offer wider exposure. Reportedly, when the commissioner asked an ESPN executive how ESPN could continue its warehousing practices in the wake of the Justice Department's investigation, the executive dismissed the idea.[21]

Clearly, though, the investigation had an effect. CSTV would soon lure the Mountain West Conference away from ESPN, and ESPN agreed to share rights to Conference USA and the Atlantic 10 with the upstart network. Shortly thereafter, CSTV would be acquired by CBS, giving it big pockets and a major media corporation to help it make inroads on cable systems; it has since metamorphosed into the all-purpose CBS Sports Network. And the following March, ESPN would launch a new network, ESPNU, that would be its answer to CSTV but – more than that – would provide more space for ESPN to show content it had under contract and thus reduce warehousing complaints. The fact that it would provide more fuel for Disney's bundle and a new revenue stream certainly didn't hurt.[22]

Today, ESPNU is in 75 million households and collects a 22-cent subscriber fee, putting another $16.5 million in ESPN's coffers every month, or $198 million a year. CBS Sports Network, meanwhile, is in only 61 million households, though it collects a slightly higher, 26-cent subscriber fee, netting just under $16 million a month or $190 million a year – and it doesn't have the deep pockets ESPN has from its myriad of other networks.[23]

* * *

The power of sports programming has the potential to create some strange bedfellows. It is such that two very different media companies can be drawn very close together almost entirely on the back of their complementary assets that they can bring to a sports contract, to the point of drawing speculation about a merger. Such is the case with the split between the CBS Corporation and Viacom in 2005, which promised to insulate the latter company from the slower-growth businesses that CBS inherited, yet which created two companies with very similar revenues – and CBS was the one better situated to take advantage of the boom in sports rights... if it weren't for most of the old Viacom's cable networks joining the new Viacom.[24]

By 2010 CBS wanted to get out from under a contract to air the NCAA Tournament that was set to lose it considerable amounts of money each year, to the point of engaging in talks to get ESPN to take it off its hands.[25] Certainly the NCAA was very interested in moving most of the tournament to cable, which not only had the potential to increase the rights fees the NCAA collected but also allowed every game to be shown nationally, without the regionalization CBS had engaged in. CBS ended up retaining the tournament by forming an alliance with Turner to show games on TBS, TNT, and truTV in addition to the CBS broadcast network. Turner had never shown college basketball before and truTV, once known as Court TV, had never shown sports of any kind before, but Turner, which was paying a larger portion of the rights fee, went so far as to start alternating the Final Four with CBS starting in 2016 (later negotiations allowed TBS to show the national semifinals in 2014 and 2015 while the national championship game remained on CBS).[26]

CBS' lack of any credible cable network prevented it from holding on to the tournament on its own, but neither was Turner in particularly good position to mount a bid without CBS. For the moment, the ability to partner with a broadcast network remains a critical piece of any effort to build a strong cable sports operation. To be sure, Turner's strategy, as an owner of general-entertainment networks with almost-vestigial sports programming, has generally consisted of limiting itself to high-profile, big-ticket items like the major sports, but that didn't prevent it from losing the rights to its portion of the NASCAR schedule, due in part to monetary losses. Since the NCAA Tournament deal, Turner has repeatedly looked for other properties to put on truTV, including a push for NHL rights, but hasn't been able to secure any other properties to put on the channel.[27]

CBS' broadcast network and Turner's cable networks have talked about alliances for other sports rights, and CBS and Time Warner present complementary pieces in other ways as well - the two entities each own half of the CW network - with the only real point of competition between their respective television networks being the premium-cable networks HBO and Showtime. Even so, you'd expect any talks of an actual merger between the two companies to be limited to a very superficial analysis by a poster on a message board, yet it's something respected financial analysts have discussed since the start of the NCAA Tournament alliance.[28] There are a whole host of reasons to expect such a merger to remain limited to people's fantasies, but given just how important sports have become, it's easy to see just how enticing such a merger can look to armchair CEOs.

After all, it wouldn't be the first time sports was a driving factor behind a merger of media companies. As far back as 1995, when Disney bought ABC, Michael Eisner declared "the crown jewel of this acquisition to be ESPN" at the press conference announcing the deal, and has claimed to have valued the ABC network at zero at the time despite it being profitable and on top of the ratings.[29] Comcast's bid a decade later for Disney has also been claimed to have valued ABC negligibly, and was motivated in large part by Comcast's observation, even then, of how much money ESPN was taking out of their pockets.[30] Rebuffed in its efforts to buy ESPN, Comcast turned its attention to trying to compete with it, purchasing rights to the NHL for the network that would become Versus,and sports, specifically the ability to marry Comcast's cable outlets with NBC's broadcast network and rights to high-profile sports like the NFL and Olympics, was widely considered a major factor in Comcast's acquisition of NBC Universal.[31] More recently, in 2014 Fox made an unsuccessful bid to acquire Time Warner, and again analysts suggested a key reason was the control such a deal would give Fox over Turner's panoply of sports rights in baseball, basketball, and (at the time) NASCAR, potentially making FS1 the most credible challenger to ESPN yet.[32]

* * *

For the moment, however, none of these competitors can compete with the reach of ESPN, which has enjoyed more than a decade with a veritable monopoly over the sports landscape, one that gives it unbelievable power. To a large extent, ESPN *is* sports, or at least defines what sports is, thanks not merely to its array of sports rights but all the shows it schedules around it – shows like *SportsCenter* or *Pardon the Interruption*.

Ask NHL fans about ESPN's power to set the conversation. The league and ESPN had had a long and fruitful relationship together, and hockey effectively built ESPN2 into a network with a presence nearly on par with ESPN, but by the middle of the 2000s hockey was being increasingly shunted aside, making way for the likes of poker. In the midst of a contentious lockout that would end up cancelling the entire 2004-05 season, ESPN effectively lowballed the league and the two sides ended up parting ways. With nowhere else to turn to at the time, the NHL would end up confined to a channel then known as the Outdoor Life Network. The move attracted ridicule – what's an indoor sport like hockey doing on the Outdoor Life Network? – and had practical consequences as well, as the network had very little distribution outside systems run by its owner,

Comcast.[33] But Comcast had a method to its madness – OLN's profile had already been raised when its rights to the Tour de France allowed it to luck into Lance Armstrong's incredible post-cancer (and ultimately, too good to be true) run of seven straight Tour de France titles, and the NHL deal wound up being the foundation that allowed Comcast to eventually rebrand the network to Versus, and later, after Comcast acquired NBC Universal, to the NBC Sports Network.

But in the short term, it meant the NHL would no longer be partners with ESPN, and to hear hockey fans tell it, that meant ESPN would treat the league as a complete nonentity. Hockey highlights disappeared from *SportsCenter* and its storylines were completely invisible to the masses of sports fans for whom ESPN set the conversation.

For many in the sports media business, the launch of Fox Sports 1 was supposed to mark the biggest threat to ESPN in years. Fox had amassed what looked to be an impressive array of sports rights and made a lot of noise about competing with ESPN on day one, drawing comparisons to how it had broken up the three-network hegemony with the launch of its broadcast network and the dominance of CNN with the launch of the Fox News Channel.[34] It had its own ESPN-esque afternoon talk show, *Crowd Goes Wild*, for which it had hired Regis Philbin as the host. It had its own equivalent to *SportsCenter*, *Fox Sports Live*, for which it had imported two Canadians, Jay Onrait and Dan O'Toole, that had become stars in their native country for their offbeat approach to the usual highlight formula on TSN's version of *SportsCentre* (TSN is partly owned by ESPN).[35]

Many commenters seemed to expect FS1 to mark a substantial challenge to ESPN's hegemony[36], and though they publicly said otherwise, even ESPN seemed worried about the threat, going so far as to patch up its relationship with Keith Olbermann. Olbermann had redefined *SportsCenter* in the 90s with his legendary partnership with Dan Patrick, but had a reputation as an egotistical, explosive personality that burned bridges wherever he went, and his split with ESPN was so divisive that one executive claimed he "didn't burn bridges here, he napalmed them".[37] He'd managed to reinvent himself as a liberal commentator on

MSNBC and later Al Gore's Current network, but ultimately wound up breaking up with both of them, and it appeared he was running low on places that were still willing to work with him – until ESPN brought him in to host a weeknight highlights-and-analysis show on ESPN2 out of what Olbermann later admitted was a desire to blunt any momentum *Fox Sports Live* might build.[38]

But all the *sturm und drang* about the threat FS1 posed to ESPN turned out to be much ado about nothing, at least so far. The new network's ratings turned out to be far closer to that of the NBC Sports Network than even ESPN2, and most of its vaunted original shows drew viewership numbers in the mid-to-low five digits, dwarfed by *NASCAR Race Hub*, an unheralded part of FS1's afternoon lineup that had been a holdover from Speed, suggesting a substantial part of the new network's potential audience came from people already familiar with its former incarnation, the same people that had complained so vociferously at the launch. The staredown with cable operators over carriage fees prevented Fox from helping people not already familiar with Speed figure out where to find the new channel in the lead-up to the launch, and much of the hype surrounding the launch took place in a corner of the sports media universe few ventured into, but it's not clear it would have made much of a difference, as many of the sports events that paraded onto FS1 airwaves in the succeeding months, including high-profile college football games (including one high-profile contest between Oregon and Washington that even had ESPN's *College GameDay* setting up shop there), found themselves hurt more by moving to FS1 than the network benefitted from them.

Many of the new network's rights either involved sports with fanbases with little crossover with other sports (NASCAR, the UFC), sports entities that didn't have a passionate enough fanbase to propel FS1 to greater exposure (most of its college rights, MLS), or were based around events that came once a year at best, which wouldn't be enough to sustain year-round viewership (US Open golf, the World Cup, and ultimately, given its lack of exclusivity for any regular-season game it didn't own both teams' regional sports networks for, Major League Baseball). FS1's ratings proved so miniscule compared to the expectations Fox had set for them it ended up giving advertisers make-goods on its World Series coverage. Within a year all the network's original programming beyond *Race Hub* and *Fox Sports Live*, including the vaunted *Crowd Goes Wild*, had been cancelled, but FS1's ratings haven't progressed much since then. The ingrained habits of most viewers used to turning on ESPN for their sports news and even for sports themselves proved harder to break than most commentators, and possibly Fox itself, expected.

Fox may yet pose a challenge to ESPN in the long term, but it's clear by now that its fate will be heavily determined by Fox's ability to acquire more of the network's reason for existence in the first place, the live sports rights that can, in theory, attract a captive audience to whatever channel happens to air them. It's here that Fox truly competes with ESPN and poses a legitimate threat at the moment, simply in the form of the potential Fox might have if it managed to obtain a critical mass of sports rights, and it's here that ESPN in many ways controls Fox's destiny, using its market power to shut the upstart out of any rights that might give them too much momentum. But even when ESPN does manage to shut out Fox, it does so by paying more for rights, more than Fox can afford or at least enough to convince entities not to even give them a chance. And in this, the real winners in the emergence of potential competitors to ESPN are the sports entities that can provide the programming they all covet.

3

Printing Money

LEBRON JAMES IS, BY ALL ACCOUNTS, the greatest basketball player on the planet, the greatest basketball player since Michael Jordan retired, and probably one of the five best basketball players who ever lived. Certainly the course of his career is unlike anything that would have been possible for any earlier athlete in any sport. His transcendental talent had become widely recognized when he was still playing for St. Vincent St. Mary's high school in Akron, Ohio, when ESPN began sending cameras and announcers to cover his games, and since then his basketball career has been deeply intertwined with ESPN every step of the way. By the time he entered the NBA Draft (the NBA still allowed high schoolers to jump directly to professional basketball without playing in college first) his ESPN exposure meant he was already a ready-made star, one of the biggest stars in the league before playing a game, and ESPN was there when the Cleveland Cavaliers, less than 40 miles away from Akron, selected him with the first pick in the NBA Draft.

James spent seven illustrious years with the Cavs, winning virtually every individual accolade available to him, but he never had the supporting cast to win the sport's biggest prize, an NBA championship, only reaching the NBA Finals once. When his contract expired in 2010, James arranged the broadcast of an ESPN special, "The Decision", where he announced he was "taking [his] talents to South Beach", joining Dwayne Wade and Chris Bosh on the Miami Heat. The move turned James into Public Enemy #1 not only in Cleveland but around the country for ripping Clevelanders' hearts out on a primetime national television special, not helped by the swagger the three of them showed at a "welcome party" the next night in Miami, when James proclaimed that the team would win "not five, not six, not seven" championships. ESPN also came in for criticism for its willingness to go along with the special, even though pretty much any other media outlet would jump at the chance to air the special, which drew a bigger audience than any non-Finals game since ESPN began airing NBA games.

James would make four straight NBA Finals and win two championships with the Heat, but lost the first Finals to the Dallas Mavericks, and as Wade's history of injuries caught up with him, nearly single-handedly pulled the Heat to a grueling, borderline miraculous, second title against the San Antonio Spurs, whose best players were at their peak and winning championships before James was even in the league. The Heat made a fourth Finals in a depleted Eastern Conference in 2014, but fell in a rematch with the Spurs in five games.

Perhaps the prospect of having to carry the Heat by himself indefinitely, with no guarantee of future championships, entered into his decision in 2014 to return to Cleveland and the Cavaliers. This decision was everything that "The Decision" wasn't. Rather than a television special, this decision would be announced in a piece written with *Sports Illustrated*'s Lee Jenkins. Everything James did wrong in "The Decision", he did right this time, apologizing for the lapse in judgment that led to "The Decision", recognizing what he and his departure truly meant for the city of Cleveland, declaring he never would have left Miami for any other team, and pledging to end his career with the Cavs.[1] But while LeBron's words may have said all the right things, his actions told a different story: James signed only a two-year contract with the Cavaliers (the NBA maximum is four, five if re-signing with the same team) with a player opt-out after the first year.[2] It was easy to question James' motivations: did he negotiate this contract in order to give himself leverage to motivate Cavaliers management to put a team capable of winning a championship on the court as soon as possible? Would the basketball world have to put up with rampant speculation over what LeBron would do each of the next two years? Would LeBron rip Clevelanders' hearts out all over again if the team wasn't ready to win quickly enough?

In fact, LeBron's motivations may have been decidedly more benign, in that they in no way represented a lack of commitment to the Cavaliers or the city of Cleveland. Rather, what entered LeBron's mind was the NBA's national television contract that was slated to expire in the 2015-16 season. Anyone who was paying attention to the booming market for sports rights on television knew the NBA would be in for a massive payday when those rights came up for bid, and that meant a dramatic increase in the league's salary cap. The length of James' contract had less to do with setting up another departure within two years and more with preserving his ability to make as much money as he could as soon as he could.[3] The contract of the greatest professional basketball player on the planet was influenced by the circumstances surrounding his league's television contract.

* * *

In the aftermath of the BCS deal, some executives with sports leagues worried that ESPN would become a de facto monopoly that could drive down the price of rights fees. Even a year later, the best prospects for someone to stand up to ESPN and bid up rights seemed to be the broadcast networks, general-entertainment networks, and the then-Versus network.[4] As we saw in the last chapter, those fears proved unfounded. The prospect of ESPN and Fox competing to rack up sports rights, while also fending off advances from NBC, as CBS and Turner lurk trying to get their own piece of the action, now has sports leagues salivating at how high it could drive their rights fees. Even for those without a horse in the race, the competition between the bunch of them can often seem like something out of a soap opera.

Major League Baseball has already seen the benefits the newfound competition can net them. Already it had benefitted from the steps taken by the NFL and NBA to move to cable: its 2006 rights re-negotiations, worth roughly $712 million/year, placed almost the entire postseason on TBS, which ended its long tradition of national Braves games in favor of a general package of games on Sunday afternoons, with only the World Series and one League Championship Series remaining on Fox.

(Previously Fox and ESPN had split the postseason with Fox airing both LCS's and marquee Division Series games, effectively taking over Fox's primetime in early-to-mid October, and Fox wasn't entirely unhappy about getting its primetime back in that early part of the postseason.)[5] But by 2012 it found itself in position to take advantage of its position as programming it would be hard to replicate, certainly in the near term, on sports networks. NBC wanted a piece of the action, Fox wanted to move some of its games to what would become Fox Sports 1, ESPN wanted playoff games, Turner wasn't interested in going gently into the good night, and baseball itself wished to improve the standing of its MLB Network.[6]

MLB let its exclusive negotiating windows expire, but then started a new, informal negotiating session with ESPN during the Summer Olympics, when NBC would be otherwise occupied. MLB would incorporate all of its various rights, including international, digital, and radio rights, into a single agreement, and would lift blackouts on ESPN's Monday and Wednesday games, but ESPN would have to pay nearly double what it had been paying under the old contract for a deal not much different from what ESPN had before: ESPN kept its Sunday, Monday, and Wednesday night packages, only adding games on holidays, one game from the new Wild Card round, and any tiebreakers. Getting a piece of the playoffs was important enough that Disney head Bob Iger personally contacted Commissioner Bud Selig to emphasize the point, but nonetheless ESPN agreed to the deal, hoping more playoff rights would become available after later rounds of negotiation.[7] Doubtless the specter of NBC or Fox taking some or all of ESPN's rights if they dawdled also hung over their heads; by keeping its existing regular-season cable packages, ESPN severely reduced the value of a baseball agreement to any potential competitors, especially NBC, by locking them out of any of the most popular cable packages.[8] Baseball intended to consolidate its remaining inventory to a single partner.

Desperate to maintain its presence in baseball that helped build TBS into what it became today, Turner began talking with CBS about an alliance that could allow CBS to air as little as the All-Star Game and World Series, but baseball was skeptical about the offer. That left the remaining inventory as Fox's to lose, but Fox was unwilling to take on TBS' weak Sunday afternoon package for the price baseball was asking, so baseball ultimately split the rights between TBS and Fox. End result: Fox has two time slots every Saturday, with the vast majority of those games airing on Fox Sports 1, and splits the division series with TBS along the same league lines as the LCS, again with as many games as Fox wants, potentially up to and including every one of its LCS games, on Fox Sports 1, except for two games surrendered to MLB Network, while TBS reduces its Sunday afternoon commitment to the later half of the season. Both entities also paid double what they were before, despite TBS' reduced commitment.[9]

* * *

When NASCAR signed an eight-year agreement with Fox, TNT, and ESPN in 2006, it was coming off a contract with Fox, NBC, and TNT that produced such ratings heights many people were wondering if it was joining the ranks of the major sports. But since then, ratings for NASCAR had fallen significantly, declining each year from 2007, the first year of the deal, to 2010, though they were still a considerable force.[10] The sport was especially struggling in the young demographics that are so valuable to television advertisers.

But the larger evolution in the sports landscape since the previous deal was signed meant NASCAR still stood to profit handsomely. The 2008 BCS deal was not yet a reality, meaning the importance of cable was not yet clear; Fox had actually taken races off of FX and put its entire Sprint Cup schedule on its broadcast network, which made perfect sense at the time but was looking increasingly anachronistic as more sports moved to cable and as NASCAR ratings continued to slide. By 2011, Fox was already talking with NASCAR about potentially putting some Sprint Cup races on Speed in the future, beyond the non-points Duel races (which set the starting order for the Daytona 500) and All-Star Race.[11] The advent of Fox's plans to convert Speed to FS1 only intensified that interest, and NBC, now owned by Comcast and thus now wielding

NBCSN as a cable outlet, made no secret of its desire to get back into the sport.[12]

Fox actually ended up holding talks with NASCAR about renewing its deal a year before it really needed to, making sure not to run the risk of losing its rights to anyone else while still allowing NASCAR to put the part of the season it didn't have up for bid.[13] By October of 2012, it reached an eight-year renewal of its deal worth $300 million a year – its previous rate of $220 million a year in the previous deal, signed when NASCAR was considered a hot property, was exactly the same as in the deal it initially signed in 2001. The deal allowed Fox to keep its 13 Sprint Cup series races, some of which could now be shown on Fox Sports 1, as well as the entire Camping World Truck Series schedule that had become a Speed mainstay.[14]

But ESPN and Turner preferred to wait until their exclusive negotiating windows opened the following summer, and that ended up leaving them decidedly more lukewarm about re-upping with the sport. Ratings were continuing to decline during the first half of the 2013 season, with TNT seeing its lowest ratings in 29 years of covering the sport. Before the negotiating window even expired, both ESPN and Turner told NASCAR they would not even submit bids (and later attempted to get out of their deals a year early), meaning the second half of the season would effectively fall into NBC's lap. One might think that would leave NBC holding all the cards, but NBC eventually signed a deal worth $440 million a year for 20 Sprint Cup races and the corresponding second-tier Nationwide (now Xfinity) series races, a 54 percent increase over what ESPN and Turner had been paying.[15] After the remaining three Sprint Cup races and corresponding Nationwide races were sold to Fox (for $125 million a year, nearly half of the earlier deal), NASCAR came out of everything with an $820 million/year haul, a 46% increase from the 2006 deal.[16] Despite all the concerns about declining ratings and aging demographics, the larger movement in the sports media landscape trumped them all and allowed NASCAR to come away with a healthy chunk of change.

* * *

It's easy to see why the NBA's television contract was set to receive so much attention among people in the know both in basketball circles and among more general watchers of the sports television landscape. Not only would the NBA be set to take advantage of the skyrocketing rights fees across all of sports, but most other valuable sports rights would be locked up into the next decade by the time the NBA came onto the market, potentially making the NBA even more valuable. For Fox and NBC, the NBA would represent their last, best chance to truly make a big impact with their sports networks for the foreseeable future. In fact, when Fox made its effort to purchase Time Warner in 2014, some wondered if it was an attempt to score the NBA rights Turner looked set to renew. NBA games are particularly popular in the 18-49 demographic, making the potential windfall all the greater.[17]

The NBA began informal negotiations with ESPN and Turner as early as the summer of 2013, in part out of fears that the booming sports rights landscape represented a bubble that might burst if the league dawdled (a possibility we'll look into in more detail in the last chapter).[18] ESPN and Turner, for their part, had no interest in waiting until their exclusive negotiating windows ended and they had to compete with Fox and NBC for the rights.[19] The NBA also considered opening up a new TV package to sell to a third partner, but ESPN was adamantly against doing so.[20]

Despite the NBA's rights not coming onto the open market, the league nearly tripled its annual rights fees. New NBA commissioner Adam Silver put out feelers to Fox, NBC, and others after the 2014 All-Star Game to help establish how much money the league could expect to get on the open market, ensuring the league wouldn't leave any money on the table even renewing with its existing partners early, and ESPN and Turner didn't hesitate to agree to the numbers the league asked for. The NBA's previous deals were worth a combined $930 million a year; under the new deal ESPN alone would pay $1.4 billion a year, while Turner would chip in $1.2 billion. For the most part, the deal would be similar to the previous deal, with Turner adding 12 games on a new night with more flexibility in scheduling, and ESPN adding 15 games.[21]

All three of these leagues – MLB, NASCAR, and the NBA – reaped the benefits of the red-hot media rights landscape. MLB and the NBA saw massive increases despite little in the way of actual changes to their media deals, with the same entities signing up with them as before – as the NBA proved, just the prospect of an interloper snatching away rights was enough to entice their incumbents to pony up. NASCAR saw the biggest changes but mostly because foundering ratings scared off two of their incumbent partners, yet still saw a substantial rights fee increase. All three can attest that it's a great time to be a sports league, providing valuable programming that's impossible to replicate, and it's far from limited to those three. For collegiate conferences, the effect has been so profound that we'll look into it in more detail in the next chapter.

* * *

The biggest leagues and conferences may be salivating at having multiple competitors groveling at their feet for the valuable programming they represent, but smaller leagues, conferences, and events may benefit even more. With multiple ESPN networks, plus Fox Sports 1, NBCSN, and CBS Sports Network, there's a lot of time in the day that needs to be filled. All these channels are desperate for programming, and that's very good news for entities that might otherwise be completely ignored. This is especially the case for CBS Sports Network, which is substantially weaker than the others, and which has signed contracts with the likes of Major League Lacrosse, the National Lacrosse League, the Arena Football League, and the last, abortive season of the UFL. Smaller college conferences have also benefitted, and not just with CBS Sports Network and its college roots; the Atlantic 10 doubled its national television presence in 2012 after signing agreements with ESPN, NBCSN, and CBS Sports Network.[22] After George Mason's magical run to the Final Four and other NCAA Tournament success, the CAA managed to secure a substantial number of games on NBCSN, only to lose many of their best teams to the Atlantic 10. NBCSN also had an agreement with the Canadian Football League before that league moved full-time to ESPN.

For the Ultimate Fighting Championship, which had built a substantially larger niche of young men, the timing was perfect. UFC had become the hottest property in sports off of a combination of pay-per-view and its hit reality show *The Ultimate Fighter* on Spike TV, supplemented with smaller cards on Spike and Versus, the latter of which it inherited with the acquisition of the World Extreme Cagefighting promotion. Despite rival promotions, backed by singular stars, such as EliteXC and Strikeforce getting pushes on Showtime and CBS, President Dana White had been consistent that he would not seek a broader contract with a broadcast outlet until the time was right and a partner was willing to fully invest in and promote the sport while allowing UFC to control production.[23] The increasing value of sports properties to media companies would seem to fit the bill, and it became seemingly inevitable that the UFC would leave Spike TV after its contract ended in 2011. ESPN expressed interest, CBS made sense after the UFC acquired Strikeforce earlier in the year and inherited that company's relationship with Showtime, and Comcast seemed to be the front-runner for a time with its existing relationship with the company, but the UFC ultimately reached a seven-year deal with Fox that netted it at least $90 million a year, not quite in the league of other high-level sports and not enough for pay-per-view not to remain a key part of the business, but more than double what it had been getting from Spike and Versus.[24] The deal initially called for four cards a year on Fox, starting with a heavyweight championship fight less than three months after the deal's announcement, and six on FX, plus moving *The Ultimate Fighter* to a live model that was slated to give FX another 26 live time slots a year, and additional content for Fox's action-sports network Fuel.[25] *TUF* would ditch the live model after one season, with most of the FX and Fuel content moving to Fox Sports 1 at that network's launch as Fuel was converted to Fox Sports 2.

The need for programming to fill up time on cable sports networks has also resulted in a shift in NBC's strategy around the Olympics. Once upon a time, NBC trotted out Olympic sports once every four years and sealed them away until the next Olympics to "preserve the magic of the Olympics". Since the Comcast acquisition, though, NBC has been gobbling up rights to individual Olympic sports during the periods between Olympics, offering revenue sharing arrangements with some and rights fees to others, but offering all of them the considerable promotional value of working with the Olympic network, and NBC the ability to promote the athletes in the lead-up to the Games. It's also produced impressive ratings, with Olympic sports producing viewership in the millions on the broadcast network. To some degree, the push started before the Comcast acquisition: the three biggest Summer Olympic sports, USA Swimming, Gymnastics, and Track and Field, signed a deal with Wasserman Media Group in 2007 with an eye towards creating a new digital network, and the United States Olympic Committee also spent some time looking into the idea of creating an Olympic network, leading NBC to take a stake in a small network called Universal Sports that specialized in showing various Olympic sports.[26] Other networks also look for rights that can harmonize with rights they already have, as when ESPN struck a deal to show home matches of the Mexican national soccer team in English during the run-up to the 2014 World Cup.[27]

* * *

People have talked about soccer, the world's most popular sport, winning American hearts again and again in the past; the North American Soccer League, which boasted some of the sport's biggest stars on the New York Cosmos, lasted 16 years and enjoyed considerable success for a time before running into financial problems and folding in 1984. But the boom soccer has enjoyed in recent years seems different and more genuine. Soccer, or at least the United States national team and the World Cup, enjoys ratings once unheard of. Major League Soccer has already outlasted the NASL, but perhaps more telling is the degree to which devotees of European soccer have dwarfed the popularity of the domestic league. England's Premier League, in particular, has proven to be highly valuable programming to Fox, ESPN, and NBC at various times. It's a stark contrast from past soccer pushes that have attempted to focus entirely on domestic leagues patterned on America's major sports but, except in the Cosmos' heyday, lacking the best players, and this increased exposure to world-class soccer may have finally produced a group of devoted American soccer fans who aren't just in it as a fad. But what may be less commonly recognized is the degree to which all this can be chalked up to one company, Fox, and one man at another company, John Skipper – and is as much a story about digital cable and satellite's ability to serve niche audiences, and potentially make them mainstream in the process, as anything else.

With digital cable and satellite television on the rise, Fox Sports World launched in 1997, focused on coverage of international sports Fox had the rights to through its interests in other markets, especially British Sky Broadcasting, and the Prime group of regional sports networks it had recently acquired.[28] Soccer was the heart of the network's programming strategy from the start, with over 500 hours of live coverage per year planned when the network was announced.[29] Even in the countries where soccer was king, most of what was available on TV tended to come from each country's own competitions, but Fox Sports World was dedicated to showcasing the best soccer from around the world.[30] "A soccer fan just wants to see good soccer," said network general manager Dan Casey in 2000. When you see the English league or the [Italian] Serie A, you see the high caliber of athleticism and the beauty of the game. Just because the USA isn't there yet doesn't mean that in five to 10 years a shift won't take place."[31] Those soccer fans Fox Sports World, which rebranded to Fox Soccer Channel in 2005, exposed to world-class soccer would have a tremendous impact on the development of soccer in the United States.

But in 2001, when the rights for the 2002 and 2006 World Cups were up for bid, America was still apathetic to soccer, and it didn't help that the US had finished last in the 1998 Cup, and digital cable was still mostly a niche field, so broad-based cable networks still ruled. Soccer United Marketing, an arm of MLS, won the rights to the 2002 and 2006 Cups and resold the rights to ESPN and ABC in a package deal with MLS and US National Team games. Now FIFA was entertaining interest from multiple entities interested in winning the Cup for themselves without needing SUM as a middleman; besides Fox, NBC wanted to synergize the English-language rights with Spanish-language rights for Telemundo, which it acquired in 2002, stealing them away from Univision, for whom the World Cup had long been the Hispanic community's Super Bowl.

SUM remained interested in retaining the rights and selling them to whoever picked up the next MLS contract, and ESPN seemed mostly interested in buying the Cup from SUM again.[32] That's when Skipper stepped in.

Skipper's background was publishing, and he had played a key role in the launch of ESPN the Magazine in the late 90s, as well as overseeing the rise of ESPN.com as the dominant portal for sports on the web.[33] An assignment that required working with the people in charge of ESPN's Soccernet web site in the UK helped kindle a love of soccer within him that was solidified by watching the 2002 World Cup. In 2005, he made a push to be named ESPN's head of programming, and retaining the World Cup was part of his pitch.[34] It would not be easy: even as Skipper was pushing for the job, NBC and Telemundo looked set to win the World Cup rights, securing a handshake deal and a recommendation from FIFA's Marketing and Television Division, and when FIFA assembled for its Congress in Morocco in September, approving the deal seemed to be all but a formality, to the point NBC representatives didn't even bother to show up for the vote, assured the deal was in the bag.[35]

But Chuck Blazer, the general secretary of CONCACAF, the governing body for soccer in North and Central America, and the first US citizen to serve on FIFA's executive committee, had denounced the NBC deal as the potential death of soccer in the United States, citing NBC's apparent lack of interest in MLS and how much smaller Telemundo was than Univision. Some suspected his tirade was as much connected to rumors of Skipper's pending ascent than any genuine concern about NBC's commitment to the sport. The board unexpectedly voted to table the deal and collect a new round of bids. NBC executives were once again assured that the vote was only a minor hiccup and the board would surely approve their deal within two months, but for most of that time, virtually from the instant Skipper's promotion was made official, he was in Switzerland meeting feverishly with FIFA officials pitching them on a $100 million bid for World Cup rights and a considerable increase in ESPN's commitment to the event. Although NBC had made many of the same commitments as ESPN, FIFA never even asked them to match the offer before blindsiding them with the announcement that ESPN had spirited away the rights.[36]

Skipper was a believer that soccer could truly catch on in America, especially given the country's changing demographics, and he had big plans for the World Cup as the centerpiece of his new administration and one of the company's top priorities, intending to promote the World Cup as the landmark event it was in the rest of the world and treat it as ESPN's equivalent of the Olympics.[37] ESPN sent 300 staffers to South Africa for the 2006 World Cup to produce 65 hours of studio coverage and more than 200 hours of coverage overall, including features on the history and culture of the country, a level of pre- and post-game coverage normally reserved for *Monday Night Football*, and even sending the network's flagship show *SportsCenter* there.[38] It paid off in massively increased interest in the World Cup, especially the United States national team. The US' three group-stage matches averaged over 11 million viewers across ESPN's platforms and Univision – nearly doubling the 6.6 million they attracted four years before – and nearly 15 million tuned in on ABC alone to see the US' World Cup run finally end in the knockout stage to Ghana. And where once late-night comics might have mocked the very existence of soccer and America's interest, or lack thereof, in it, now they turned their attention to the horns called *vuvuzelas* that made a constant racket on ESPN's broadcasts.[39]

But what even Skipper didn't realize was the role international club soccer would play in soccer's emergence,[40] propelled in part by increased television exposure on Fox Soccer Channel but also by increased touring by European teams in the States during their summer offseason, playing each other and against MLS sides,[41] including a revamped MLS all-star game format pitting a single team of all-stars against top club teams from around the world.[42] Once Fox Soccer became rated by Nielsen in October 2008, it became apparent that the Premier League was more popular in America than America's own domestic league; even though Fox Soccer was in 66 million fewer homes than ESPN2, it aired ten games that season that drew a larger audience than ESPN's average for MLS games.

Media companies took notice. They had previously shied away from international soccer, fearing the morning and afternoon time slots would depress audiences, but that also meant they would represent live programming at times when there generally wasn't any.[43] Fox won the rights to the prestigious UEFA Champions League, long an afternoon time-filler for ESPN, in 2009, and began airing the final on the Fox broadcast network;[44] as for the Premier League, ESPN began sublicensing games from Fox, and in April 2012, ESPN attracted over a million viewers for the "Manchester Derby" between Manchester United and Manchester City, two teams vying for the Premier League title, the most-watched Premier League match on cable – but not the most watched on any platform; Fox had attracted larger numbers to its broadcast network for matches pitting Manchester United against Arsenal in January and Chelsea on Super Bowl Sunday.[45] The avid audience for the Premier League in the states also attracted interest in other areas; six of the league's 20 teams, including premier clubs Manchester United, Liverpool, and Arsenal, were in American hands by the 2013-14 season,[46] while MLS, which had attempted to court youth soccer players at its launch, pivoted to embrace a more European model of soccer fandom based on older fans with more of a connection to the team.[47] And with the increased competition for the sports cable dollar, America loomed as a new and potentially lucrative source of revenue for top soccer competitions.

* * *

ESPN, Fox, NBC, and Univision once again convened in Switzerland to compete for the TV rights to the 2018 and 2022 World Cups in 2011, and this time there was no doubt over the value of the property. ESPN and Univision were widely considered the front-runners to retain the rights, but neither did. Fox paid around $475 million for English-language rights, more than ESPN and Univision combined had paid in the previous cycle and nearly $100 million more than ESPN's bid, while NBC's Telemundo broke the bank with a $625 million bid for Spanish-language rights.[48] In the days before Fox's all-sports network plans came to light, it seemed like the greatest moment of triumph for Fox Soccer for

Fox to win the World Cup; even if Fox Soccer didn't air many matches from the main World Cup, the numerous ancillary tournaments Fox also won the rights to would provide valuable programming over the summer, positioning Fox in general and Fox Soccer in particular as the absolute hub of the soccer world.[49]

Certainly it had a strong case to be considered the home of European club soccer, with the Premier League and Champions League joined by matches from Italy and occasionally France. Its main rival was GolTV, a significantly smaller operation started in 2003 that required a subscription to a Spanish-language package on many cable operators and only boasted 15 million households across both languages, but which boasted matches from Spain and Germany among others (sublicensing some of the former to ESPN), meaning it had quite possibly the three most prominent and successful European clubs outside England, Barcelona, Real Madrid, and Bayern Munich.[50] Then Al Jazeera, backed by the deep pockets of the Qatari royal family, stepped in and completely upended the marketplace.

For most Americans, Al Jazeera is mostly known as the outfit that aired Osama bin Laden's video messages in the years following the 9/11 attacks, which has given it an indelible association in the public mind with terrorism, not helped by the association the Arab world as a whole has with terrorism. In fact, however, Al Jazeera has developed a reputation outside America as one of the most respected news organizations in the world, with remarkably even-handed and in-depth reporting of issues in the Arab world; its provision of airtime to bin Laden is an outgrowth of its commitment to give airtime to just about every perspective imaginable, including pro-Israeli, pro-Saddam Hussein, and pro-democracy, including providing some of the best coverage of the 2012 Arab Spring, and as a result it has drawn the ire of seemingly every ruler in the Arab world, all despite being founded by and, for at least its first decade, utterly dependent on the money of, the Emir of Qatar.[51] In addition, Al Jazeera has established a presence all over the world over the past decade, since the launch of Al Jazeera English in 2006, but its association with bin Laden meant it would face a decidedly uphill struggle to crack the American market, already harder to crack than most other countries because of its relatively decentralized panoply of cable and satellite companies.[52] How could it overcome its association with terrorism and land a place on American cable lineups? For Al Jazeera, the answer started with soccer.

Al Jazeera was already active in the market for international rights for top European leagues, but over the course of 2011 and 2012, Al Jazeera spirited away the North American rights to the Spanish, Italian, and French leagues, and eventually added the United States' road World Cup qualifiers. With these rights, cable operators would have no choice but to carry its beIN Sport network.[53] In 2013, Al Jazeera purchased Al Gore's Current network, intending to turn it into Al Jazeera America; it's an open question whether the plan would have succeeded if it weren't for the inroads beIN Sport had already made on cable systems.[54]

The effect of Al Jazeera's soccer play was to decimate GolTV and take away a significant part of Fox Soccer's depth. But while Al Jazeera was one factor, NBC may have played a bigger role in sealing Fox Soccer's fate. Now merged with Comcast, and thus with the NBC Sports Network now in its portfolio, NBC saw a lot more potential in acquiring all aspects of the soccer world, and signed a three-year deal with MLS to take the package of games that were airing on Fox Soccer in 2011, putting the games on a network in nearly twice the households than Fox Soccer and on broadcast television for the first time since 2008.[55] But NBC was set to take aim at the heart of Fox Soccer's portfolio.

* * *

With increased interest in the Premier League across the board, ESPN and Fox, submitting a joint bid that mostly preserved their status quo, were joined by NBC, Al Jazeera, marketing agency IMG, which would sublicense the games to interested networks, and Discovery Networks, interested in using Premier League games to juice up interest in its Velocity network, when the rights came up for bid in the fall of 2012. NBC's bid was initially thought to be underwhelming, as they had just picked up the rights to Formula 1 racing, previously on Speed, which would compete for many of the same timeslots. Similar timeslot considerations worked against beIN Sport, since the Premier League played at many of the same times as the Spanish and Italian leagues.[56] But NBC stepped up with a bid of over $80 million a year, over triple what Fox had been paying, to snatch away the rights.[57]

Just like that, NBC had sealed the fate of Fox Soccer, a victim of its own wild success, as the network that had built up the Premier League to the point where it became valuable enough for NBC to take it away. But NBC's commitment to the Premier League went beyond merely outbidding ESPN and Fox. NBC had its sights on pushing the league far further than Fox and ESPN had taken it, right into the center of the American sports conversation and as tentpole programming for NBCSN. It would show all 380 matches live on one of its cable networks or on a special suite of part-time "Extra Time" channels it offered cable operators that carried NBCSN for no extra cost, augmented by over 600 hours of studio coverage and other original programming that would rely heavily on authentic British voices. 20 of those matches would air on the NBC broadcast network, a considerable achievement for a league that had no broadcast presence stateside just a few years before. And in the build-up to the start of the 2013-14 season, NBC plastered New York with billboards and subway wraps featuring every team in the league and ran TV spots starring *Saturday Night Live*'s Jason Sudeikis as an American football coach cluelessly attempting to take the reins at storied club Tottenham Hotspur.[58]

The result was something hailed as perhaps the best coverage *any* sport received in the United States, and it worked out very well for NBC as well.[59] By 2014, the Premier League was actually attracting larger audiences to NBCSN than the NHL, the league the network had previously revolved around.[60] Fox Soccer was all but forgotten as NBC received much of the credit for improving the popularity of the Premier League in the United States. Certainly the Premier League seemed in line to receive a substantial boost in its rights fee despite relatively little time passing since the last time the contract came up for renewal. Despite bids from Fox and beIN Sports (and helped by the Premier League forbidding joint bids), in 2015 NBC and the Premier League renewed their deal for another six years, twice the length that had previously been the norm for

Premier League contracts, with the annual rights fee reportedly doubling to the point of NBC paying a full $1 billion over the life of the deal.[61]

But while Fox may have lost its club-league rights and was shutting down Fox Soccer, that didn't mean it was giving up on all soccer that wasn't the Champions League or World Cup, or even that it wasn't willing to get back into the European soccer universe. Fox picked up the rights to air the German Bundesliga in 2015, and had its sights on getting MLS back as well. MLS had timed its agreement with NBC to coincide with the expiration of ESPN and Univision's deals, and intended to condense its TV rights deals to a single partner in each language, as well as a consistent time slot for games, when those rights came up for renewal after the 2014 season.[62] Although ESPN was interested, it wasn't interested in claiming the entire package, so ESPN and MLS reached out to Fox on a joint bid. Fox was interested as long as its package was equal to ESPN's. Despite continued anemic ratings, the two set out their willingness to pay as much as $75 million a year, a massive increase over the roughly $23 million/year ESPN, NBC, and Univision were combining for, and that was enough for NBC to pull out of negotiations entirely in January 2014. Despite having a clear field, negotiations dragged on for another five months over a wide variety of issues, especially a groundbreaking deal for ESPN to offer the league's out-of-market package over the Internet. Under the terms of the deal, and a $15 million deal the league signed with Univision, ESPN and Fox would each have games on Sunday evenings, while Univision's UniMas network would have an exclusive package of Friday night games plus two exclusive playoff games, with English commentary available on SAP, establishing it as a peer of the league's English-language partners. Most other matches would air on Saturdays. ESPN and Fox would alternate the MLS Cup and All-Star game with Univision airing games in Spanish.[63]

* * *

Television has long had an impact on the biggest sports, but with sports increasingly becoming more important as programming for cable networks than in their own right, nearly every one has contorted itself to extract more money out of its partners, even in ways the fans may not like but will watch anyway. Such was the case when the NCAA considered expanding the basketball tournament to 96 teams during its 2010 renegotiations, as well as when baseball introduced its new wild-card games – in both cases motivated at least in part by a desire to increase inventory to sell to television networks. No doubt the evolution of the BCS to the new College Football Playoff was motivated as much by the desire to extract more money out of a TV partner as by the outrage surrounding the BCS system. Even smaller sports have been affected, and in their case the effect can be quite profound.

In 2010, a team funded by Oracle chief Larry Ellison won the America's Cup, the world's oldest and most prestigious yachting competition, allowing it to set the terms for the next Cup. Yacht racing had been on television before – ESPN's coverage of the 1987 America's Cup, the first in the over-century-old history of the Cup to be defended by a syndicate other than the New York Yacht Club, was a key milestone in its development and credibility – but by the 2000s the sport, once more popular than golf or tennis, had fallen well behind those sports when it came to television rights fees and sponsorship revenue.[64] Ellison hoped to create a truly television-friendly event that would bring the sport to a wider audience, to appeal to the "Facebook generation instead of the Flintstone generation", in the words of Russell Coutts, who Ellison named head of his racing team, Oracle Team USA[65], and they convinced Comcast to reach an agreement to put the races on NBC and NBCSN.[66] Ellison and Coutts created a series of promotional races, the America's Cup Series, run throughout 2012, with plans for an international sailing league running 12 to 14 events a year, and promised that upwards of a dozen challengers would race in the Louis Vuitton Cup, which determines the challenger of the America's Cup.[67] Coverage of the race itself would be enhanced with on-board HD cameras and 14 microphones on each boat.[68] The centerpiece of Ellison's plan was the AC72, a large but lightweight catamaran, powered by winged sails, that hydrofoils across the water, appearing to rise into the air, at speeds close to 50 miles an hour.[69] The boat could also be raced in a wider variety of weather conditions, giving networks greater guarantees they would actually see a race on a given day, and within view of spectators on the shore.[70] But it was because of the AC72 that things started going very, very wrong.

Although the idea was to cut the costs of fielding a team, the opposite effect occurred – teams found themselves spending over $100 million building and testing the boats.[71] More disturbingly, the AC72 proved to be downright dangerous. Oracle's team saw their boat capsize during training in October of 2012; no one was injured, but the boat was severely damaged.[72] Between the risk and the expense, Ellison's promise of over a dozen challengers failed to materialise; only three teams signed up for the Louis Vuitton Cup[73], causing sources of fundraising to evaporate and the City of San Francisco left with a shortfall of as much as $20 million to cover its costs[74]. Then in May, a British sailor and former Olympic gold medalist, Andrew Simpson, drowned when his boat capsized and trapped him underneath, sparking widespread debate over whether the AC72 was too dangerous to sail. Certainly the boats were so fast and difficult as to almost neuter the importance of skill and tactics in favor of simply keeping the boat upright.[75] Simpson's team, the Swedish-backed Artemis Racing, ended up skipping the first month of the Louis Vuitton Cup, resulting in the farcical spectacle of most of the Vuitton Cup consisting of one boat sailing around the course alone, further exacerbated when one of the other challengers, Italy's Luna Rossa, sat out its own first race in protest of rules changes it had an unheard challenge of.[76] Frustration mounted when the first three races of the Vuitton Cup finals were effectively won by the team that *didn't* suffer a mechanical failure.[77]

But in the end, the America's Cup not only provided stunning visuals for television but a compelling storyline, as Oracle Team USA mounted an incredible comeback from an 8-1 deficit, one loss away from losing the Cup, to knock off Emirates Team New Zealand and retain the Cup. Even though Team USA had only one American sailor and consisted mainly of Kiwis, even though part of the reason it was down so far was because it was docked two points after attempting to cheat in a preliminary event, and even though even the announcers on the broadcast credited the people behind the scenes for reworking Team USA's boat more than anything else for the comeback, it was hard for those watching on television not to get caught up in the patriotism and root for the United States and its scrappy sailors to finish the comeback.[78] Where there is competition, real, unscripted competition, people will watch and they will get invested, especially if they feel like one side is representing "them". And that's something media companies are more than willing to give them - even if they change the nature of the competition in the process, something that, as the next two chapters show, even America's most popular sports aren't immune to, precisely because of their popularity.

4

Big Man on Campus

HOW ESPN BECAME COLLEGE FOOTBALL'S MOST POWERFUL ENTITY –
AND FUNDAMENTALLY CHANGED IT IN THE PROCESS

E VEN FOR A NATION AS FOOTBALL-OBSESSED AS OURS, football fanaticism runs bigger in Texas, whether in high school, college, or the NFL, and perhaps no football player is more Texas than Johnny Manziel. For all his football excellence – of which there is plenty – Manziel attracts nearly as much attention for his swagger, partying ways, and bending of the rules. Before he'd even taken a snap in college, he'd attracted national attention for posing shirtless for a mug shot after getting arrested for his role in a bar fight.[1]

The product of a family rich in Texas oil wealth, Manziel grew up in Tyler, Texas, but moved to the town of Kerrville for high school.[2] At Tivy High School, Manziel achieved folk-hero status, drawing comparisons to all-time quarterbacks like Brett Favre and Drew Brees, as his senior year proved to be one of the best in the history of Texas high school football – 44 touchdowns passing, 30 running, and accounting for over 5,000 yards of offense. But he still wasn't highly recruited due to concerns about his height and whether he was a true quarterback; ESPN considered him the 78th-best quarterback of his class, and the University of Texas, his personal favorite school, reportedly was more interested in his abilities on the baseball diamond than the football field, and to the extent they did want his football abilities, allegedly wanted them at defensive back. He initially committed to the University of Oregon, but eventually switched to Texas A&M.[3] A Texas A&M message board took to referring to him as "Johnny (expletive) Football"; cleaned up to "Johnny Football", the moniker was destined to stick to him for the rest of his career.[4]

Despite the bar fight arrest, A&M coach Kevin Sumlin named him his team's starting quarterback for the 2012 season, and he proved to have as amazing a run in college as he had in high school. In November, he propelled the Aggies to an upset win over #1 Alabama that made him a household name across the nation,[5] and finished the season with over 4600 all-purpose yards, a Southeastern Conference record, and became only the fifth player in NCAA history and first freshman to pass for 3000 and rush for 1000 yards in a season, something he achieved two games sooner than any other player. Although he wasn't even on the radar for the Heisman Trophy before the Alabama game, he ended up becoming the first freshman in history to win college football's most prestigious award.[6]

In 2014, he declared for the NFL draft, and after he wasn't selected in the top ten picks, it seemed like fate was delivering Manziel and all his swagger to the Dallas Cowboys, the personification of Texas swagger in the NFL. The Cowboys passed on him, and eventually the Cleveland Browns, having already passed on him twice, traded up to pick him with the 22nd pick, in part because, according to ESPN's Sal Paolantonio, the team's owner was walking the streets of Cleveland when a homeless man told him to "draft Manziel".[7] Manziel proceeded to sign a 4-year, $8.25 million contract with the Browns, but that paled in comparison to the degree to which Texas A&M had benefitted from his presence before he'd ever collected a dime.[8] During the 2012-13 fiscal year alone, Texas A&M received $740 million in donations, $300 million more than their previous high and nearly as much more as the next-best total raised by any Texas university, $453 million by the University of Texas over the same period.[9] The school put that windfall towards a $450 million renovation of Kyle Field envisioned to be the biggest in Texas. On the field, 247Sports.com named Texas A&M the fifth-best recruiting class of 2014; Rivals.com had them sixth.[10]

To hear the school's athletic director Eric Hyman tell it, what made the hoopla over Johnny Football possible, as much as anything Manziel did on the field, was something Texas A&M did a year before he ever set foot on campus. In 2011, the school announced it would be moving from the Big 12 Conference to the SEC starting with Manziel's freshman season, and as Hyman put it, "If we were in the Big 12, I don't know that Johnny Manziel would have won the Heisman." Though ESPN has contracts with every major college conference, perhaps no college conference is more important to ESPN than the SEC, and Texas A&M reaped the exposure benefits instantly, with *College Gameday*, ESPN's Saturday-morning pregame show, visiting College Station for A&M's home opener against Florida. ESPN followed Manziel's exploits all season long on football Saturdays and on its *SportsCenter* and *College Football Live* shows, and its regular "Heisman Watch" segments tracked how Manziel was doing in the Heisman race. A&M forbade freshmen from giving interviews, but during the last week of the regular season, the school and ESPN booked an interview between Manziel and ESPN's Scott Van Pelt that became a featured story on *GameDay*.[11] Such is the power of ESPN that, in the vacuum of any strong, central authority of college sports, ESPN has come to virtually run every aspect of college football, right down to the life and death of conferences like the Big 12.

* * *

No one could have imagined just how much the *NCAA v. Board of Regents* decision would end up changing college football. The colleges who brought the suit simply wanted more control over the television contract, and for most of the 80s the CFA didn't offer much that was different from what the NCAA had been offering. But ESPN began offering more and more games to a nationwide audience, and in 1991 Notre Dame broke from the CFA and signed a contract to air its games nationally on NBC. The SEC and Big East followed suit in breaking from the CFA in 1995, and the floodgates opened.[12] College football was no longer a regional phenomenon played out on Saturdays throughout the fall; now it was a national sport played nonstop for three months.[13]

Before 1984, the national championship was a sideshow, something that people paid attention to and debated over but that was of secondary importance to people's regional rivalries and conferences. Every year the AP and coaches' polls were taken at the end of the season and whoever got the most votes was declared the national champion. It was an extra crown to wear at the end of the season on top of the prizes that really mattered, winning your conference or at least winning your rivalries and going to a bowl game. Now people could follow the best teams and conferences all season long, and the sport's basically nonexistent national championship, in a sports landscape littered with playoffs and certain championship games, became unacceptable. After co-champions were crowned in 1990 and 1991, the conferences that housed the CFA schools (the Big Ten and Pac-10 had separate contracts) plus Notre Dame formed the Bowl Coalition to attempt to force a "national championship game" between the top two teams in the nation. This was superseded by the Bowl Alliance in 1995 and finally by the Bowl Championship Series in 1998 following the CFA's demise. The BCS managed to get the Big Ten, Pac-10, and Rose Bowl on board, putting decades of the Rose Bowl's tradition of pitting Big 10 and Pac-10 champions against one another at risk (or throwing it out entirely every fourth year, at least at first), but meaning for once it could claim to really and truly be the true national championship of college football.

Except it wasn't. Despite many tweaks to the formula over the years, the BCS only focused attention on just how much college football wasn't set up to crown a true national champion. Controversy over the national champion – and if not that the championship game matchup, and if not that the teams in the other BCS bowls – occurred nearly every year of the BCS' existence, and beyond that teams from the so-called "mid-major" conferences were utterly precluded from playing for the national championship. Their ability to play at the level of the major conferences had long been in doubt, but a series of high-profile wins over major-conference teams on the occasions they did make BCS bowls made more people wonder whether they – or at least, the Mountain West's Utah, TCU, and BYU, and the WAC's Boise State – really did deserve to play for national championships. Calls for a true playoff mounted over the years, and eventually the commissioners relented, instituting the new six-bowl, four-team College Football Playoff system starting in 2014.

ESPN also created proliferation in the bowl system in general. There were only eleven bowl games in 1975, sixteen in 1983, and nineteen as late as 1994 (and eighteen for the next two years); for perspective, there were 107 teams in Division I-A in 1994, and any team with a winning record was eligible for a bowl, so you would expect 53-54 teams to be eligible for 38 invitations, most of them going to members of the power conferences. By 2000 there were 25 bowls; luckily Division I-A had grown to 116 teams as schools sought the vast amounts of television money pouring into college football's top division, so there were 58 teams to fill the 50 spots. In 2002 three new bowls were added, bringing the total to 28, but only one team had joined I-A, so the 58-59 teams now had to fill 56 spots - in other words, you were nearly guaranteed a bowl if you finished with a winning record. Then the NCAA decided to add a twelfth game to FBS teams' schedules and allow 6-6 teams to go to bowl games, meaning the way was clear for *more than half* of teams in FBS to go to bowl games; four games started up in 2006 alone, opening 64 bowl spots for the 119-team FBS. Then starting in 2013, a further flurry of teams entering the FBS ranks expanded their number to 127 by the 2015 season, with one in transition. Naturally, although the new CFP removed the BCS Championship Game from the slate of bowl games, several games lined up to take its place; in 2015, there were 40 bowls offering spots to 80 teams, but only 77 teams at 6-6 or better, necessitating the NCAA to allow 5-7 teams with strong Academic Progress Rate scores to participate in bowls.[14]

* * *

ESPN and NCAA v. *Board of Regents* also shattered tradition and stability in the very makeup and identity of conferences. In 1984, no major college conference had more than ten teams, and most of their lineups had remained the same for decades. But in the 1980s, many members of the Southwest Conference, made up mostly of Texas schools, were hit with NCAA sanctions, including SMU's infamous "death penalty" in 1987. In 1992, Arkansas left the SWC for the SEC, which had found a loophole in the NCAA bylaws that would allow it to split into two divisions and hold a conference championship game if it had 12 members, and so added then-independent South Carolina as well to hit the 12-team mark. That inspired Texas, Texas A&M, Texas Tech, and Baylor - half of the SWC's then-membership - to join with the members of the Big Eight conference, including Oklahoma and Nebraska, to form the Big 12 conference, complete with their own title game, starting in 1996. The remaining four schools fell into mid-major conferences.

Television money and the BCS meant your conference defined your prospects. The more appearances on national television your conference, and thus your team, had, the more visibility you had in the public eye and the more attractive your school was to recruits. And if your school was a member of one of the six "BCS conferences", the financial benefits couldn't be counted; the worst team in a BCS conference made much more money off the BCS than the best team in a non-BCS conference could ever hope for. Independence – there were 26 independent schools in the 1990 season, five of which were ranked, more than any single conference – was no longer a viable option unless you were Notre Dame, whose independence survived only because of a combination of being one of the five most storied programs in the country (if not *the* most storied), its alumni being dead-set against joining a conference for any reason, and the fact NBC was willing to pay it to air its games and only its games.

The Big East, a basketball conference that had been formed primarily with monetary considerations in mind and greatly benefitted from ESPN's money and exposure, only formed its football conference in 1991, adding five schools to fill out an eight-team football lineup, meaning only three of its prior members were members of the football conference. Though it enjoyed BCS status (thanks to initially having powerhouse Miami and later adding some of the better teams from Conference USA like Louisville), the Big East saw repeated defections to the ACC and the tension between its football and basketball sides ultimately caused it to split in two. Conference USA itself was only formed in 1996, composed mostly of independents whose previous non-football-sponsoring conferences had just merged. The WAC briefly expanded to 16 teams at the same time, taking in three of the SWC's refugees, but that proved to be too unwieldy a size and it soon broke in two, with half its schools leaving to form the Mountain West in 1999; the MAC, meanwhile, added two schools in 1997 and also started staging a conference title game.

By 2007 only three independents remained in FBS – Notre Dame, Navy, and Army – and Army had spent several years in Conference USA.

As early as 2004 Notre Dame and Navy were joined as the only independent schools by Florida Atlantic, which had just made the move to what was still called Division I-A and would join the Sun Belt the following year.

* * *

But 2007 would also completely and fundamentally redefine the nature of television money and make what conference you were in more important than ever. That year, the Big Ten, in association with Fox, launched the Big Ten Network. The Mountain West had launched its own network the previous year, but the BTN was the first network devoted to and owned by a major college conference. Much like the professional leagues that launched and controlled their own networks, the Big Ten would control half the advertising and subscription revenue for the network that aired their games, rather than just collect a rights fee. It was something ESPN didn't want to see catch on: shortly after the BTN was unveiled, ESPN effectively bribed the SEC away from starting their own network by paying them over two billion dollars over 15 years, taking control of virtually their entire inventory, and giving them one of the most widely-distributed syndication packages in the country.[15] Within three years, the BTN was making almost as much money for Big Ten schools as the conference's contract with ESPN, and all told, Big Ten schools were making $22 million each per year – more than *three times* as much as a school in any other conference, BCS or no, outside the SEC.[16] For all its tradition and history, the Big Ten was now, more than anything else, a moneymaking alliance.

With Big Ten schools making so much money, the Big Ten could have its pick of just about any school in the country, just about all of whom would leap at the chance to get in on the action. In the past, even when driven by television money, realignment had been based primarily on geography and rivalries: the four Texas schools were a natural addition to the Big Eight, besides the existing bitter rivalry between Texas and Oklahoma; the additions of Arkansas and South Carolina were natural outgrowths of the SEC's existing footprint; the Big Ten itself had added

Penn State, a natural fit to its Midwestern roots. Now all that mattered to schools was the value of the conference's television contract, and all that mattered to conferences was how an addition could maximize that value. If the Big Ten could add Texas and the bounty of television households it added to the Big Ten Network (and an inroad into those fertile recruiting grounds), or add a school that could help it make inroads into the lucrative New York market, it would. Too much "geographic fit" was now actually a bad thing, if it didn't help the BTN get into any new households.[17]

Even the Big Ten's role as a conference became less important to its identity than its television contracts. It could easily expand to a 16-team "superconference", maybe even 20, doubling the size of any conference from just a generation earlier, despite there still being only 12 games in an FBS season (and some of those necessarily nonconference games), to say nothing of the impact such an unwieldy conference would have on other sports, including basketball. Indeed, the Pac-10 came close to recruiting three Texas schools, Colorado, Oklahoma, and Oklahoma State to form a superconference itself, with the arrangement only falling apart when Texas A&M flirted with joining the SEC instead, Texas decided it didn't want to surrender all its television rights to the conference, and ESPN guaranteed the value of the Big 12's contract to keep it together, leaving the Pac-10 with only Colorado.

The Big Ten ultimately decided to add Nebraska, a team from a small market but a football powerhouse with a national following and another natural geographic and cultural outgrowth for the conference, while the Pac-10 added Utah to complement Colorado and, led by a new commissioner from outside the world of college sports, set out to completely reshape the market in its upcoming rights renegotiations, both in how much money it would rake in from the growing competition over sports on television and in the value they sought to bring to their own take on a conference network, and how much of that value they would retain for themselves.

* * *

Like the professional leagues discussed in the last chapter, college conferences have benefitted handsomely from the red-hot sports rights market. But there's a lot more at stake for college conferences in the age of realignment. More than merely being a windfall for a conference's schools, a good rights deal can make or break a conference's very existence – especially when TV rights control a school's ability to improve its facilities, lure the best staff, and attract high-profile recruits. If a conference finds itself too far behind its rivals in television revenue, it will inevitably fall behind on the field as well, which will only exacerbate the revenue gap when the TV contracts come up for renewal.

In 2009, the then-still-Pac-10 conference, at the time sitting at fifth place out of the six power conferences in television revenue and looking at poor timeslots for its games compared to other conferences, hired Larry Scott as its commissioner, who had just spent six years dramatically increasing the revenues of the Women's Tennis Association as its chairman. Scott, who first got on the Pac-10's radar when he told the ATP, the men's tennis tour, that it would have to merge with the WTA if it wanted Scott as its chairman, looked at the Pac-10 as a money-making enterprise first and foremost, more than a mere academic alliance, and as an outsider wasn't afraid to explore every possible avenue to increase the league's profile and revenue, even if that meant annexing six Big 12 schools.[18]

After the Pac-16 plan fell apart, Scott and his consultant, Chris Bevilacqua, who had helped to co-found CSTV, set about talking to school presidents about a new kind of rights deal, explaining how ESPN could use SEC games to propel distribution of its ESPNU and ESPN3 networks, potentially making that billion-dollar deal look like a bargain. Scott hoped to convince the schools to stop handling so many rights and marketing deals themselves and let the league handle them – an especially tall order for the Los Angeles schools, USC and UCLA, that were more valuable than the conference's non-California schools. The schools' athletic directors, Pat Haden of USC and Dan Guerrero of UCLA, eventually told Scott they would agree to centralize their rights and live with revenue sharing if he could deliver a rights deal worth $175 million per year.[19]

Scott felt that college sports rights were dramatically undervalued – ESPN's new *Monday Night Football* deal would pay $1.9 billion a year for 18 games, while ESPN was paying less than a billion for nearly 2,000 college football and basketball games. He also knew that Comcast had just bought NBC and was desperate for programming for its NBC Sports Network, and ESPN was just as determined to stop NBC from getting it. So he told ESPN, NBC, and Fox that he wanted a substantially higher price per game than was the norm – indeed, after the Big 12 was reported to be receiving a $90 million/year offer from Fox, Scott was emboldened to ask for the richest contract in all of college sports. And as much as they might not like it, they would not really have much choice but to go along, especially with Turner waiting in the wings as a potential fourth bidder.[20] Adding Colorado and Utah actually worked out pretty well for Comcast's interest, putting the Pac-12 in two states where Comcast was a dominant cable provider, something the Pac-16 plan wouldn't have done. ESPN, which had paid so much to stop the SEC from launching its own network, even told the Pac-12 that it was interested in partnering with them on a network, as were Fox and Comcast.[21]

Comcast told the Pac-12 it was willing to pay $225 million per year for the rights, $50 million more than Haden and Guerrero's demands, more than what the SEC was collecting from CBS and ESPN, and more than ESPN or Fox were willing to pay individually. At a time when rumblings about Fox starting a sports network of its own hadn't yet appeared, such a deal would give Comcast, seemingly the biggest contender to pose a threat to ESPN, valuable rights to a BCS conference and considerable momentum. Spurred on by Bevilacqua, ESPN's John Skipper contacted Fox's Randy Freer to talk about teaming up on a bid to snatch Pac-12 rights away from Comcast, one that would come out to $3 billion over 12 years, or $250 million a year.[22]

What made the deal look especially massive was that that $3 billion gave ESPN and Fox the rights to just 44 football games and 68 men's basketball games, just barely over the number of SEC football games alone ESPN and CBS were set to combine for. The Pac-12 had held fully half its football inventory for its own network. No partnership had been agreed to as part of the deal, and Scott and Bevilacqua were increasingly enamored of the idea of going it alone rather than forming a partnership, allowing them to keep all the money for themselves but exposing them to risk if the network underperformed and effectively tasking the conference with building its own media company. After securing distribution with the nation's cable operators (but not satellite providers, Verizon FiOS, or AT&T U-Verse), they announced the Pac-12 Networks, a collection of one national feed and six regional feeds, one for each of the conference's natural geographic rivalries.[23]

By the end of the network's first year, it had lined up distribution and sponsorship arrangements with Dish Network and U-Verse, was negotiating for a deal with Verizon, and posted a profit that emboldened the conference's confidence in its business model.[24] DirecTV was still holding out when it merged with AT&T in 2015, and the merger didn't do much to break the impasse, reportedly because AT&T wanted to expand its sponsorship and infrastructure relationship with the Pac-12 in a way that wasn't really possible.[25] Nonetheless, since launching the network the Pac-12 has raked in more revenue than any other conference, though that figure doesn't include production costs for the networks.[26]

Meanwhile, the Pac-12 deal marked the start of an unlikely partnership between ESPN and Fox that would have ramifications beyond one deal. The two entities would team up again and again, even after Fox made clear its plans to go after ESPN with the launch of Fox Sports 1. They struck a similar partnership around the Big 12 to what they had with the Pac-12, and as mentioned in the last chapter, teaming up in an ill-fated bid for English Premier League rights. After Fox won the rights to the World Cup, ESPN even invited them to study how ESPN produced the 2014 World Cup in Brazil.[27] More indirectly, ESPN's decision to lock up all its Major League Baseball rights may have also made things easier for Fox to retain its portion of the package by chilling NBC's interest. Whether because of Skipper's relationship with Freer, forged over the Pac-12 deal, compared with his chillier relationship with his counterparts at NBC,[28] or from a more business-oriented perspective, ESPN preferring that if it had a competitor, it wouldn't be one owned by a cable operator it would have to negotiate with for carriage,[29] ESPN effectively built Fox up as its own potential competitor at the expense of NBC.

* * *

The Pac-12's massive contract from ESPN and Fox, and the money they stood to make from the Pac-12 Networks, made the SEC's position look less enticing. The SEC was quite possibly the most popular college conference, certainly the most successful, but it was now stuck with a contract less valuable than what the Pac-12 had, and with the Big Ten Network becoming more successful at scoring distribution, it became apparent that the Big Ten would eclipse the network-less SEC in revenue as well, and pull away from it as the BTN's subscriber fees increased.[30] Texas A&M had flirted with joining the SEC before, but when it saw how much money rival Texas stood to make from the Longhorn Network, including from subscribers in its own backyard, it was more ready than ever to pull the trigger, and the conference was more than willing to expand into the nation's second-most-populous state and into the fertile recruiting grounds of a state where high school football is a religion if it would help provide suitable pretext to renegotiate its deal with ESPN. With Missouri, representing another populous state in new territory for the conference, also in the fold, the SEC went back to the negotiating table, and this time it was determined to launch a network, even if partnering with ESPN would be the only way to do so.[31]

The biggest obstacle faced by an SEC network would be the packages of games ESPN had sublicensed to Fox's regional networks and Comcast's CSS network. The CSS deal wouldn't expire until 2014, and Comcast reached out to ESPN about the possibility of partnering on an SEC network created by converting CSS, but ESPN was intent on running the channel on its own; the Fox deal would expire a year later, in 2015. The SEC, like the Pac-12, would also need its schools to give the SEC rights to games they had held themselves, including one football game per year per team offered on pay-per-view, and sold to various other agencies.[32] Once those issues were cleared up, in May 2013 the SEC and ESPN announced a 10-year extension of their existing deal, running through 2034, that included the launch of the SEC Network in August 2014, in time to pick up the expiring CSS package and by that point just 15 months away, and with AT&T U-Verse already on board.[33]

Other conferences also took notice of the Pac-12's deal. The ACC might be the single most valuable conference in college basketball – boasting the sport's most storied rivalry between Duke and North Carolina – but its football teams were well out of the national conversation, and that was what drove the value of its media rights deal in 2010. The ACC wanted $120 million a year from ESPN, substantially less than what the SEC had scored from ESPN and CBS, but ESPN wasn't even willing to pay that much.[34] Interest from Fox resulted in the package being bid up to $155 million a year, still well short of the SEC's haul with the Big 12 and Pac-10 still yet to step up to the plate. ESPN would control the ACC's entire bucket of football and basketball rights, instead of acquiring the basketball rights from syndicator Raycom; now Raycom would sublicense football and basketball games from ESPN.[35] Fox, which had previously aired a package of Sunday night basketball games on its regional sports networks, would no longer air ACC games; instead, Raycom would create a package of games it would syndicate to RSNs itself[36], and the Sunday night basketball package would air on ESPNU.[37]

After the Pac-12 and Big 12 deals made the ACC's deal look woefully small-time, the conference added Syracuse and Pittsburgh from the Big East with an eye towards renegotiating its deal with ESPN. They were able to increase their haul to a level on par with what the Pac-12 secured from Fox and ESPN, in exchange for additional inventory and adding four years to the deal, taking it through 2027.[38] But without a conference network, the ACC's revenue per school would remain well short of the Big Ten and Pac-12, so even after renegotiating the deal the conference continued to hold talks about launching a network, especially after adding Notre Dame in non-football sports. But ESPN, already in the process of getting the SEC Network, which would have considerable geographic overlap with an ACC network, off the ground, has remained lukewarm to the idea.[39] Another obstacle is the fact that, unlike in the SEC where ESPN handled all syndication itself, any ACC network would have to acquire rights to games currently in syndication back from Raycom, as well as the regional sports networks Raycom has also sold games to.[40]

The spectre of ESPN and TV money in general had hovered in the background throughout this round of conference realignment, but what happened in the ACC put it squarely in the foreground. ESPN saving the Big 12 was one thing, but the move of Syracuse and Pittsburgh to the ACC had the opposite effect on the Big East. That conference had accepted the broad outlines of a $130 million/year offer from ESPN, nearly quadruple what it had been getting, despite some concerns about leaving money on the table, but rejected it unanimously after the Pac-12's deal with ESPN and Fox was announced.[41] It then watched two of its most prominent schools defect to the ACC – and then listened to Boston College's athletic director make comments about the move that included the money line "TV – ESPN – is the one who told us what to do". The AD and all parties involved quickly backed off the comments, but for many bloggers it seemed an admission that ESPN was pulling all the strings on conference realignment and, in this particular case, may have given the Big East the proverbial "offer they couldn't refuse" and the departures of Syracuse and Pittsburgh were the metaphorical horse's head in their bed.[42] In the aftermath, the Big East effectively divorced from itself, the conference's Catholic schools seceding and winning the rights to take the Big East name with them, while the remnants that were left behind – those that didn't decide they didn't want to join after all – were left to take much less money from ESPN and go forward as the American Athletic Conference.

In this round of realignment, longstanding rivalries were thrown by the wayside in the name of chasing the almighty dollar. The "Backyard Brawl" between West Virginia and Pittsburgh was quite possibly the biggest college football rivalry in the Northeast, with only World War II interrupting it since 1919. Didn't matter: the Big 12 needed teams to make up for defections and decided West Virginia had the best combination of a strong school and a strong football program known nationwide despite being hundreds of miles from any other team in the conference, but of course had West Virginia stayed in the Big East it would have lost Pittsburgh to the ACC anyway. The "Border War" between Kansas and Missouri reflected a bitter rivalry between those states that dated to before the Civil War. Didn't matter: Missouri headed to the SEC to serve as a companion school to Texas A&M because the conference valued the population of the state and the value the school could bring being enough to make up for having another mouth to feed.

While all this was going on, the Big Ten, despite sitting at twelve teams (in a much-commented-on irony, the Big 12 sat at ten), the sweet spot to hold a conference championship game, decided they needed to expand further, and while in the past Penn State and Nebraska had been good cultural fits for the rest of the conference, this time they added Maryland and Rutgers, two schools on the eastern seaboard a good distance away from any other Big Ten schools, Maryland a rising basketball power that had recently started a budding intra-ACC rivalry with Duke but facing massive financial problems, Rutgers a school that had played in the first-ever college football game and had had a brief flowering of success but was still an uninspiring school with an apathetic at best fanbase. More than anything else, the addition of Maryland and Rutgers showed how the priorities had changed: more than anything else, it was about preventing the ACC, fresh off the Syracuse and Pittsburgh additions, from having an undisputed claim to the Northeast and putting the BTN on cable systems in the big markets of Washington, DC and New York City respectively. Sources suggested that if the BTN found its way on basic cable in those markets as well as the Philadelphia and Baltimore markets, totaling 15 million households, it could make as much as $200 million in additional subscriber fees, though it was highly unlikely the BTN would add all of those households and $100 million was more realistic.[43]

* * *

No sport has been influenced more by television, and specifically ESPN, over the last few decades than college football, and the proof is printed right on the tickets – or rather, it's in what's *not* printed: the kickoff time. The dates and opponents may be scheduled months or years in advance, but for most of the season, nearly every Saturday game in a power conference has its kickoff time up in the air, waiting for its TV partners to inform them what games will air when and on what networks, which occurs twelve days before game day, in some cases only six. Other sports and leagues have embraced this notion of "flexible scheduling", but none have taken it as far as college football, where fans (and coaches, and players, and school officials) have literally no clue when their game will kick off until less than two weeks in advance.[44]

College football, in other words, has become a made-for-TV event. After the *Board of Regents* decision, ESPN convinced smaller conferences to break from tradition and play games on Thursday; today, Thursday is a destination night populated mostly by the biggest conferences, and ESPN has populated most of the week from Tuesday to Saturday with college football. ESPN has even gotten into the business of playing matchmaker, finding schools with holes in their nonconference schedules and booking matchups between them to create attractions people will watch every week of the season. [45] More recently, ESPN has helped create a number of neutral-site games to raise the profile of the opening weekend of the regular season.[46] In an age where schools are constantly maximizing their wins in order to increase their chances of qualifying for bowls or playing for the national championship, such ESPN creations are just about the only place where quality nonconference matchups happen in the regular season outside of regularly scheduled rivalries. ESPN even owns the software used by virtually every school – and even competing networks – to schedule games, known as the Pigskin Access Scheduling System (PASS).[47]

The untold story of the "BCS busters", namely TCU and Boise State, was just how much ESPN had played a direct role in their success because of the schools' willingness to play games when ESPN asked them to, even if it fell in the middle of the week and heavily inconvenienced fans. Those games meant exposure, exposure that could be golden for a school that couldn't otherwise count on it. TCU was mired in the dumps a few years after being left behind by the Southwest Conference's collapse, but it built its way back up by accommodating ESPN and playing all throughout the week, even playing on Friday and thus competing against high school football, a religion in Texas. It paid off: even after the Mountain West left ESPN in 2006, TCU had such success it made repeated trips to BCS bowls, even the vaunted Rose Bowl, and eventually made it back to the big time, rejoining several of its fellow Southwest Conference-mates in the Big 12 in 2012, where they scored a Thanksgiving-night upset win over mighty Texas. [48]

Boise State followed the same formula upon joining the Western Athletic Conference, a conference that had weekday slots to fill on ESPN, in 2001, just five years after entering Division I-A. Before long, Boise State scored a landmark victory over Oklahoma in the 2008 Fiesta Bowl, and the WAC's rights payments from ESPN were the envy of most other non-BCS conferences. But once Boise State decided to make even more money in the Mountain West, it was the beginning of the end for the WAC. Its rights fee from ESPN plummeted to less than a third of its former value, and as the Mountain West lost teams to other conferences, it repeatedly raided the WAC's best schools, and soon the WAC became almost unrecognizable. [49] With only seven football-playing schools left, 2012 was the WAC's last year even sponsoring a football conference, and now as a non-football conference it's populated by such schools as Seattle University, which only recently even returned to Division I.

Louisville was one of the first to boast of the benefits ESPN provided it. In 1995, it had just joined Conference USA, and decided to construct a new, state-of-the-art football stadium to replace one that was pushing 40 years old. After finishing 1-10 in 1997, it hired a new coach that brought a television-friendly pass-happy offense to the football team, a ticket Boise State would also use to attract ESPN's attention. Conference USA signed a contract in 2001 that made it the first conference to colonize Tuesday and Wednesday nights for football, but most of its schools balked at the notion of going so far against tradition, at a time when even Thursday night games were only grudgingly accepted. Louisville, then mostly a commuter school, was not one of them. They played as many as five or six games in the middle of the week the first two years of the contract, or half of their entire schedule. The school effectively had to blaze its own trail to prepare for such an unusual schedule, but it paid off in exposure and in wins. Louisville became a national name in a way it never had been before, and by 2006 it not only found itself in a BCS conference (the Big East), it wound up going 12-1 and playing in (and winning) the Orange Bowl. Two Thursday night games against other national-caliber opponents that year became some of the highest rated college football games in the history of ESPN, convincing more prominent schools Thursday nights were worth the disruption.[50]

In 2014 Louisville joined the vaunted Atlantic Coast Conference, and with it came much more television money, four times what it was making in the Big East – but even beyond that is the ability to hit up local businesses and alumni for more donations to improve the athletic department's facilities off the back of its national-caliber programs. And on-field success has also built Louisville into an academic power as well: better students and professors, more students living on campus, more scholarships, more academic achievements.[51]

ESPN has also gotten into the business of owning many of its own bowls, because it knows how important bowl games are to filling up its December schedule, no matter what teams play in them. The nine bowls it owns are some of the lowest-rated of the season, and many might not exist without ESPN propping them up. But prop them up it does, because even the lowest-rated bowls still attract millions of viewers, viewers even ESPN would struggle to attract any other way, viewers drawn to the live programming that is ESPN's biggest strength.[52] Those millions of viewers are now one of the biggest rewards of trips to bowls, which can help a mediocre program draw recruits and stay where they are or even move further up the chain.

It's often been said that the vast majority of schools lose money on bowl games – the payouts to schools are wiped out by extravagant ticket guarantees and travel expenses. Even the biggest bowls can end up taking a program for a ride. But it's still easy to see why a school whose team goes 6-6 leaps at the opportunity to go to a bowl, even a tiny one: besides the exposure the game gives to recruits and others watching on television, it also serves as a vacation and reward for current players.[53] But Andy Schwarz, an economist specializing in antitrust law, says the supposed money-losing bowl enterprise is as much about creative accounting as anything else. In most BCS conferences, the payout for going to a bowl goes directly to the conference, not the school, to be distributed evenly among all members; the conference also pays for many of the expenses of a school that goes to a bowl game. As an example, though it was widely reported that Virginia Tech took a financial bath on its trip to the 2011 Orange Bowl, Schwarz calculates that the school would have made a $19.2 million profit if it didn't have to share revenue with the conference. Even with revenue sharing, though Virginia Tech claimed to take a $420,000 loss on the game, it actually made a $1.2 million profit – because Virginia Tech didn't even count its share of ACC bowl revenues, only the amount the ACC paid the school to cover expenses, effectively making it impossible for the school to make a profit on paper. (And that figure only includes Virginia Tech's share of its own Orange Bowl revenue – its profit doubles to $2.4 million when its share of other ACC schools' bowl revenues is counted.)[54]

In general, success in college sports has become a high-stakes game of blackjack for schools increasingly facing tight budgets and rising tuition costs. Every school seeks to match the rise of Boise State in football or Gonzaga in basketball, becoming a national name that makes money directly for the university and gets their name into the minds of potential students. Most end up losing money on the enterprise. According to the NCAA, of 345 Division I schools, only 24 end up making a profit, all FBS schools,[55] although this may undercount the total; a USA Today analysis of data from public schools for the 2013-14 school year found all 50 public schools in a power conference, plus five other Division I programs (two of them non-FBS), were self-sufficient before various payments to the school.[56]

* * *

With so much at stake, academics is increasingly left by the wayside. The NCAA's insistence on referring to its players as "student-athletes" – and its incessant commercials during the NCAA Tournament that, at one point, proclaimed that "most of [them] will go pro in something other than sports" – increasingly rings hollow. Once a way to help build healthy bodies as well as healthy minds, college athletic departments are now professional sports teams within academic institutions – except they don't have to pay their players.[57]

It's becoming increasingly difficult to defend the amateur status of student-athletes, once considered the core principle of collegiate athletics, when seemingly everyone else is making money from the system hand over fist. Not that student-athletes are necessarily coming away empty-handed; these days it seems like a program and its alumni should be assumed to be paying its players under the table until proven otherwise, and the NCAA seems to be a bunch of Keystone Kops, seemingly helpless to enforce its own rules (if not actively looking the other way) and its punishment seemingly arbitrary and capricious, if not completely random, when it does come.[58] Even Manziel, with his oil-money parents, ran into trouble with the NCAA when it was alleged he was paid for signing autographs. The NCAA has recently passed rules allowing schools to pay for a student-athlete's "full cost of attendance" above and beyond a player's scholarship, room and board, but for many, it's far from enough.

Ed O'Bannon was a star player on UCLA's 1995 national championship team before having a short NBA career. One day, he discovered that his likeness was being used on NCAA-branded video games, yet he wasn't seeing a dime in revenue from them. He brought a class-action suit against the NCAA that, along with others, could have a tremendous impact on the NCAA's money flow and how college athletes are treated. United States District Court Judge Claudia Wolken ruled in 2014 that the NCAA's rules on amateurism violated antitrust law and issued an injunction requiring member schools to pay their student-athletes, including name, image, and license rights. However, in 2015 a three-judge panel of the United States Court of Appeals, while upholding the underlying ruling, only required NCAA schools to pay for cost of attendance, on grounds that anything more would "transform NCAA sports into 'minor league status'", leaving unanswered the question of whether it already was.[59] Certainly the National Labor Relations Board seems to think it might be: in 2014, one of its regional directors ruled that Northwestern football players meet the definition of "employees" and so are allowed to form a union - implicitly allowing the same for all private universities - but the full board declined to hear the case due to its unprecedented nature and the fact it wouldn't apply to public schools.[60] Nonetheless, the fights have established an important beachhead for potential future legal challenges.

Lost in the increasingly heated debate over the treatment of student-athletes is the fact that the entire reason the NCAA's claims of being an educational, amateur enterprise ring so hollow, and why the whole issue has come to a head to begin with, is because of the millions if not billions of dollars pouring into collegiate athletics that have already wiped out the purity of college sports the NCAA claims to be defending in the eyes of all but the most idealistic, deluded, or self-interested observers. That money is coming in partly to fill time on ESPN and other networks, but it wouldn't be nearly as much if college sports weren't so incredibly popular, with college football providing America's most popular sports programming outside the NFL and Olympics.[61]

Similarly, the NCAA will point out that if football or basketball stars were really so exploited by not being paid beyond the costs of their scholarship, they could play in minor leagues or, in the case of basketball, abroad, or if they wanted to, the NFL or NBA could start their own developmental leagues akin to the minor league baseball system.[62] But players don't go to those leagues, and the NFL shut down its developmental league, NFL Europe, in 2007, because no one cares about them – nor do they really care all that much about minor league baseball, for that matter, despite its own history and tradition. But they care mightily about their college teams, and in turn, those audiences allow players to build their brand and starpower and grow their exposure in ways nothing else out there can.[63]

And the reason that people care so much about college sports is the connection between the team and the school that inspires people to root for "their school's" team regardless of who the players are and in spite of the fact all the players would much rather be in the NFL or NBA. That passion has inspired, and continues to sustain, a multibillion dollar industry that has severed the very connection that built it. It often seems that big time college athletes don't care one whit about the school they attend beyond the team that represents it and only go to class because the conditions of their scholarship demand it. They are only there to develop their game and their brand for the professional leagues.[64] In essence, big-

time college sports consist of developmental teams for the NFL and NBA
(that those leagues don't have to pay for) that have sold their naming
rights for a fanbase. Jerry Seinfeld's crack about how professional sports
fandom, especially in the post-free agency era, amounts to "rooting for
laundry", is all the more apt in modern college athletics.[65]

That professional sports leagues have managed to survive and thrive
in the post-free agency era in spite of Seinfeld's observation suggests the
same could be true of college athletics if the players were acknowledged as
paid employees. Still, what could happen if the façade were lifted on the
system and college sports became, if they weren't already, professional
teams whose only difference from the actual professional teams were the
quality and limited career of the players and the mostly arbitrary
connection to the school you attended? (At least professional teams have
to have some sort of connection to a location; many college teams play
well off-campus and some share arenas or fields with pro teams.) The
NCAA – and ESPN – might not want to find out.

5

King of Sports

M ARK SHAPIRO HAD HAD ONE OF THE most meteoric rises in the history of the cable business. He'd had an internship at NBC before he'd even graduated college in 1992, and by the following year he'd already risen to the rank of associate producer when ESPN came calling for him to serve as a production assistant on radio host Jim Rome's talk show for the launch of ESPN2. Within a decade, he'd been appointed head of programming for the entire ESPN family of networks at the age of only 32, tasked to reverse a trend of declining ratings. His solution was a motley collection of original programming unlike anything any sports network had seen before. Some of it worked (*Pardon the Interruption*), some of it didn't (*Beg, Borrow and Deal*).[1] One show, however, would underscore the challenges facing ESPN for years to come, well beyond original programming and well after Shapiro's departure, like no other: *Playmakers*.

Born of Shapiro's desire to target women and other casual viewers who might not have that much interest in sports, *Playmakers* was ESPN's first venture into scripted content - and still the only, for reasons *Playmakers* would make apparent. The series depicted the behind-the-scenes salaciousness of the fictional Cougars team, but the team's antics were anything but fictional: producer John Eisendrath based the series on the real-life problems besetting the National Football League at the time, but hidden behind a veil of fiction to avoid legal problems (the NFL logo and name were nowhere to be found). *Playmakers* covered everything from substance abuse and drug testing to spousal abuse and even homosexuality - issues no one was talking about in the context of the NFL at the time.[2]

While *Playmakers* may have been insulated from legal retribution, ESPN was far from insulated from the power of the NFL. Then-Commissioner Paul Tagliabue felt the show traded in negative stereotypes of African-Americans in general and NFL players in particular, without balancing it out with any sort of positive portrayal, and decided to go straight to the top, to then-Disney head Michael Eisner, informing him that as a contractual partner with the league, ESPN had "an obligation to present NFL football, NFL players, NFL teams in a way that makes it a valuable, credible, respected product...People want to watch sports where they can respect the athletes. This program leads them to have a view of the athletes that leads them to disrespect the athletes." Representatives of the league began insinuating that ESPN's deal to air NFL games would be at risk if the show continued to air, and despite being a critical and ratings success, ESPN decided to cancel *Playmakers* after one season. Shapiro later called it "the first time in history that a show was canceled for being too good."[3]

"Lawyers and doctors can get written about, cops can get written about, even the President of the United States gets written about. Powerful people get fictionalized on television all the time, and that's just the way it is. But for some reason, sports leagues can't accept that that is also going to happen to them," Eisendrath told journalists James Andrew Miller and Tom Shales in 2011 for their seminal history of ESPN, *Those Guys Have All the Fun*. "I think that the NFL, like Major League Baseball and the NBA, is a monopoly. A monopoly is by definition a bully. They can bully anybody they want. That's the power that they've been given. Maybe that's why there are very few things to which we grant monopoly status in this country."[4]

Two years after Eisendrath's comments saw print and a decade after the *Playmakers* scandal came and went, the NFL's power to bully ESPN reared its ugly head again in a much bigger way. Mark Fainaru-Wada was already one of sports journalism's most famous figures for his book *Game of Shadows* exposing the BALCO lab that had supplied steroids to numerous baseball players, including Barry Bonds; his brother Steve Fainaru had won a Pulitzer Prize for his work reporting on the Iraq War. By 2012, the two of them were reporters for ESPN's *Outside the Lines*, where their reporting on concussions and the NFL had led to a deal for a book, *League of Denial*, that would look into what the league knew about the concussion issue, when they knew it, and the steps they took to prevent anyone else from knowing. PBS' *Frontline* approached them to make a documentary based on the book, and their bosses at ESPN agreed, eventually reaching a deal that would apply *OTL* co-branding to the documentary.[5]

Though it wasn't originally their idea, the documentary became a point of pride for many at ESPN, something to point to if people questioned whether ESPN could truly report objectively about its own business partners. During a Television Critics Association panel to promote the documentary on August 6, 2013, ESPN senior coordinating producer Dwayne Bray explained that ESPN "is sort of a bifurcated company. You do have the business partners on one side, but you also have the editorial production side. And our journalism has been very strong on this issue and so strong that we partner with *Frontline*. *Frontline* is about as ~ it's the gold standard, I've said before, of long form investigative documentaries....we made a conscious decision when we were presented with this opportunity to literally get in bed with *Frontline*."[6] But that same panel would ultimately start a chain of events that would render Bray's words hollow.

At the panel, Frontline unveiled a trailer for the documentary with the tagline "Get ready to change the way you see the game" and several provocative quotes from people interviewed for the documentary, both regarding the topic of concussions ("I'm really wondering if every single football player doesn't have this") and the power of the NFL ("You can't go against the NFL, they'll squash you"), which made high-ranking executives at ESPN and the NFL uneasy.[7] Two weeks later, ESPN announced it was removing the *OTL* branding from the documentary, citing concerns over its lack of editorial control over the finished product, despite the partnership being in place and the documentary in the works for over a year.[8] ESPN President John Skipper later explained that he felt the trailer was too sensationalistic and the comment about "every single football player" suffering brain damage was too "over-the-top".[9]

All parties involved vehemently denied that the NFL had pressured ESPN into pulling its name from the documentary, but the following day the *New York Times* published a report suggesting that was exactly the case, noting that a week before the decision to pull ESPN's branding came down, commissioner Roger Goodell and NFL Network president Steve Bornstein met with Skipper and ESPN executive vice president for production John Wildhack for lunch near NFL headquarters, where the NFL executives voiced their displeasure at the direction of the documentary.[10] According to Miller, who contributed to the piece, the NFL didn't directly put pressure on ESPN to pull their name from the documentary, but expressing their displeasure was all that was needed.[11]

Both PBS and the Fainarus insisted the documentary would go forward completely intact with or without ESPN branding, and not only did ESPN insist it would continue to report hard on concussions but when the time came for the documentary to come out ESPN actually promoted it quite heavily on its airwaves, but the damage had been done.[12] So far as most observers were concerned, ESPN had chosen its business relationship with the NFL over its journalistic integrity, much as it had chosen that business relationship over *Playmakers*. Whether or not the NFL could have actually afforded to seriously punish ESPN for either incident was an open question; no other entity was likely to pay nearly as much for *Monday Night Football* as ESPN, and in the case of *League of Denial* ESPN may have been motivated as much by the desire not to inflict collateral damage on college football, which it's so reliant on for its programming schedule, as any pressure on the NFL's part.[13]

Still, both incidents showed that for as much power as ESPN wields over college football, it may well be at the mercy of the almighty NFL. NFL games are the single biggest reason ESPN collects such massive subscriber fees from cable customers, and that's an apple cart ESPN is loath to upset. The same goes, to a lesser extent, for the NFL's other television partners, which include three of the biggest media companies in the world. By 2012, NFL games drew audiences over 150% higher than primetime shows on the broadcast networks, meaning NFL games were, ultimately, the heart of the other three broadcast networks.[14] Put them together, and it's easy to see how the NFL might be able to, to some degree, shield itself from criticism from the entities most able to have that criticism heard. Perhaps the trailer was right: "You can't go against the NFL, they'll squash you." If the NFL could squash ESPN going against it, what chance would anyone else have?

* * *

A year after the *League of Denial* controversy, the NFL once again came under fire for its treatment of a sensitive topic regarding its players, and while it may not have posed the existential threat of the concussion issue, it proved to be all the more public. On February 15, 2014, Ray Rice, then the star running back for the Baltimore Ravens, and his fiancée Janay Palmer were arrested for a fight at an Atlantic City Casino, what Rice's attorneys characterized as a "minor physical altercation". Four days later, gossip website TMZ released security footage of Rice dragging Palmer's limp body out of an elevator, making Palmer look much more like a victim than an equal perpetrator, and police acknowledged the existence of additional video showing Rice knocking Palmer unconscious. Rice and Palmer were married a little over a month later, after the charges against Rice were upgraded to aggravated assault from simple assault and the charges against Palmer dropped. Rice subsequently reached an agreement to enter a pretrial intervention program that could result in the whole thing being removed from his criminal record.[15] Any meaningful punishment would now be in the hands of the NFL, which under Goodell's tenure had showed little hesitation in punishing players severely for merely being accused of a crime, over and above whatever the legal system came up with.

But in July, Goodell announced that Rice would be suspended only two games – for many, a laughably short span of time given the severity of the crime and Goodell's use of far more punitive suspensions for seemingly lesser crimes, including a full season's suspension for Cleveland Browns running back Josh Gordon for marijuana possession. The outcry over Goodell's punishment of Rice led Goodell to adopt a new policy on domestic violence that would include a six-game suspension for the first offense and a lifetime ban for the second, but that outcry was nothing compared to that which flared up just after the first week of the season, when TMZ revealed more security video, this time depicting an argument between Rice and Palmer in the elevator ending in Rice punching Palmer and knocking her out. Even though this second video only added visuals to what was already known and reported, it still underscored the insufficiency of the league's initial punishment, and left Goodell to feebly extend Rice's suspension to the entire season - *after* the Ravens had already released him.[16]

The Ravens and the league claimed they hadn't seen the second video until TMZ released it, in spite of the league's efforts to obtain it, and Goodell claimed Rice had been "ambiguous", if not outright lying, about what happened in the elevator before his initial suspension. But almost immediately, holes started appearing in the league's version of events. The Associated Press claimed that someone at the league *did* receive the video showing what happened in the elevator and left a voicemail calling it "terrible", while ESPN reported that Rice had been honest and forthright with both the team and the league about what happened, something Ravens GM Ozzie Newsome also affirmed.[17] Reporters had claimed the league had the tape even before its public release and given accounts of it accurate enough in the details to raise further questions. The Rice controversy also put a spotlight on how the league treated others accused of domestic violence, including the Carolina Panthers' Greg Hardy and the San Francisco 49ers' Ray McDonald, and even other crimes, such as Minnesota Vikings' star running back Adrian Peterson coming under fire for child abuse.

Were it not for TMZ, the Rice case might have gone much the same way as the Hardy and McDonald cases initially seemed to go, and whatever problem the NFL had with domestic violence would have remained completely unknown. The most damning report to come in the aftermath of the second tape, the report that someone had received it and left a voicemail about it, came from an entity with perhaps the least interest in maintaining a relationship with the league. NFL reporting is generally a far less weighty affair, focusing on who's getting signed, who's injured, and other information about the games themselves, feeding the league's quest to be a 24/7/365 sport and a voracious appetite among fans for information that might help them get an edge in their fantasy leagues. The NFL has spent lavishly on esteemed reporters to work for their own web site and network, and even the top reporters who work for other outlets - ESPN's Adam Schefter (formerly of NFL Network), Fox's Jay Glazer, *Sports Illustrated's* Peter King (who appears on NBC's weekly pregame show) - often work for outlets that themselves have every incentive to "protect the shield". The Rice scandal only seemingly caused many of these reporters to turn on the league because the league had itself fed them a narrative that quickly proved untenable, forcing them to choose between the league and their own reputation; King had initially reported that the league had seen the elevator video, but after it was released and the league denied seeing it before, King claimed his source only assumed the league had obtained the video and that King himself never followed up on it, making him look like a chump and a shockingly shoddy reporter before the AP even affirmed King's initial report. Even then, criticism on the largest platforms was strangely muted. On the pregame for the first game of CBS' brand-new *Thursday Night Football* package, days after the release of the elevator video, host James Brown gave a critically acclaimed speech urging greater attention on the issue of domestic violence and the larger issue of society's treatment of women - but one devoid of any criticism of any specific people, certainly anyone in the league offices.[18]

As the controversy grew and grew, and calls mounted for Goodell to resign or be fired, no matter how bad it got Goodell remained justifiably confident his job was in no realistic danger. He maintained the support of the owners throughout everything. But the reason the owners continued to stand by Goodell as the controversy swirled, by all accounts, was because of all the money the league was making under his watch, including a 10-figure deal with DirecTV for the Sunday Ticket out-of-market package signed shortly before the release of the elevator video. But as we've seen, any commissioner of any reasonably popular sports league could make millions of dollars in TV revenue in their sleep in this day and age - billions, in the case of the absolute ratings juggernaut that is the NFL. Nor could Goodell take credit for said unspeakable popularity; the groundwork for that was laid by Goodell's predecessors in the commissioner's office, Pete Rozelle and Paul Tagliabue, by forces outside the league's control, and by an unassuming figure in the league offices, predating Goodell's tenure, who may wield more power over the league's network partners than anyone else in the league.

* * *

One of the most powerful men in sports or television is someone even hardcore fans of both have probably never heard of. He is not the head of a major sports league or someone with a high position at a major network, yet he can almost singlehandedly control the fates of three of the four major networks as well as ESPN. That means executives from the four companies, men most would consider extremely powerful in their own right, regularly make trips to his office every year to beg him to give them what they want. He is Howard Katz, the NFL's senior vice president of broadcasting and media operations, and he is the man who sets out the NFL's schedule each year.

The NFL is unique among American professional sports leagues in that it spreads out its TV rights across four different partners, accounting for (almost) every single one of the league's games. NBC airs games on Sunday nights, ESPN on Monday nights, while CBS and NFL Network share Thursday nights. The remaining games go into one of two Sunday afternoon windows (except on Thanksgiving), with CBS airing AFC games and games with an AFC road team, and Fox airing NFC games and games with an NFC road team. On any given week, either Fox or CBS will have a doubleheader, allowing them to show two games in almost every market, one at 1 PM ET and one at 4:25 PM ET; the other network will have a "singleheader", airing one game in each market at either 1 PM or 4:05 PM ET. (The NFL does not allow a network to air a game opposite a home game for a market's local team, so if the local team happens to be playing a home game on the singleheader network, the doubleheader network will only show one game in the timeslot the local team isn't playing in. In addition, both networks have doubleheaders in the last week of the regular season.) Generally most games will kick off at 1 PM ET with only a smattering of games in the late slot (often as few as one on the singleheader network and two on the doubleheader), mostly games hosted by West Coast teams and one game of national interest to showcase in the late doubleheader slot.

Thus every network has a place to showcase the most attractive games to a national audience, and every network wants to make sure they have games that are as attractive as possible. NBC's Sunday night package is supposed to be where all the biggest, marquee games go, but considering how much CBS and Fox pay for NFL rights they're not about to let NBC hog all the biggest games all of the time. They'd also point out that the late doubleheader game on either network generally actually gets slightly bigger ratings than *Sunday Night Football*, for reasons ranging from the tougher competition in primetime to the presence of multiple games engaging multiple fanbases.[19] (NBC can counter with its platform being truly national with no regionalization.) Meanwhile, ESPN may try to lobby for a better schedule for its Monday night games, but realistically even at best its package is generally treated as second-class to the Sunday games on the widely-distributed broadcast networks and doesn't have the flexibility to move away from a weak matchup late in the season that NBC has, but it still works to get as much out of its NFL package (and as much fuel for its subscription fees) as it can, looking for big-market teams that can pop ratings and teams that might not be valued that highly by broadcast networks but have the chance to have hugely successful years.[20] The Thursday package, meanwhile, is heavily restricted by the NFL's desire to limit and balance the amount of disruption its mid-week location causes to team schedules by having each team play there once, limiting its ability to house showcase games.

Balancing the concerns of all these entities, not to mention other concerns of the teams, is Katz's job,[21] and during Super Bowl week, the NFL's biggest showcase and the biggest spectacle of the year on all of television, what should be the high point of the year for whatever network shows it, all the network executives make sure to make time to meet with Katz and make their case for the games they wish to have for the upcoming season and why they should be the ones to get them.[22] (The games themselves are effectively determined as soon as the regular season ends, but when those games take place are not.) Katz takes all the requests from the networks and the teams, including stadium availability that the NFL may not have complete control over, as well as principles the NFL itself prefers to follow, and inputs them all into a series of high-tech computers running the NFL's own proprietary software, which runs through trillions of possible combinations virtually nonstop from the end of the season. Katz and his team assess thousands of potential schedules looking for the best one, then start the computers again looking for an even better one, until Katz and the league are satisfied with what they have.[23]

Katz has proved to be a masterful schedule maker since his first season at the helm in 2005.[24] Katz was originally the chairman of Don Ohlmeyer's Ohlmeyer Communications until Ohlmeyer sold it to ESPN in 1993, at which point Katz took an executive position there; considered by many to be Steve Bornstein's successor as the head of the company, when he didn't get the job he became head of ABC Sports in what he perceived to be a step up, only to find that ABC Sports was well in the process of withering away to nothing and becoming overshadowed by ESPN.[25] Longtime Fox Sports president David Hill credits Katz's broadcasting background for ensuring the creation of schedules that benefit all the league's TV partners every week of the season, "showcas[ing] the best of the league in every available window", and credits him more than anyone else for the league's unmatched and continued ratings dominance in the face of declining ratings across the rest of television, a sentiment former CBS and NBC heads Sean McManus and Dick Ebersol concur with.[26] Under Katz, the NFL, already the most powerful brand in American sports, has become the ultimate reality show, a seventeen-week drama playing out across four or five networks (depending on how you count NFLN), followed by four or five more weeks during the playoffs (depending on how you count the Pro Bowl), with must-see television in every important timeslot; almost without exception, the games that can produce the highest ratings are placed in the timeslots with the biggest audiences. Monday Night Football may have become a classic piece of Americana during the 70s and 80s, but it's under Katz that Sunday Night Football has become the most-watched show on all of primetime television, even as it's lagged behind Fox and

CBS's late-afternoon packages. College football may be a made-for-TV event, but it has nothing on the NFL in terms of either ratings or just how much it's oriented for television right down to the kickoff times of every single game.

The structure of the league's TV contracts has increasingly aided the development of a TV-friendly schedule. Flexible scheduling allows NBC to keep its schedule interesting and important as the season goes along, avoiding lackluster matchups and showcasing games that may have flown under the radar when the schedule was set, while CBS and Fox can choose to showcase any game it has the rights to in the late time slot and can "protect" one game each in five out of six weeks, from the eleventh to the sixteenth week, from moving to NBC and thus ensuring marquee games for their own packages deep into the season.[27] The most recent TV contracts, which came into effect in 2014, provide even more flexibility: NBC can flex a limited number of games as early as the fifth week of the season, while CBS and Fox can "cross-flex" a limited number of games between them.[28] The NFL's commitment to flexible scheduling, so important to the made-for-TV drama the league provides, is made possible by its TV deals that give its national TV partners rights to all its games; other professional leagues must balance their national TV deals with making sure local TV partners receive valuable games as well, and as we'll see in the next chapter, local TV deals are plenty lucrative in their own right.[29] The principles the NFL has used to set the schedule itself has also helped: in recent years the NFL has scheduled all divisional matchups in the last week of the regular season, which due to the structure of the league's tiebreakers, maximizes the number of games with importance to each team, especially with games with impact on one another placed in the same time slot when possible, maximizing the drama as late into the season as possible and inflating ratings even higher.[30]

* * *

Nothing shows the power of TV money to shape a sport quite like the NFL. Forget the introduction of the Red Zone channel or the recent move to 4:25 ET starts for its late-afternoon doubleheaders. Consider that, in the face of the ongoing controversy over concussions and player safety more generally, the league has expanded its Thursday-night slate, previously eight games, to a full season, meaning every team will have to play after only three days' rest once a season, and continues to toy with the idea of expanding the regular season to 18 games, meaning more wear and tear on players' bodies. But two more games means collecting another pound of flesh from the TV partners, and an expanded Thursday night slate means the possibility of selling some of it to a cable outlet – possibly one like Fox Sports 1 or NBCSN that would fall over itself to get the valuable programming of the NFL, even if the quality of play on Thursday nights has tended to be poor.

The NFL first tested the waters for selling an eight-game package of Thursday night games in 2011, in the middle of a contentious lockout of the players, in hopes that new revenue could help smooth out the bad feelings engendered by the lockout. Comcast, which had previously sought the package of games that went to NFL Network in 2005 for Versus, and Turner, looking to put TNT back in the NFL game or add sports programming to truTV, were considered the front-runners, while Fox's efforts to put games on FX were hindered by clauses in its contracts with cable operators hindering Fox's ability to raise FX's rates. ESPN was also expected to take a look, and even Viacom was speculated to get in the game on behalf of Spike TV. All told, analysts expected an eight-game Thursday night package to fetch $700 million a year, and the league was reportedly interested in using the talks to shore up NFL Network by giving management responsibilities or even an ownership stake to the winning bidder.[31]

But after renewing its *Monday Night Football* deal with ESPN, commissioner Goodell put Thursday night talks on the back burner, in part because it wasn't able to get an 18-game schedule, meaning any new Thursday night games would have to be taken out of CBS and Fox's packages in the next negotiations with them. Any talks about a new Thursday night package would be put on hold for at least a year and wouldn't take effect until the new TV deals did in 2014. But most analysts were confident when the talks did resume, they would pick up where they left off with Comcast, Turner, Fox, and ESPN all expressing interest.[32] If anything, by that point Fox Sports 1 would become a reality, making Fox that much more credible a contender.

But the following February, the league announced that NFL Network's slate of games would expand to 13 games, effectively taking up most of the season, which seemed to put the kibosh on selling part of the Thursday night package to another partner, at least for the foreseeable future. Steve Bornstein, the head of NFL Network, cited two reasons for the move: breaking Time Warner Cable and Cablevision's ongoing reticence to carry NFL Network, and establishing the popularity of a full season of Thursday night games. Splitting the package would probably cut off any chance of getting the holdouts on board, and while the existing games were quite popular, their numbers were a shadow of what ESPN's Monday night games were getting.[33] The more popular the NFL could establish Thursday night games were, especially once football fans developed more of a habit of tuning in earlier in the season, the more money they could squeeze out of a bidding war for half of the season, and getting more widespread carriage for NFL Network would be key for that.

Time Warner Cable and Cablevision did get on board by a few weeks into the 2012 season, and the NFL finally opened bidding for an eight-game Thursday-night package in January 2014. But there were some big surprises. For one thing, any deal would only be for a single year. For another, the NFL mandated that anyone broadcasting the games simulcast them on NFL Network, diluting a lot of the value of the package.[34] Perhaps more surprising, although Turner was one of the entities asked to bid (but quickly rejected), the league made known its preference to air games on a broadcast outlet, not a cable channel, if possible – cutting out the possibility of benefitting from cable subscription fees or of propping up the networks that were a major source of interest in the package in the first place.[35] Fox would be bidding for its broadcast outlet, not FS1; NBC would be bidding for its broadcast outlet, not NBCSN; even ESPN, an outlet with substantially larger distribution than NFL Network even with Cablevision and Time Warner Cable on board, would be bidding for ABC, not ESPN. Once again, the NFL's concern was to increase the prominence of the package rather than completely cash in right away, while keeping one foot in the territory of keeping the full season of games on NFL Network. Even with Time Warner Cable and Cablevision on board, Thursday night games were averaging less than ten million viewers – which by the NFL's standards is unacceptably disappointing – and the league wanted to make Thursday as much of a destination night as possible, and that meant the maximum audience that only a broadcast network could provide. With the right partner, the league could even raise the profile of NFL Network as a whole beyond the Thursday night slate.[36]

Ultimately, CBS won the bidding as much to avoid having to compete with Thursday night games on a rival network, which could dilute their top-rated Thursday primetime slate, than to have the game themselves.[37] The cincher for CBS' bid was their promise to produce the games that aired on NFL Network exclusively on top of their own, allowing the NFL to save on running its own production unit, and put their lead broadcast team of Jim Nantz and Phil Simms on all 16 games. That, coupled with CBS' Thursday primetime strength and commitment to promote the games, convinced the NFL to pick their bid over bids that actually offered slightly more money; notably, insiders thought NBC, which had the most to gain and could synergize not only with their Sunday night package but with their games on the opening week of the season and on Thanksgiving, had the inside track to win the bid before it was actually announced.[38]

Things did not work out quite as the NFL hoped; the first few games of the new package were highly uncompetitive blowouts, and CBS' eight-game slate fell substantially short of the 12 rating the network guaranteed to advertisers, which the league offices took as a sign that ratings could get higher if the games were more competitive.[39] (One could argue that the uncompetitive games were a natural result of the short rest before Thursday night, but the NFL did seem to get particularly unlucky: it set a new record for the biggest blowout in the history of the franchise three weeks in a row.)[40] The league has exercised its one-year option and given CBS and *Thursday Night Football* another year to establish its bona fides before taking the property on the open market under the same terms as before, including the same one-year option.[41] They were rewarded with a comeback win by Peyton Manning and the Denver Broncos over the

Kansas City Chiefs in the package's first game of the season, which attracted the highest audience in the package's history of over 21 million viewers, peaking with nearly 23 million – still below what NBC's Sunday night package drew the first week.[42] All told, the seven games to air on both CBS and NFL Network the first two months of the season averaged 17.6 million viewers, a jump of 5% and nearly a million viewers from 2014 – amounting to a jump of only six-tenths of a ratings point to 10.9, still over a point behind what CBS guaranteed that first year.[43] Still, reports are the NFL is ready to take the package to the open market this offseason, and Fox, CBS, NBC, and Turner have all voiced interest that could bring the value of the package to over $600 million, double the $300 million CBS paid this year.[44] Stay tuned.

6

All Sports are Local

J EREMY LIN IS NOT SOMEONE YOU WOULD initially tag as a basketball superstar. Born of Taiwanese immigrant engineers, Lin, at six-foot-three, doesn't come off as the most athletic or flashy of players, and for a long time he wasn't the best shooter either. Nor does he fit the quintessential "jock" stereotype: besides his ethnicity, he was raised in Palo Alto, in the shadow of Stanford University, where he had a GPA over 4 in high school, and graduated from Harvard with a 3.1 GPA and a degree in economics.[1]

Lin led Palo Alto High to a 32-1 record and an upset state championship win over national powerhouse Mater Dei in 2006, but every college team he spoke with, including Stanford (literally across the street from Palo Alto High), wouldn't give him a scholarship, telling him to try out as a walk-on (someone who tries out for the team as a normal student). Even Harvard assistant coach Bill Holden wasn't impressed by his first impression of Lin, only warming to him when he saw Lin play a competitive game in an AAU tournament against Division I prospects.[2] Holden convinced him to come to Harvard, and Lin made the All-Ivy League first team his last two years, including finishing as one of 11 finalists for the Bob Cousy Award for the best collegiate point guard his senior year, and had the highest career steal total in Ivy League history.[3]

Again overlooked by NBA scouts, Lin was signed as a free agent by the Golden State Warriors, in what some termed a marketing stunt for Lin's hometown team, becoming the first American-born player of Taiwanese or Chinese descent in NBA history, and only its fourth Asian-American. But after a season where he saw less than twenty minutes of game action, he was cut in December 2011. The Houston Rockets picked him up but cut him after twelve days, and the New York Knicks subsequently claimed him off waivers, but had him play in the NBA's Developmental League in January. By February, after the Knicks returned him to the active roster, Lin was sleeping on his brother's couch, wondering whether he would make it to February 7, when his league-minimum contract, less than $800,000, became guaranteed.[4]

On February 4, with the Knicks ravaged by injuries and sitting at 8-15, Lin came off the bench in a game against the then-New Jersey Nets, and proceeded to score 25 points, an NBA record for a player from Harvard, and 7 assists. Two nights later against the Utah Jazz, Lin became the first player to score 28 points and record 8 assists in his first NBA start since Hall of Famer Isiah Thomas in 1981, becoming, almost literally overnight, a nationwide, and soon worldwide, sensation known as "Linsanity". Lin became a point of pride for Asian-Americans across the nation, and his devout Christian faith tapped into that demographic as well, but Americans of all stripes found themselves falling in love with his underdog story.[5] Lin propelled the Knicks to a seven-game winning streak, including a game against the Lakers where he outplayed future Hall of Famer Kobe Bryant, and 109 points over his first four starts, the most by any player since the ABA-NBA merger.[6]

Two games after the streak ended, star Carmelo Anthony, who had been out over the entire course of Linsanity to that point, returned to the Knicks' lineup,[7] and while the Knicks went 2-2 over their first four games with Anthony and Lin playing together,[8] they proceeded to go on a six-game losing streak afterwards, costing coach Mike D'Antoni his job, with interim replacement Mike Woodson initially planning to de-emphasize Lin.[9] A little over a week later, Lin began feeling soreness in his knee, an MRI revealed a tear, and Lin eventually opted to have surgery, ending his season and marking the final end of Linsanity.[10] That offseason, Lin became a free agent and everyone expected the Knicks' profligate owner, James Dolan, to match any offer he was given, no matter how lavish. Rockets GM Daryl Morey, upset over letting Lin slip through his fingers, offered a three-year, $25 million contract including a "poison pill" giving Lin $14 million of that money in the third season, the Knicks opted not to match, and just like that, Linsanity had left the Big Apple.[11] Lin never quite reached the heights of Linsanity again, spending most of his tenure in Houston as a backup to James Harden, who the Rockets acquired shortly before his first season, and was traded to the Lakers before the poison-pill season, where he struggled even more in an offense that didn't suit his skills.[12] In the 2015 offseason, he signed a two-year, $4.3-million contract with the Charlotte Hornets, after getting rebuffed when he offered to return to the Knicks.[13]

In the end, no one may have benefitted more from Linsanity than Dolan. When Lin first came off the bench, the MSG network that carries the team's games, and was at the time part of the same business unit as the Knicks, had been absent from Time Warner Cable lineups for the entire year to that point, and with the Knicks' struggles there was no real reason for that to change. TWC claimed that MSG, after initially calling for a 6.5% hike in subscriber fees TWC might have been able to live with, got greedy and began asking for a 53% increase over fees that were already sky-high at an estimated $2.48 for MSG and $2.17 for sister network MSG Plus, something MSG denied, and also tried to use the negotiations to prop up the music network Fuse it also owned.[14] With fans across New York clamoring for the sides to reach a resolution so TWC customers could see Linsanity on TV for themselves, TWC and MSG reached an agreement on February 17. The following August, in MSG's first full quarterly report since the TWC agreement became official, the company reported a 20% rise in affiliate fees to $167 million, mostly on the back of the deal.[15] If one assumes the company would have only seen the 6.5% increase TWC initially prepared to accept, then MSG reaped a nearly $19 million windfall from Linsanity that quarter alone from TWC subscription fees alone, on pace for over $75 million a year for the entire life of the deal – more than the entire contract Lin received from the Rockets. Dolan could have easily matched the Rockets' offer, but chose not to – because he was already set to make many millions off Lin for years to come.

* * *

In 2014, shortly after Major League Baseball's All-Star break, sports business journalist Maury Brown looked at the ratings for baseball games on regional sports networks and discovered something astounding. In 12 of the 24 US markets where at least one baseball team's RSN wasn't mired in carriage disputes with providers - exactly half - baseball games were the most-watched programming in all of primetime television from the start of the season up to that point. Another seven, bringing the total to 19, ranked in the top three in their respective markets, meaning they beat at least half of the Big Four broadcast networks, and in every single one of the 24 markets, baseball games ranked among the top eight shows in all of primetime (The Chicago White Sox, the only team not mired in a carriage dispute to fall out of their market's top eight, finished ninth, but share their market with the Cubs.)[16] When he looked again a year later, the White Sox were the only team not in a carriage dispute outside the top *seven* shows in primetime, and in all 24 markets, baseball games on regional sports networks were the most popular programming on cable - and even in Houston, the one market where carriage disputes kept baseball out of the top spot, the team was still #2 in cable and #7 in all of primetime. In fact, the White Sox were the only team outside the top four spots on cable even *including* teams in carriage disputes, with the Oakland Athletics the only other non-carriage-dispute team outside the top two.[17]

Throughout this book, we've been discussing the value of live sports on a national basis, how it built ESPN into a powerhouse and has major media companies scrambling to imitate it, but to put a twist on a common phrase from another field, all sports (or at least all professional team sports) are local, driven by passion for local teams more than by interest in the league as a whole, and Brown's data suggests that, at least in the vast majority of the home markets of Major League Baseball teams (and admittedly, during the summer when entertainment programming is less potent), local teams and the regional sports networks that show them are more popular even than the almighty ESPN - and might be more of a motivation for fans to sign up, and stay signed up, for cable. The money regional sports networks collect in subscription fees backs this up as well. As we've seen, MSG was charging cable companies over twice as much for *each* of its networks as any national cable network that wasn't ESPN or TNT even before the TWC dispute, and its rates were actually par for the course - SNL Kagan estimated that regional sports networks *averaged*

$2.49 a month in 2012,[18] more than twice the $1.21 TNT was charging as the second-most expensive non-3D national cable network.[19]

The power of regional sports networks was already recognized in the early 90s, when some wondered if the various RSNs could challenge ESPN's dominance if they found some way to come together, especially when Liberty Media consolidated its ownership of the Prime network by buying out its partner, Bill Daniels, and turned its eye to the SportsChannel joint venture of Cablevision and NBC, which, if combined, could amass nearly as many subscribers as ESPN had at the time.[20] Challenging ESPN was Rupert Murdoch's plan when he partnered with Liberty to rename the Prime networks as "Fox Sports Net" and started airing a national baseball game of the week across them on Thursdays, and then took a 40% stake in the SportsChannel networks and brought them into the FSN fold as well.[21]

But the thing that was supposed to be such an asset for Fox Sports Net, its wall-to-wall coverage of local teams, ended up being a liability. Carriage of national programming was heavily dependent on what each local network happened to have on that night, which was merely an annoyance for talk or highlight shows, but which proved fatal for the network's ability to rope in national sports events. The Pac-10 conference signed a deal for FSN, not ESPN, to be its national television partner, and lived to deeply regret it.[22] Even if Fox could have controlled every regional sports network in the nation (or at least, RSNs covering the entire nation), Fox Sports Net could never be a truly national service. The regional sports market centered around local teams is fundamentally different from the national market centered around entire leagues.

But while the regional sports market may not be as obvious, it may be all the more cutthroat. There is no ESPN-like monopoly here; despite an abortive effort to launch "ESPN West" around the Anaheim Angels and Mighty Ducks in the 90s, ESPN has absolutely zero presence in the regional market (unless you count the Longhorn and SEC networks).[23] Fox tried to build such a monopoly and even seemed to have succeeded for a time, but it took a lot of work to get there and it was rather short-lived, as the FSN empire slowly lost teams and networks as the 2000s progressed. The biggest reason for that collapse was the gigantic step the bombastic owner of America's richest sports team took in 2002, a step that proved to have national implications and may be a bigger part of his legacy than the many, many other things he did on and off the field.

* * *

By all appearances, New York Yankees owner George Steinbrenner was on top of the world. The days when his mismanagement of the team, including his repeated hiring and firing of Billy Martin as the team's manager, was so notorious as to result in his getting barred from baseball were a distant memory. Now the Yankees, with a 1996 World Series championship under manager Joe Torre already in their pocket, had a team so dominant it was almost on par with the legendary "Murderer's Row" teams with the likes of Babe Ruth and Lou Gehrig. The team's success vindicated Steinbrenner's 1988 decision to accept a massive $493 million offer to televise Yankees games on MSG, a deal some said was so irresponsible it would destroy the still-nascent cable industry as well as baseball itself with a Yankees team richer than any other club could dream of.[24] But it was not all joy in Mudville. The expiration of the MSG deal in 2000 was looming. A titanic clash between billionaires was approaching, one that would set off a chain of events that would not only make the 1988 deal look like pocket change, but fundamentally change the economics of sports.

Cable operator Cablevision already owned the SportsChannel Networks when it and partner ITT bought the Madison Square Garden corporation in 1995, giving it ownership of the arena, Knicks, Rangers, and the MSG Network, ending a long fight over carriage of MSG on Cablevision systems. Two years later, with ITT facing a hostile takeover attempt from Hilton Hotels, Cablevision outbid numerous other media companies for their share of MSG, giving Cablevision and its head Charles Dolan, James' father, a monopoly over the seven MLB, NBA, and NHL teams in the nation's largest media market, and accelerating existing plans to merge SportsChannel with the MSG Network.[25] The Yankees, though, had the power to singlehandedly change that calculus if it decided to reach a deal with ESPN or Time Warner.[26]

One year after Cablevision picked up full control of MSG, and with Steinbrenner struggling for cash flow and wondering about his ability to pass the Yankees down to his heirs, *Newsday* reported that Cablevision was engaged in talks with Steinbrenner to buy the Yankees.[27] Those talks hit a stumbling block in part because Steinbrenner wanted to remain in control of the club for at least 15 years, and because Cablevision alienated MSG executives by pitching Steinbrenner on control of the Knicks and Rangers.[28] After about a year of off-and-on talks, Steinbrenner instead merged the Yankees and the then-New Jersey Nets to form a company called YankeeNets, creating powerful leverage in TV negotiations with Cablevision by allowing any potential competitor to MSG to have two teams and year-round programming instead of just one. Uniquely, the Nets' owners would maintain control of their team just as Steinbrenner did his.[29]

Cablevision offered the Yankees a whopping $100 million a year to renew their rights, but Steinbrenner wanted control of the product and its distribution. He was enamored of the idea of launching a regional sports network that was completely controlled by the team.[30] He attempted to move the team's rights to a company 95% owned by the team and 5% owned by a subsidiary of IMG,[31] but MSG won an injunction on grounds that it was an attempt to circumvent MSG's right of first refusal.[32] The two sides continued negotiating well into the fall of 2000, when Steinbrenner went back to IMG and struck a one-year deal without a right of refusal, threatening to leave Cablevision helpless to prevent the Yankees from leaving MSG after the 2001 season even if they matched.[33] MSG did match, but also filed suit in order to preserve their right of refusal.[34] The two sides eventually reached a settlement resulting in MSG getting the rights for 85 games for free while YankeeNets retained the remaining 65 non-nationally televised games to sell to an over-the-air station or MSG, but also had the right to pay MSG $30 million to take back their 85 games in order to launch a network,[35] which they did.[36]

On one level, the Yankees' decision to launch their own network wasn't any different from what MSG had always been with the Knicks and Rangers, but the Yankees were a far more powerful brand than either of them, and what they did had implications throughout all of baseball (to a much greater degree than the Boston Red Sox, which had owned 80% of New England Sports Network since the 80s, but only put about half their schedule on what was a premium network at the time).[37] YankeeNets sold 40% of the network, known as YES (Yankees Entertainment and Sports), to a group of investors including Goldman Sachs for $340 million (making more than ten times the money back they paid MSG right from the start), implying the whole network was worth $850 million, which may have been an understatement.[38] YES would also ask for $2 per subscriber, the biggest rate of any RSN at the time in the nation's largest market[39], a rate so high some cable operators would end up dropping MSG and still raise their rates.[40] The new network, as it turned out, would be announced the day before 9/11.[41] That tragic day caused the nation to rally around New York, and for a couple months at least, around the Yankees, normally the most hated team in baseball outside New York. But YES laid the foundation for the Yankees to be hated more than ever.

For baseball commissioner Bud Selig, the news couldn't come at a worse time, when the sport was embroiled in controversy over the yawning chasm between the haves and the have nots (a controversy which meant the prospect of a labor stoppage would haunt YES' first season, and a chasm which the Oakland Athletics' ability to overcome would turn into the basis for the book and movie *Moneyball*), and there was no bigger have than the Yankees – just the $30 million in ransom they paid MSG was worth more than five teams' combined TV contracts.[42] Steinbrenner could insulate much of his revenues (an estimated $9.8 million the first year) from whatever revenue sharing scheme Selig and the other baseball power brokers cooked up, since they accrued to YES and to YankeeNets, not the Yankees themselves.[43] Pretty much every team in baseball found themselves wanting to follow the Yankees' lead just to keep up.[44] That meant the implications of YES for the cable industry spread beyond New York and to every cable system in the country, all of which wanted YES to fail, lest all of them find themselves dealing with their own YES's.[45]

The Yankees were about to go toe-to-toe with Cablevision, as well as Time Warner Cable and Comcast, one more time, and the stakes would be bigger than ever – and the time frame tighter than ever with the new network launching in just six months. But the allure of the Yankees would prove too powerful. Despite Cablevision and Time Warner Cable wanting to relegate YES to a premium channel or pay tier,[46] YES eventually reached a deal with DirecTV, allowing Yankees fans stuck with a cable provider not carrying YES to put up a satellite dish to get the Yankees, and Time Warner Cable and Comcast soon followed suit. Only Cablevision continued to hold out for the network's first year, and even they got on board for Year 2 after submitting to binding arbitration.[47] As if the success of YES wasn't bad enough, the arbitration panel required Cablevision to place YES on expanded basic – Cablevision had offered its own New York-area RSNs as premium channels, and placed YES on a tier with them the first year – effectively killing the distribution of RSNs anywhere but on widely distributed packages.[48]

Pandora's Box was now wide open. Cable operators were right to fear that others would follow in YES' footsteps. The success of YES influenced all the in-house outlets to follow, be they league-owned networks like the NFL Network, networks owned by college conferences like BTN, or other teams' in-house organs.[49]

* * *

YES didn't just undermine baseball's efforts at revenue sharing because of its ownership structure, or even because of the size of the market it could lean on. The combination of the size of the market and the depth of its dedication to the Yankees created a perfect storm that made YES a must-have for DirecTV, Time Warner, Comcast, and ultimately, Cablevision. The depth of Yankees fandom was something MSG knew well: even with the Knicks and Rangers, it had less than two million subscribers before the 1988 Yankees deal, but by the time YES launched it had ballooned to eight million.[50] Teams in smaller markets, that might have less passionate fanbases, could more easily be bullied by cable operators with national footprints, meaning YES's strategy was less viable, even discounting the smaller scale, for small-market teams. The Kansas City Royals and Minnesota Twins learned that the hard way: over the next two seasons, they respectively launched the Royals Sports Television Network and Victory Sports One, but neither was able to gain any carriage. VS1 folded six months into the 2004 season, and the Royals shut down RSTN and went back to Fox in 2007.[51] But one of the cable operators YES had just gone to a bruising war with had a different idea, one that would make it a beneficiary of the Yankees' strategy instead of a victim.

Comcast was already in the regional sports network business. After purchasing a majority interest in the Philadelphia Flyers and 76ers, they moved their rights and those of the Phillies off of the premium PRISM service and the basic-cable SportsChannel and onto a new service called Comcast SportsNet in 1997, which became, at the time, the most expensive regional sports network in the country at $1.50 per subscriber.[52] And in 2000, Comcast purchased Home Team Sports, which carried the major-league teams in Baltimore and Washington, from Viacom, and rebranded that as Comcast SportsNet as well.[53] Comcast greatly expanded its footprint with the acquisition of AT&T Broadband, the shell of the legendary TCI empire, in 2002, and wanted to extend its nascent RSN empire as well.[54]

Fox still dominated the RSN market, but rumors swirled that the Dolan family, whose Cablevision was still Fox's partner, wanted to get out of the cable business, so Comcast reportedly worked on a deal that would have Comcast purchase Cablevision's stake in FSN, and the five former SportsChannel networks it shared with Fox under the Regional Programming Partners banner, for Cablevision stock Comcast owned. Three of those networks, in Chicago, the San Francisco Bay Area, and New England, were in areas Comcast served, and a fourth, in Florida, could potentially complement the CSS network it co-owned with Charter (the fifth was in Ohio, and MSG and FSN New York were separate from RPP).[55]

The Chicago network's relationship with its teams wasn't in the best shape. The city's two baseball teams, the White Sox and Cubs, had their eyes on the success the Yankees were having with YES and were considering breaking away to start their own network, exercising an out they had with FSN at the end of 2003. Jerry Reinsdorf owned both the Sox and basketball's Chicago Bulls, so the Bulls were likely to go where the Sox went, and the hockey Blackhawks would represent valuable additional programming for any new network. The four of them had been in discussions about forming a new network even when they signed their

Fox deal in 1999, and Comcast had already been in discussions with the Tribune Company, the Cubs' owners, about such an enterprise earlier in the year.[56] Were the four teams to form their own network, they could pool risk across the four of them and have a better chance of making it than any of the baseball teams that had gone it alone.[57]

Comcast's talks with Cablevision morphed into offering to buy just the channels in Chicago and San Francisco, conditioned on the Chicago teams staying with the network.[58] But on September 29, 2003, the four Chicago teams informed FSN of their intention to leave in a year's time. A spokesman for the White Sox claimed it was just to leave all their options open rather than wait for the natural expiration of the contract, but FSN Chicago general manager Jim Corno got the impression from the teams' communication that their relationship had come to an end, and some felt Comcast was already deep into negotiations with them.[59] Comcast could form a new RSN directly with the teams, or buy FSN Chicago at a discount and sign up the four teams that way.[60] Two months after the split, the teams and Comcast announced they would take the former option. Comcast would reportedly own 30% of Comcast SportsNet Chicago, with the remaining 70% divvied up among the teams.[61]

Meanwhile, the Sacramento Kings had a problem of their own. Despite being one of the most successful teams in the NBA and a perennial title contender, their TV deals with FSN Bay Area and local broadcast stations brought in only $5 million a year, including less than $1 million from FSN Bay Area and limited ability for promotion due to that network's favoritism towards the Golden State Warriors.[62] After that deal expired, the Kings spent the 2003-04 season without a cable partner entirely, with just 56 out of 82 games on the area's ABC affiliate.[63] But before the 2004-05 season started, the team reached an agreement to start another new RSN with Comcast.[64] And barely two weeks after the new Chicago RSN launched, Comcast announced it would team up with Time Warner Cable on a new RSN with the New York Mets.[65]

The arrangement the Chicago teams, and eventually the Mets, reached with Comcast established the future of what the team-owned network would look like going forward: a partnership with a larger media company that could secure carriage on at least one system and possibly more, though some teams would continue to go it alone, a trend that would ultimately unravel what Fox tried to build with Fox Sports Net. It also established Comcast as what would be the biggest beneficiary of this trend, a pattern it repeated in numerous other markets across the nation. Though Comcast didn't have the ambitions to create a national "network" of the sort Fox had tried to build, preferring its RSNs to have more of a local focus, nonetheless Comcast left 2004 with the foundation of an empire that could go toe-to-toe with Fox - an empire, incidentally, that would ultimately include Fox's Bay Area and New England RSNs.[66]

* * *

Houston is one of the ten largest media markets in the country, but when it comes to sports rights it has long been in the shadow of the larger Dallas-Fort Worth metroplex. Houston-area sports teams had long aired, along with other Texas teams, on one of the oldest RSNs in the country, founded in 1983 as Home Sports Entertainment, later becoming a member of the Prime network and a founding Fox Sports Net member. As with the Chicago-area teams, the Astros and Rockets had flirted with the idea of leaving FSN Southwest before, announcing plans to leave FSN in 2002 and form their own Houston Regional Sports Network, but Fox sued the teams for breach of contract, and the teams ended up signing a new contract that resulted in the creation of a separate FS Houston RSN in 2005. But as with the Chicago teams, the prospect of following the path of so many teams before them and owning and running their own RSN was too juicy to ignore, and the contract contained an out clause after the 2012 season that seemed like a golden opportunity. It didn't hurt that the dominant cable provider in the area was Comcast, the company that was making a mint across the country by giving ownership stakes in RSNs to teams - or that AT&T, hoping to juice up interest in its U-Verse service, had been expressing its own interest in starting an RSN. AT&T attempted to partner with Dish Network on a Detroit-area RSN in 2008 and was looking to try the same tack in Houston.[67]

It wasn't hard to figure out that the most likely outcome would involve the Astros and Rockets leaving for Comcast and their own co-owned RSN. Looming over Fox's head was the fact that just about every team in the country wanted to follow the path blazed by the YES Network and paved by the Chicago teams, there were no shortage of companies willing to help them accomplish it, and quite a number of those teams had their rights coming up for renewal in the coming decade. Fox had long resisted giving up a stake in any of their regional sports networks, but now, at the other end of I-45, it pulled an about-face. In September 2010 Fox signed a 20-year contract with the Texas Rangers, starting in 2015, that tripled the team's rights fee – and gave the team a 10% stake in FS Southwest. It would stand as Major League Baseball's largest television deal for all of a month, until the Astros and Rockets announced their deal with Comcast. A year later, Fox gave a 25% stake in Fox Sports West and a $95 million rights fee to the Los Angeles Angels of Anaheim, in spite of the Angels' second-class status in the Los Angeles market, showing the Rangers deal wasn't an aberration for Fox. Even small market teams would be able to cash in, despite the failures of the Royals and Twins a decade before – the higher penetration of digital cable and increased competition from Verizon's FiOS and AT&T's U-Verse created a friendlier marketplace than in 2003. The San Diego Padres, wrapping up their contract with Cox Communications, finagled a $50 million annual rights fee and 20% stake in a new regional sports network from Fox.[68] The money involved was rising so fast that teams that had recently signed TV deals were regularly the ones most active in the free agent market. The Rangers received a $100 million upfront payment as part of its deal with Fox and promptly spent it on Japanese pitching phenom Yu Darvish; the Angels signed Albert Pujols, the best player in baseball during his tenure with the St. Louis Cardinals, to a 10-year, $240 million deal after signing their deal with Fox.[69]

Throughout all of this, there was another team that seemed poised to cash in most of all – though it didn't exactly have the looks of it at the time. While the Astros and Rangers were cashing in, the once-storied Los Angeles Dodgers were becoming a laughingstock, as the team and its finances became embroiled in a contentious divorce between owner Frank McCourt and his wife Jamie. The McCourts had long talked about the creation of their own regional sports network similar to YES, but the path to such a network wasn't clear; it would be difficult to find another team to provide year-round programming for the channel, and since Fox already owned two networks in the market it would be hard to find a partner for the enterprise.[70]

But in early 2011, Time Warner Cable, the Southland's dominant cable provider and a company known more for its fights with sports networks than its ownership of them, stunned the sports world with a deal to start a new regional sports network to carry Los Angeles Lakers games for the next twenty years – as well as a second RSN, the first Spanish-language RSN in the country – after a whirlwind three-month negotiation. TWC was now firmly established alongside Comcast as a player for sports rights in markets where it owned cable systems, and the Dodgers would seem to be marquee programming to provide year-round content for the new network, or anything else TWC had up its sleeve.[71]

One of the many things that turned up during the divorce proceedings was Frank McCourt's use of the Dodgers to pay off his personal finances, and McCourt's attempt to use the club's deal with Fox to shore up its finances served as an example of it in real time; at one point McCourt attempted to reach an agreement for a long-term extension, but Selig rejected the deal after McCourt attempted to condition a divorce settlement on it,[72] noting that the deal's structure would effectively "mortgage" the team's future to alleviate McCourt's short-term financial desperation even though the settlement was set to potentially trigger a court-supervised sale of the team that meant McCourt wouldn't own the team at any point of the deal.[73] That set the stage for the ultimate indignity, as the Dodgers declared bankruptcy; they tried to get the bankruptcy court to allow them to sell TV rights during the bankruptcy proceedings, but this time they attempted to circumvent Fox's exclusivity, leading them to file a suit as well, while MLB made clear it would reject any deal. [74] After reaching a divorce settlement, McCourt reached an agreement with MLB to sell the team at auction, with McCourt likely needing the club to fetch $1 billion to pay off all his debts – more than the then-MLB record $845 million paid for the Chicago Cubs. But for a team that was once one of baseball's marquee franchises in the nation's second-largest market about to take advantage of the television rights boom, $1 billion would be a quite reasonable starting point.[75] The team eventually sold for *two* billion to a group backed by Guggenheim Partners and with Los Angeles sports legend Magic Johnson as its public face.[76]

It initially looked like the Dodgers and Fox would come out of their exclusive negotiating window with a 25-year, $6 billion deal that could have included a Dodgers-branded channel.[77] Part of the reason the deal was never reached was a disagreement with Major League Baseball over whether or not guaranteed dividend payments in the channel should count towards the rights fee and thus towards baseball's revenue sharing plan.[78] Eventually the Fox deal fell apart and the team reached an agreement with Time Warner Cable to launch a new channel wholly owned by the club; although TWC wouldn't have an ownership stake, it would pay nearly $8 billion over 25 years, assume most of the risk, and handle ad sales and negotiations with other distributors, a structure designed to avoid triggering Fox's matching rights by having the team technically launch a channel on its own without most of the drawbacks of that approach.[79] Los Angeles would also become the only market in the top six not to have any locally-produced baseball games on over-the-air television, despite having more antenna-users than any other market, as the new network would keep all the Dodgers' games for themselves and not show any on local station KCAL as they had in seasons past.[80]

But both the Houston teams and the Dodgers may have proven the unwitting victims of a turn in the regional sports network market. CSN Houston launched at the same time as the Lakers network at the start of the 2012-13 NBA season, with Lin, prior to the Rockets acquiring Harden, at the center of ad campaigns for the network, but while TWC SportsNet quickly signed up most of Los Angeles' major providers (with Dish being the only major exception) within the first month of the season,[81] CSN Houston wasn't so lucky, remaining carried only on Comcast and a handful of smaller providers, not any satellite providers or Verizon or AT&T – and it didn't help that providers like Suddenlink and DirecTV were reaching agreements with Comcast for the NBC stable of channels but not CSN Houston.[82] The standoff continued into the spring and the start of baseball season, to the point that the network offered a free preview for the month of May, but only a few small providers took up the offer.[83] Instead, by June DirecTV and AT&T felt they had weathered most of the things that would have put the most pressure on them with little effect on their subscriber numbers, in fact seeing increases compared to the network's October launch, and now had most of the leverage in the dispute. Indeed, Comcast and the Rockets were reportedly pushing to reduce the channel's $3.40 asking price, one of the highest in the country, but the Astros were resistant.[84] That made the situation in Houston one with tremendous ramifications for the rest of the country. By September 2013, before the network was even a year old, Comcast filed an involuntary Chapter 11 bankruptcy petition against the network, blaming "total gridlock" among the parties owning the network.[85]

According to the Astros, the network was solvent as far as they knew, but the team hadn't been paid rights fees since June and Comcast filed for bankruptcy days before a team-imposed deadline to pay up the fees to avoid the Astros taking their rights back and selling them to another party. But according to Comcast and the Rockets, that threat *was* a threat of insolvency; if the Astros took their rights back, the Rockets would be obligated to do the same, which would result in the network being shut down and its assets being liquidated in a "fire sale". Comcast also accused the Astros of "sabotaging" the network by refusing to accept the lower-priced carriage agreements, but the Astros claimed that those agreements would have resulted in the network operating at a loss, which would have eventually forced the Astros to give up their stake in the network. The Astros saw themselves as having more at stake in the network's success than anyone: the Rockets' rights fee was enough to put them in the upper echelon of NBA teams, but in baseball, the lack of a salary cap and greater popularity of team-owned networks made the stakes much higher, and meant the Astros actually needed the network to turn a profit to be competitive. That meant the network's structure, which gave the Astros veto power over affiliation agreements rather than allowing Comcast and the Rockets to outvote them, was in their view necessary to protect the team's value and their investment in the network.[86] The bankruptcy judge allowed the Astros to negotiate with third parties on a new business plan for the network,[87] which the Rockets took over after the Astros sued Comcast.[88] A week into the new year, the Rockets asked for and received an extension to pursue "significant momentum" in talks with potential partners,[89] and as close as a day before a scheduled hearing believed they were close to a solution, but in February the judge officially placed the network under Chapter 11 bankruptcy protection, while raising the possibility Comcast could still be shut out of the network entirely.[90]

All of this amounted to a bad omen for SportsNet LA, as Time Warner Cable, fresh off bruising negotiations for the Lakers networks, was now about to ask Los Angeles-area cable and satellite providers to pay hefty carriage fees for a sports network once again – a reported $5 a month expected to escalate to $8 over five years, reportedly a record and, according to DirecTV chairman Mike White, more than twice the rate of other baseball teams – and those providers reportedly were balking before negotiations even began over the channel.[91] They were willing to offer the network on a sports tier or as an a la carte offering, but TWC said that would not be an option.[92] Many expected the dispute to resolve sometime around Opening Day or a few weeks thereafter, as had been the case for the Lakers network.[93]

But instead, the opposite happened, as on April 4, mere days into the season, TWC announced that DirecTV had "ended serious negotiations" over the channel, though DirecTV denied it.[94] That would mean legendary Dodgers announcer Vin Scully, a DirecTV customer, wouldn't be able to receive the network in his own home. With other providers also holding out, it also raised the prospect that the two sides would remain at odds in the long term, especially if DirecTV was using the Dodgers to take a stand against the cost of sports rights.[95] By May, DirecTV began offering partial refunds to subscribers upset over the lack of Dodger games.[96] But DirecTV, like Dish with the Lakers network[97] and like the providers in Houston, was seeing little customer turnover as a result of not carrying SportsNet LA,[98] and even had some customers contacting them in support of their position.[99] By late July, the tide had turned so much that TWC stated its willingness to send the case to an arbitrator.[100]

Time Warner Cable was expecting providers in the Los Angeles area, not exactly known for the rabidity of its sports fans, to pay for two of the ten most expensive regional sports networks in the country, each of which offered only one major league team, when virtually all of the other RSNs in the top ten offered at least two.[101] The end-run around Fox likely effectively precluded putting Dodgers games on the Lakers network, and while Dodgers president Stan Kasten made noise about "the best way to serve the fans" being to run a network with "Dodger-only content 24-7",[102] what it ultimately meant was that people in the Los Angeles area were being shut out of Dodger games because of cable operator unwillingness to carry two expensive RSNs and Time Warner Cable Deportes on top of two Fox Sports RSNs and Pac-12 Networks.[103] "It is really hard to understand why everyone needs their own channel when they didn't need one before," Andy Albert, senior vice president of content acquisition for Cox Communications, told the Los Angeles Times.[104]

What made the SportsNet LA dispute especially ominous was that the Dodgers, unlike the struggling Astros or Lakers, had an exciting, playoff-bound, potentially World-Series-contending team with potential stars like Yasiel Puig or Clayton Kershaw, not to mention that each season for the legendary Scully could be his last. If none of that could propel carriage for SportsNet LA, it wasn't a good sign for other teams looking to cash in with lucrative regional sports network deals that now looked considerably shakier. (In fact, the network ended up simulcasting the final six games of the season on local broadcast station KDOC.)[105] The CSN Houston and SportsNet LA disputes, which resulted in the Astros and Dodgers being the two teams that failed to break into their respective markets' top nine shows in primetime when Brown did his assessment of MLB ratings, looked to be a turning point in cable operators' struggle over the cost of sports programming, something they had complained about since ESPN started collecting subscription fees and which had become an increasingly pressing issue, as they finally became confident they could call the bluff of expensive regional sports networks.[106]

It eventually became apparent that converting CSN Houston to a straight rights-fee model, with the Astros and Rockets giving up their stakes in the network, would be the easiest way to fix the network's problems, with Comcast expressing interest in taking full control of the network and AT&T and Fox also making pitches.[107] In August, the network filed a reorganization plan that would make the network wholly owned by AT&T and DirecTV, by that point in the process of their merger, and cancel the interests of the network's current partners; with AT&T and DirecTV in the fold and Comcast's existing carriage agreement being honored, the network, now expected to be converted to DirecTV's Root Sports brand, would finally have carriage in a majority of Houston-area homes.[108] After Comcast agreed to allow the plan to go forward while Comcast focused on recovering a $100 million startup loan it had given the network,[109] CSN Houston became Root Sports Southwest on November 17, ending its run at just over two years.[110] No such relief would be forthcoming for SportsNet LA, however, as the dispute raged on into a second season, only breaking when the proposed Charter-Time Warner Cable merger came with an immediate carriage agreement for Charter's existing LA-area customers,[111] and still no other carriers have crossed the line and reached an agreement, even as Scully has admitted the 2016 season will likely be his last.[112]

For many, the CSN Houston and SportsNet LA disputes could mark a turning point in the debate over sports on television, one with the potential to upend everything discussed in the preceding chapters. It marks the potential popping of the long-inflating sports rights bubble and the undermining of the entire business model on which it rests, as the cable industry for the first time failed to accept the constant increase in subscription fees that has fueled the entire machine. Though it's a trend that's being accelerated by continuing technological change, in many ways it's the inevitable end result of the tension between cable operators and programmers over subscriber fees, a tension that goes a long way in explaining the AT&T-DirecTV and Charter-TWC mergers, as the importance of sports to the television industry and its reliance on subscriber fees has come to take over the entire media landscape.

7

Fighting for Scraps

CHET KANOJIA HAD BEEN THE HEAD of Navic Networks, a startup offering set-top box technology that tracked audience demographics and allowed networks to tailor their advertising to them in real time. Navic's data showed that at any given moment, roughly half of cable TV viewers were watching local broadcast stations. Kanojia reached the conclusion that if people could reliably get broadcast television signals on any device with the ability to time-shift shows and enjoy the social nature of the Internet, it might make people more willing to drop cable and satellite TV. So after selling Navic to Microsoft in 2008, Kanojia formed a new startup, Bamboom Labs, promising to stream free, over-the-air signals over the Internet to connected devices.[1]

It would not be easy. Copyright laws give the holders of copyright to TV programs the exclusive right to determine how to distribute it. Bamboom could not simply put up an antenna and retransmit the shows it picked up to customers without obtaining a license from the networks first. Numerous other startups, such as Ivi TV, had tried to do the same thing and wound up on the wrong end of infringement lawsuits that put them out of business. But Kanojia felt he had found a solution that would pass legal muster: in each market, he would put up a huge array of teeny-tiny antennas and rent them out to customers. The customers would be in control of the antenna, not Bamboom, so the situation would not be fundamentally any different from someone putting an antenna on their roof. Furthermore, programming wouldn't be distributed outside the local market and there would be severe restrictions on customers' ability to share programming or watch it on multiple devices. Kanojia had reason to believe the argument would pass legal muster: Cablevision had won a court ruling supporting a similar system for its cloud-based DVR service. It was enough to convince venture capitalists to give Bamboom $4.5

million in seed financing in April 2011, allowing it to begin beta tests in the New York City area.[2]

Ten months later, Bamboom, now named Aereo, scored a major coup when IAC/InterActiveCorp gave it $20.5 million in further funding, allowing it to prepare for a full-fledged launch in New York in March 2012. IAC's chairman, Barry Diller, joined Aereo's board of directors and became the public face of the company. Diller had played a key role in the launch and rise of the Fox network and was now prepared to go on the front lines in a bitter legal fight against his own creation, hoping to free the networks' content from, as he put it, the "closed cable-broadcast-satellite circle" that refused to let any of its content out to Internet streaming services.[3]

As Aereo prepared to launch in full in New York in March 2012, broadcasters and other businesses representing all four major networks, Univision, and PBS filed two suits in federal court in New York, alleging copyright infringement.[4] In July, a judge denied a motion for a preliminary injunction that would have forced Aereo to shut down while the case was litigated, stating that the plaintiffs had not shown their likelihood to win on the merits of their case and that there was reason to believe the Cablevision precedent would hold.[5] Broadcasters promptly appealed, and Cablevision itself filed a brief laying out what it saw as the differences between its own case and Aereo.[6] But a three-judge panel of the Second Circuit agreed with the lower court.[7] Ultimately over two years of litigation in New York and elsewhere ensued, where the underlying cases were rarely if ever actually resolved because broadcasters refused to accept judges' rulings just to keep the lights on at Aereo while they were, eventually resulting in broadcasters appealing the case – still only looking for an injunction – to the Supreme Court, a move Aereo welcomed as a means to hopefully put a stop to broadcaster litigation.[8]

The legal question was whether Aereo was engaged in a "public performance" under copyright law, but the case would really turn on the question of what Aereo actually was. Aereo claimed it was little more than a mechanism for the delivery of the over-the-air broadcast content from personal antennas people already have the right to receive for free – no different from setting up an antenna and attaching it to a TV and

Slingbox, only over a longer distance. But from a consumer point of view, there wasn't much difference between picking up broadcast content from a service like Aereo or from a cable operator. So from the broadcasters' point of view, Aereo was effectively operating as a cable operator that had found a loophole in the rules to allow it to claim not to be. At the top of their mind was the prospect that cable operators might decide to set up Aereo-like systems to get away with not paying them either[9] - and on that front Aereo was not helped by the brief in its defense by the American Cable Association, a consortium of smaller cable operators, that suggested its members might consider an Aereo-like system[10], or its own flirtations with adding cable content if it won. Aereo claimed it was trying to comply with the law, not circumvent it.[11] Diller claimed his backing of Aereo wasn't an attempt to kill broadcast TV, touting its value as a conduit for local news.[12] Rather, he claimed his goal was moving the "centricity" of video away from the "closed" systems of cable or satellite to the "open" Internet system.[13] Given that video was moving to the Internet anyway, Kanojia argued that Aereo was "the only logical architecture that exists".[14]

The Court ultimately ruled 6-3 against Aereo, saying that Aereo was, indeed, engaging in a public performance in spite of the technological steps Aereo had taken to avoid that. The dissenting justices, Scalia, Thomas and Alito, argued that the majority could only rule that way by subjectively deciding that Aereo "looked like cable TV".[15] Aereo shut down its service shortly thereafter as it began looking into next steps[16] and called on their customers to write their members of Congress[17]; it eventually decided to file the necessary paperwork to be recognized as a cable company entitled to a statutory license[18], but Diller had suggested there was no value in going that route[19], and the Copyright Office indicated it did not believe Aereo qualified for such a license, though it did not outright reject its application.[20] Within six months of the high court's decision, Aereo had filed for Chapter 11 bankruptcy[21]; a subsequent auction of many of its assets, which Aereo hoped would raise $4 million to $31.2 million, ended up raising just over $1.5 million, most of it from Tivo, who paid $1 million for the Aereo trademark and customer lists.[22] Aereo eventually reached a settlement that paid the broadcasters $950,000.[23]

The Aereo case illustrated just how much technology, and the Internet specifically, had begun breaking down many of the assumptions of the television industry, a phenomenon we'll get into in more detail in the last chapter. But for the average American that may have been hearing about or trying to follow the case, there was a more fundamental question that rarely seemed to be answered. If broadcast television is available over-the-air for free, what damages could Aereo possibly be inflicting on broadcasters? Why were broadcasters so committed to preserving the cable ecosystem? Why wouldn't they accept Aereo's argument that Aereo was simply extending the reach of their signals? The answer has to do with a piece of law, originally intended simply to allow broadcasters to share in some of the boons of the cable television revolution, that has now become so critical to their business – thanks in no small part to the growing importance of sports to the television industry – that, as the Aereo case showed, they are perfectly willing to destroy the village in order to save it.

* * *

By the late 80s and early 90s, the impact the rise of cable was having on the television landscape was already quite profound, and at the time, direct-broadcast satellite services were in their infancy, meaning the monopoly power many cable operators had was absolute. If you wanted any of the smorgasbord of new channels cable had opened up, in most cases you had exactly one option, and in turn potential programmers would have to deal with that one option or face nonexistence in the areas that company served. There was already concern about the threat the rise of cable might pose to the broadcast industry, and Congress had adopted must-carry rules requiring cable operators to carry all signals in a given area.[24] But for many broadcasters, particularly the network affiliates that had the most in-demand programming, it wasn't enough.

The subscriber-fee model pioneered by ESPN was already common enough that broadcasters were already smarting over the fundamental inequity that cable operators weren't similarly compensating them, despite the greater popularity of programming on broadcast. To broadcasters, cable operators were building an empire on the backs of their programming without paying them, then turning around and using those revenues to compete against them, especially for sports rights.[25] In 1990 the National Association of Broadcasters attempted to float a proposal that would allow cable operators to choose between carrying broadcast signals and paying broadcasters accordingly, or not carrying any broadcast signals at all, but the proposal went nowhere in Congress, and smaller, independent stations refused to give up the strong must-carry rights they enjoyed.[26] The Congressional effort to impose tougher regulation on the cable industry stalled in the face of opposition by the Bush administration, so the following year NAB went back to Congress with a new proposal: this time, broadcasters could decide whether they wanted to negotiate with cable operators for compensation, or forego such compensation and invoke their must-carry rights.[27] Spearheaded by Sen. Daniel Inouye (D-Hawaii), this was fundamentally the form retransmission consent took in the bill that eventually became the Cable Television Consumer Protection and Competition Act of 1992, passed over President Bush's veto on October 5.

The new retransmission consent marketplace was slow to develop. Most broadcast stations stuck with their long-standing must-carry rights, and CBS, which had been at the forefront of pushing for retransmission consent, found themselves faced with a united front of cable operators when they attempted to charge for their signal. The other networks fared better by using retransmission consent as leverage to give cable networks a broad launch: ABC with ESPN2, Fox with FX, and NBC with the forerunner to today's MSNBC.[28] This remained the state of the retransmission consent marketplace well into the 2000s: a subsidy for the launch and continued carriage of cable networks.

But in the later part of the decade, the growth of direct-broadcast satellite services, and later telco services such as Verizon's FiOS and AT&T's U-Verse, gave broadcasters more leverage to demand cash payments from cable and satellite operators, now that customers' only alternative was no longer using an antenna and not paying broadcasters anything.[29] Satellite and telco providers paid up knowing they couldn't win customers away from cable without local stations, emboldening broadcasters to take a harder line to get cable companies to pay up lest they lose customers to the satellite and telco services that were already doing so – especially as they pushed for carriage of high-definition signals.[30] This came just as a number of factors greatly transformed the economics of the broadcasting industry and made retransmission consent more important than ever. Not the least of these developments was the 2008 BCS deal with ESPN, which shined a spotlight on the necessity of broadcast networks to find a way to replicate ESPN's dual-revenue stream if it hoped to continue to compete for sports rights, and which coincided with the Great Recession wreaking havoc on advertising revenue. "We need to have a business model that enables us to compete with the ESPNs and the TNTs and USAs that are doing more original programming and buying more sports programming," said News Corporation Chief Operating Officer Chase Carey. By 2009, Fox and CBS were making renewed pushes for direct payments for their owned-and-operated stations' signals.[31] Retransmission consent revenues grew over tenfold over six years, from $215 million industrywide in 2006, the year CBS started pressing cable operators, to $2.4 billion in 2012.[32]

But in order to properly benefit, networks would have to collect money from all their stations, not just their owned-and-operated ones. For most of the history of television, networks paid their affiliates to put their programming on the air and sell national advertising off it, a system the networks were already pushing to reverse earlier in the decade. By 2009, networks were pushing for as much as half of what their affiliates were collecting in retransmission consent,[33] as well as inserting themselves into negotiations directly, arguing that they could negotiate a higher price out of cable operators than affiliates were doing on their own.[34] Some affiliate owners, many of whom had been out in front when it came to collecting cash from cable operators, chafed at this development,[35] but others saw the networks as "partners",[36] recognized the importance of sharing retrans revenues to the networks' continued ability to retain tentpole programming,[37] and that major network programming was the big reason major network affiliates could rake in so much cash.[38] But many affiliate owners found that sharing revenue with networks effectively caused the retransmission consent stream to dry up as far as they were concerned.[39] SNL Kagan estimated that affiliates were giving up 45% of their retransmission consent revenue in 2014, but projected it to rise to 50% by 2019 if not sooner, with networks pushing for much higher percentages.[40] As much as individual stations may have led the way, the renewed push for reverse compensation made it increasingly clear that retransmission consent was working primarily for the networks – which, after all, were on the front lines of fighting to avoid losing their programming advantages to cable.

Cable operators almost immediately called for Washington to step in, complaining that retransmission consent rules, now that cable no longer had an effective monopoly, were tilted in favor of broadcasters, as broadcasters could threaten to and actually black out programming if operators did not meet their rate demands. Because stations that requested retransmission consent were still required to be shown on the basic tier of service, the increased push for retransmission consent fees forcibly increased everyone's cable bill. Moreover, retransmission consent, which had been explicitly sold as a means to protect local stations and allow them to continue to produce local broadcasting, with NAB explicitly promising national networks would play no role in retransmission consent negotiations, had effectively become a subsidy for the broadcast networks, as increased demands for compensation resulted in stations cutting the local programming retransmission consent was supposed to protect. Meanwhile, while retransmission consent and other provisions of the 1992 Act successfully staved off consolidation of cable networks in the hands of cable operators, it only replaced it with consolidation of cable networks in the hands of the media conglomerates that owned the networks. The result, Time Warner Cable Executive Vice President Melinda Witmer told Congress in 2012, was that cable subscribers were "literally paying billions of dollars to subsidize content that the broadcasters make available for free both over-the-air and via the Internet."[41]

Yet for supposedly being tilted in their favor, the state of the marketplace was not exactly friendly to the broadcast industry; besides the decline in local programming, Witmer noted that cable channels were now showing programs like *Monday Night Football* and the BCS that used to be on the broadcast networks, which she alleged was because media companies were using retransmission consent to prop up their cable networks.[42] Of course, she conveniently omitted that cable operators were, at least nominally, still paying more for ESPN, the network airing those two things, than for any broadcast network. If the retransmission consent marketplace was "tilted" in favor of broadcasters, it was only because it *had* to be in order to correct for the larger marketplace factors favoring cable networks. Broadcast television could only remain an economically viable avenue for programming compared to cable networks – and only barely so at that – if it could continue to collect retransmission consent fees, and that meant, among other things, broadcasters had to hold on to their automatic placement on the basic tier, lest customers forego a tier that included their stations in favor of one of those free avenues for their programming, especially the over-the-air route that was the definition of being a broadcast station.

This, then, is the challenge posed by Aereo and what caused it to strike such fear in the broadcast business. Aereo upended the assumptions underlying the retransmission consent regime and exposed the glaring hole in the middle of it, showed that retransmission consent was always no more than a band-aid for the problem it was trying to solve, and in the process exposed just what broadcasters had given up, or at least were willing to lose: their very identity. The prospect of Aereo or a cable operator offering ESPN to subscribers but not paying the retransmission consent fees that allowed them to be competitive with ESPN was so unacceptable to the broadcast networks that as they continued to lose the early court challenges, they revealed their willingness to destroy the village in order to save it. In April 2013, shortly after the Second Circuit panel's ruling, Carey threatened to pull Fox programming off the airwaves and offer it only to cable subscribers if they didn't get their way with Aereo, and the other networks seemed to approve of his bluster, with Univision chairman Haim Saban admitting he too had looked into the possibility[43] and Moonves intimating he could make a similar move later in the month.[44] Broadcast networks could never truly achieve parity with cable networks so long as there remained the possibility of people getting their content free, over-the-air, with an antenna – in other words, so long as they continued to have the very thing that made them broadcast, as opposed to cable, networks - and as technology continued to develop it would only get easier for people to get their cable networks without paying for the broadcast ones.

Carey inadvertently laid out the paradox in a 2011 News Corporation earnings call: "In many ways, I think a broadcast network should look like a cable network and it should have two real meaningful streams of revenue, subscription and advertising, as we look for this to be a significant part of the revenue for that broadcast business."[45] The unanswered question was, if "a broadcast network should look like a cable network", why wasn't it one, and what was it really gaining by being a broadcast network? If the broadcast networks were willing to become cable networks if they didn't get their way with Aereo, why hadn't they done so already, other than that they couldn't get away with it?

* * *

In the early days of cable, getting carriage on a system was as simple as providing a unique service that could entice people to sign up for cable to begin with. Eventually large swathes of the country decided to get on board, while the spots available on the systems started to fill up, and new cable networks had to provide more of a value proposition to justify bumping out another network. Meanwhile, the carriage-fee marketplace opened up a whole new business model for the most popular cable channels to make money in the business. The advent of direct-broadcast satellite and digital cable in the late 90s opened up a wide swath of new territory for new networks to conquer, most of them, as noted in Chapter 2, extensions of existing networks. By the end of the 2000s, most cable systems sported far more channels than were likely to be particularly popular. But around that point, a new Darwinian competition was taking shape, one created not by channel space but by money, specifically the constantly rising price of carrying ESPN and the explosion in the broadcast retransmission consent marketplace.

As broadcast networks began taking a harder line on retransmission consent, many in the industry wondered where the money to pay them would come from. Many expected weaker cable channels to see pressure on their carriage fees and potentially go out of business.[46] When most cable networks kept collecting their carriage fees as before, some suggested that the balance would come out of cable company profits - or consumers' cable bills.[47] In the end, both of them took some of the hit: cable operators' video margin declined 14 points from 71.4% in 1999 to 57.8% ten years later, but the next 14-point decline only took half that long, hitting 43.4% in 2014, although some of the reasons for that will be covered in the next chapter.[48] Meanwhile, the average cable bill soared 39% from 2010 to 2015, reaching $99.10.[49]

Increasingly, cable networks have sought to justify charging higher fees (or being carried at all) through marquee programming that viewers won't want to miss - enough to call their cable operator and complain if said operator drops the network at an inauspicious time, if they don't switch to a cable operator that's still carrying it.[50] Sports, of course, is at the top of the list of this sort of marquee programming, but for networks without it creating something that viewers become attached to is much tougher, and comes with its own expenses. Many networks that once relied heavily on movies and reruns, while still using such things to fill out lower-demand times, have invested heavily in original programming, hoping to turn their network into a brand with cachet as shows like *The Sopranos* did for HBO. AMC and FX are the most famous and successful at the tactic with shows like *Mad Men*, *Sons of Anarchy*, and *The Walking Dead* - shows that have racked up Emmy nominations and wins, as well as large audiences - but even more unlikely networks have dived into the game. The History Channel put a lot of money into reality shows like *Pawn Stars* and *American Pickers*, but ventured into scripted drama in 2013 with *Vikings*.[51] Such shows can appear more central to carriage disputes than the networks they air on, with headlines such as "Dish subscribers could lose 'Mad Men' in dispute", not even mentioning the network at issue, common.[52]

Unencumbered by the need to make a profit from ads alone, and freed from FCC restrictions on language and other content that bedevil broadcast, cable networks have given showrunners considerable creative freedom to make high-quality, critically acclaimed shows that they can brandish in front of cable operators and that attract a devoted audience, no matter how small, willing to cancel their cable subscriptions if they can't get their show, and the result is what many have dubbed a new golden age of television. *Mad Men* never attracted an audience on par with its critical acclaim and Emmy nominations, but it helped AMC increase its subscriber fee to 40 cents a month by 2012.[53] *The Walking Dead*, on the other hand, has become the most popular scripted show not only on cable, but on all of television in the 18-49 demographic, and with the network fresh off of launching the spinoff *Fear the Walking Dead*, AMC is on pace to nearly double its 2010 ad revenues in 2015.[54]

* * *

All this shines a new light on the race to build up new sports networks laid out in chapter 2, and shows that more is at stake than just sports. As much as the likes of CBS, Fox, and NBC may want a powerful sports network for their own sake, they also want a popular network cable companies can't afford to drop. That way, they can force those companies to carry a bunch of other, far less popular, channels.

The vast majority of channels on your cable lineup are owned by a handful of companies. As of July 2015, the cable network in the most households is Food Network, owned by Scripps Networks Interactive, which also owns HGTV, the Travel Channel, the Cooking Channel, and DIY Network. In second place is Discovery Channel, whose owner, Discovery Communications, owns TLC, Animal Planet, and numerous smaller networks. USA is owned by Comcast, which also owns NBC, E!, Syfy, MSNBC, CNBC, Bravo, the Weather Channel, Oxygen, and the Esquire Network, besides NBCSN and the Golf Channel. Cartoon Network is owned by Time Warner, which also owns TBS, CNN, HLN, TNT, HBO, Cinemax, truTV, and TCM. The Disney Channel's namesake owns, besides ESPN and ESPN2, ABC Family, Disney XD, and others – as well as A+E Networks, another joint venture with Hearst (split 50-50 this time) named for the A&E network and which also owns History, Lifetime, and smaller networks like FYI. AMC is owned by AMC Networks, which also owns IFC, We, and Sundance. Fox owns FX, Fox News, the National Geographic Channel, Fox Business, and various spinoff networks, to say nothing of Fox Sports 1 and 2. Nickelodeon is owned by Viacom, which also owns Comedy Central, Spike, MTV, VH1, TV Land, BET, CMT, Logo, and numerous MTV and Nick spinoffs.[55]

The network with the largest distribution Nielsen tracks (meaning mostly that it's a commercial network) not owned by one of these eight companies is the Hallmark Channel, with over 12 million fewer homes than Food Network – and we haven't even gotten to any cable networks owned by CBS, a company relatively less reliant on cable networks but which still owns Showtime, Pop (formerly TVGN), and the CBS Sports Network.[56] The broadly-distributed commercial networks not owned by one of these companies can be counted on one hand, and most are owned by formidable corporations themselves. A cable company that wants the popular channels – ESPN, TNT, USA, Fox News, Comedy Central, AMC, Discovery, and Food Network, on top of any others these companies happen to have – has to carry the lesser ones.[57] With retransmission consent, Disney, Comcast, Fox, and CBS can also tie carriage of their broadcast networks, namely their owned-and-operated stations, to carriage of their cable networks and vice versa. The result is a situation where a cable company's hands are tied as much as the consumer's are.

Programmers deny actually requiring operators to take smaller channels in order to carry the popular ones; rather, they merely offer discounts on popular channels if carriers take the smaller ones.[58] But in 2013, Cablevision filed suit against Viacom, claiming they wouldn't consider a proposal that included just the popular channels, and would have assessed a penalty of over a billion dollars, more than their entire 2013 programming budget, if Cablevision had carried only the popular channels.[59] The dispute raged on for the better part of two years, only being settled in October 2015, after Cablevision had agreed to be acquired by the Dutch company Altice.[60]

Smaller networks not affiliated with the big media companies supported Cablevision in its suit, and with good reason.[61] With the big media conglomerates owning so many channels, any network not owned by one of these companies, and thus unable to leverage the other networks in the company's portfolio, faces a major uphill battle, and often selling out to one of the big conglomerates is the only way to survive, as when the Sundance Channel was sold to AMC in 2008.[62] Even with the power of the NFL behind it and even with a package of live games, the NFL Network still had difficulty finding its way onto cable packages without the backing of a major media conglomerate; at the nadir of the network's carriage in 2008, the league was talking with ESPN and Fox about partnering with them to help with carriage.[63]

Tennis Channel and Bloomberg Television fought long, bruising legal disputes with Comcast, accusing Comcast of favoring their own networks over those owned by other parties, with Tennis Channel winning an FCC decision mandating Comcast increase the network's distribution[64] only to see it overturned by a federal court[65] and Bloomberg winning a court order requiring Comcast to place them near major news networks, namely CNBC and MSNBC, on their channel lineups.[66] Even Discovery Communications complained to the FCC about finding it harder to get good terms for their channels once the owners of broadcast networks started taking greater advantage of retransmission consent.[67] MLB Network had more success by tying its carriage to that of the out-of-market Extra Innings package; it initially announced an exclusive deal for the network and Extra Innings with DirecTV, before striking the same deal and giving up some equity in the network to cable operators under congressional pressure, allowing it to have what was, at the time, the biggest launch in cable history in 2009.[68] NBATV also had success increasing its distribution by tying its fortunes to the out-of-market League Pass package.[69] Since the NBC/Comcast merger, some networks have taken advantage of Comcast's pledge to carry minority-owned networks to gain a foothold in carriage – even if the minorities that own them aren't exactly strapped for resources, like Magic Johnson's Aspire network, Sean "Diddy" Combs' Revolt network, or Robert Rodriguez's El Rey network.[70] Some startups have even reportedly gone so far as to pay cable operators for carriage, including Newsmax TV on DirecTV[71] and beIN Sport.[72]

Even for media conglomerates, launching a new network from scratch is increasingly a losing proposition, certainly not if it doesn't have valuable sports programming. A network that isn't catching on with audiences or giving cable operators reason to fork over more money – or even one that might be redundant with a new programming concept that the suits think will be more valuable - is prone to being converted wholesale into something else, as happened with Fox's sports networks to become Fox Sports 1 and 2 and FXX. It's pretty much the only way they introduce any new programming concepts these days. The newest national non-premium English-language channel any of the eight companies listed above have launched from scratch is the Fox Business network, launched in 2007. In the eight years since, Discovery Home and Leisure, a network primarily about home improvement in the vein of HGTV, was converted to Planet Green, a network about "green" living, and then to Destination America, a network billed as targeting "middle America" with America-centric programming. Fuel was subject to rumors of a sale to Viacom[73] and conversion to a UFC-centric or NASCAR network before being converted to Fox Sports 2. Fox Soccer was converted to FXX even though that placed the network next to other sports channels on channel lineups and in many cases on a sports tier. G4, a network originally about video games but increasingly becoming a generic male-oriented channel, was slated to be converted into the Esquire network, only for owners Comcast to decide to convert the Style network instead out of concern for Style's alleged demographic overlap with other networks in the portfolio, letting G4's carriage whittle away to nothing. Discovery Health was converted into the Oprah Winfrey Network with most of the channel's former programming being merged into FitTV, and Fox Reality Channel was converted into Nat Geo Wild, Fox and National Geographic's answer to Animal Planet.[74]

* * *

With media conglomerates asking for more and more money out of cable operators for retransmission consent and sports networks, negotiations for carriage have become increasingly contentious. Blackouts of channels have become a not uncommon phenomenon, and even when they don't happen both sides will often take their case to the media and the public as deadlines loom. Retransmission consent, in particular, has been a particularly nasty battleground that has left sore feelings at cable companies; retransmission-related blackouts increased from 51 in 2011 to

127 in 2013, according to a group of cable companies pushing for retransmission consent reform.[75] Time Warner Cable and Cablevision, the last holdouts for NFL Network, have been especially notorious for going to war with media companies over sports rights and retransmission fees.

When these carriage battles happen, broadcast stations trying to get retransmission consent have limited leverage compared to cable networks. When some of the earliest cable operators to fight retransmission consent fights directed people to network Web sites, networks started cutting off access to Web site feeds for people who got their Internet from a cable operator in a carriage dispute – often with collateral damage – and more recently networks have moved online streams of their feeds to the TV Everywhere model discussed in the next chapter. But broadcast stations still do not change the fact that their content is available free, over the air, and from the beginning cable operators have advised customers to put up an antenna to receive broadcast stations that are being blacked out on the cable provider.[76] Indeed, Time Warner Cable went so far as to give away antennas[77] and suggest customers use Aereo during its 2013 dispute with CBS.[78]

High-profile programming is usually quite visible in these disputes, either putting pressure on the cable operator to do a deal or getting pre-empted. A dispute between Disney and Cablevision saw ABC's New York station go dark early in the morning of March 7, 2010, and the two sides didn't reach an agreement and put the station back on Cablevision customers' screens until 14 minutes into the Academy Awards that night.[79] CBS's owned-and-operated stations remained off Time Warner Cable systems for a month in 2013 before a deal was done days before the start of the NFL season.[80] Turner Broadcasting cut Dish customers off of CNN, Cartoon Network, and related networks in October 2014; about a month later, with the deadline for the popular TNT and TBS networks – including TNT's NBA coverage – looming within a couple of weeks, the two sides reached a short-term extension that kept all the networks on the air into 2015,[81] and struck a long-term agreement with that deadline approaching at the start of April, as TBS prepared to show the NCAA Final Four.[82]

Usually, programmers are able to make cable operators the bad guy for depriving customers of popular programming, while cable operators, already unpopular and blamed for poor service and sky-high cable bills, find it hard to court sympathy.[83] TWC acknowledged that the 2013 CBS dispute accelerated subscriber losses, while CBS boasted that it wasn't harmed one bit.[84] So cable bills inexorably go up, and not just to protect cable company profits. The average price of DirecTV service increased 20% from 2009 to 2013, but DirecTV's programming costs rose 45% over the same period.[85]

Comcast has generally kept quiet on both the retransmission and sports fronts, though. Although it did shunt NFL Network to a sports tier, engaged in a lengthy carriage dispute over Big Ten Network, and complained about the rising cost of sports rights,[86] after it started work on the merger with NBC, which gave it more cable networks and a stake on both sides of the retransmission consent debate, Comcast mostly completed deals with programmers with a minimum of fanfare. Initially, this was to avoid raising the hackles of regulators in order to get the deal approved,[87] but even after the merger was completed Comcast showed much more sympathy for the plight of programmers than when its COO Steve Burke could say with a straight face that Comcast could simultaneously try to keep the cost of sports rights down as a cable operator while bidding them up as a programmer.[88] In 2013, Comcast and Fox negotiated for over a month after their agreement expired at the end of 2012 without interrupting service or engaging in any public sniping until reaching a deal.[89]

As disputes have grown more contentious, and factors that will be explored in the next chapter have shaken up the landscape, carriage disputes have lasted for longer and taken on deeper implications. Suddenlink Communications, a cable operator in mid-size markets centered on the Midwest, dropped Viacom channels in October 2014, and the dispute raged on so long that by late February, CEO Jerry Kent raised the possibility that Viacom's channels might never return, saying the company had "moved on".[90] Others also raised the possibility of limiting their channel selection. "Mathematically, we're probably not going to be able to carry all the major [programmers] long-term, because we just don't want to raise prices to $100 a month," said Dish chairman Charlie Ergen.[91]

* * *

It's easier for a cable company to resist carrying a network when it doesn't carry it already, even when an established company is behind it - recall how companies mostly launch new national networks by rebranding old ones. That means every launch of a new sports network, namely league-owned, conference-owned, and regional sports networks, becomes a battleground as no cable operator wants to give in and carry an expensive network they'll likely be stuck with in perpetuity. As much as cable operators grandstand over the increasing costs of ESPN, it's the launch of these new networks where they do much of their substantive fighting over the cost of sports.

The YES Network did not quite cause a revolution right away, as the failures of the Royals and Twins networks indicate. Five years later, NBATV and NFL Network remained poorly distributed. Even with Fox on its side, the Big Ten Network looked like folly when it launched in 2007 without much distribution beyond DirecTV, owned by Fox at the time. None of the top eight cable operators carried it, and the dispute with the two biggest, Comcast and Time Warner Cable, was one of the nastiest the industry had ever seen, with the principals exchanging quite heated barbs. The cable operators feared the Big Ten Network could set a precedent that would lead to the floodgates opening; "What's to stop there from being a Wolverine network next?" Witmer asked at an industry conference. Commissioner Jim Delany had to work hard to keep the conference's schools unified at a time when many of them wanted to shut down the project. But Fox eventually got the cable operators on board by leveraging its regional sports networks, and the BTN soon started making enough money to prove the cable companies' fears well-founded.[92]

Virtually from its inception, DirecTV aligned itself closely with sports, touting its sports coverage heavily in advertising, led by its exclusive carriage of the NFL's Sunday Ticket out-of-market package. But even DirecTV has its limits when it comes to the rising cost of sports, especially since, unlike Verizon, AT&T, and cable providers, it doesn't sell Internet or home phone service, at least not directly, and therefore doesn't have that as a revenue stream.[93] In 2009, it blindsided executives at Comcast by taking its then-Versus network off the air.[94] The network remained off the air for the entire NHL regular season, with a deal only being reached right before the playoffs. DirecTV also had rancorous, public negotiations with YES Network and Fox two years later, although no networks went off the air then. As mentioned in the last chapter, DirecTV is at the epicenter of the CSN Houston and SportsNet LA disputes, and also hasn't carried the Pac-12 Networks since their launch. DirecTV even assessed a $3 surcharge to customers in markets with multiple regional sports networks in an attempt to shine a light directly on the issue.[95] All this led to some speculation that DirecTV would give up its Sunday Ticket exclusivity, especially with the value of the package diluted by the expansion of the Thursday night schedule and NFL RedZone being made available to cable operators,[96] but DirecTV and the NFL reached an eight-year extension worth $1.5 billion a year.[97] One motivating factor for DirecTV to do a deal with the NFL: a clause in the agreement for AT&T and DirecTV to merge allowed AT&T to walk away if DirecTV didn't renew its Sunday Ticket deal.[98]

Notably, however, Disney has been largely immune to these carriage battles. Even though ESPN is Public Enemy #1 when it comes to the rising cost of sports rights, it's still too powerful for cable operators to even risk going to war with them. ESPN cut it close enough in carriage talks with Time Warner Cable in 2010 that both sides started public posturing, but most deals since then have been made with a minimum of discord, including pacts with Comcast in 2012[99] and DirecTV in 2014,[100] and a 2014 agreement with Dish that came six months after their original agreement expired without a blackout.[101] While ESPN had trouble getting carriage for the Longhorn Network at first, that didn't last, and the SEC Network had one of the biggest launches for any cable network ever, as ESPN used the expiration of its carriage agreements for its other networks to get carriage for its new ones. ESPN did have some trouble getting ESPNU off the ground, eventually allowing cable operators to pick it up in exchange for moving ESPN Classic, which was seeing plummeting ratings and was the subject of numerous rebranding or merging rumors, to a sports tier.[102]

* * *

As the stakes go up in carriage negotiations, both sides try to get every ounce of leverage they can. For cable providers, that often means buying other cable companies in order to make sure you control as many subscribers as possible. AT&T explicitly cited controlling programming costs as a factor in its acquisition of DirecTV,[103] although Comcast and Charter denied that their respective acquisitions of Time Warner Cable would have a similar effect, because none of the companies serve the same places.[104] In 2003, shortly after Comcast acquired AT&T Broadband, the top ten pay-TV providers accounted for nearly 86 percent of the market;[105] by 2010, after Verizon and AT&T had entered the market, that number went up to about 91.6 percent.[106] If all proposed mergers go through, that number will go up to over 95% - and just six companies will control nearly 90%.[107]

There's less opportunities for programming providers to combine, but it probably isn't a coincidence that Fox went after Time Warner after the Comcast-TWC and AT&T-DirecTV mergers were announced – more leverage for cable and satellite providers means less for programmers.[108] Broadcasters, however, have consolidated like mad in a rush to increase their retransmission consent leverage, and unlike cable companies are upfront about retrans leverage being the driving factor in their mergers.[109] In 2010, the largest station owner not to have a presence in New York was the Sinclair Broadcast Group, with stations in 21.6% of the country, good for ninth among all station owners.[110] By 2015, Sinclair had improved to 37.5%, behind only Ion Media Networks, Tribune, and CBS, while Gannett and Media General had increased their respective holdings to over 22% - and Tribune, previously at 35.1%, had improved all the way to over 44%, well over the official FCC cap of 39%, thanks to an FCC rule allowing UHF stations to count only half towards the cap.[111] (The rule had its origins in the days when UHF suffered serious competitive disadvantages to VHF, as noted in Chapter 1, but those factors have gone away; in fact, many former VHF stations are actually physically located on UHF in the age following the 2008 digital transition, as its propagation characteristics are usually superior.)[112] In 2010, the ten largest station owners to own a substantial number of Big Four stations combined to reach 255% of the country; today their combined reach is 307%, about the same number as the top 15 in 2010.[113]

Within a market, FCC rules forbid owning more than two stations in a market, at least one outside the market's top four, and don't even allow that much if there would otherwise be less than eight "independent voices", but even before the FCC allowed the owning of multiple television stations at all in 1999, Sinclair became infamous for finding ways to exploit the rules by having a shell corporation own the second station in a market, to the point that the Rainbow PUSH Coalition raised formal objections that led to Sinclair being assessed a $40,000 fine.[114] The American Cable Association documented 36 instances of supposedly-separate stations coordinating retransmission consent negotiations in 33 markets in 2010, which went up to 46 pairs in 41 markets just two years later.[115] By 2014 Free Press identified 80 markets where a company controlled two stations in the top four.[116] That year the FCC announced it would start cracking down on the use of such sharing agreements to circumvent ownership rules, but because the rules govern the number of *stations* one company may own or control in a market, there was nothing stopping Sinclair from gutting a station they couldn't acquire of its programming (or shutting it down entirely) and moving it to a digital subchannel (broadcasters' way of taking advantage of the same expansion of channel capacity digital opened up for cable) of a station they do own, as they did with some stations they were slated to acquire when the new rules came down.[117] The National Association of Broadcasters has proposed removing the eight-voices and top-four rules entirely, arguing that they are unnecessary in an age of increased competition from cable networks and the Internet.[118]

Cable companies are paying high prices for ESPN and regional sports networks that they pass on to all of their customers, no matter how much or how little of those networks they watch. With media companies looking to get their own piece of ESPN's lucrative subscriber fee income, cable companies looking to get on the other end of the equation by starting their own regional sports networks, and sports leagues, teams, and conferences looking to fully or partially cut out the middleman, the cost of sports rights is skyrocketing, a cost all these networks, new and old, pass on to cable companies. Needing to pay for all these sports networks that have launched in the last decade-plus, as well as retransmission consent fees for broadcasters looking to avoid losing their own sports rights to the cable networks, cable companies have engaged in increasingly heated showdowns with programmers, which have left customers caught in the middle, losing channels when the two sides can't agree and seeing their rates go up when they do. It's a seemingly unstable situation built on an unfair business model, and one might wonder if anything might be done about it. In our final chapter, we examine several forces that could shake things up, and may already be doing so – and indeed, stand poised to undermine the entire structure of cable television as it has existed for close to 40 years. In the short term, however, those forces are only underscoring the importance of sports to the television industry – and in the process, uncover the real reason for their importance, a reason that even the parties involved seem to be at best dimly aware of.

8

Breaking Free

O N MAY 2, 2015, Floyd Mayweather and Manny Pacquiao, the two biggest draws in boxing and arguably the two best pound-for-pound fighters in the world, faced off in Las Vegas in what was dubbed the "Fight of the Century". It was supposed to be a triumph of boxing's relevance, or at least a last gasp, for a sport that was once a mainstay of broadcast television in the days of Marciano and Ali, on par with baseball and horse racing among America's most popular sports, but which had since suffered decades of decline and increasing irrelevance (especially outside the Hispanic community), with virtually all the sport's biggest fights long consigned to premium cable and pay-per-view, its championships split among at least four and as many as ten different organizations with a claim to "world" title status, and dominated by bombastic and questionably-ethical masters of personal promotional fiefdoms such as Don King and Bob Arum, all allowing many championship matches to turn out to be carefully-arranged mismatches hardly worth the $30 pay-per-view fee.[1] But instead it proved to be emblematic of all the issues facing the sport.

Actually, the problems began with the date itself and the events leading up to the fight taking place on it. Reports that Pacquiao had signed a contract for the fight had circulated as early as December 2009, but were quickly debunked. Negotiations broke down soon thereafter over Mayweather's request for Olympic-style drug testing, including blood tests right up to the weigh-in (according to Arum, Pacquiao feels having his blood drawn weakens him), which Pacquiao's camp said suggested Mayweather was trying to duck the fight to preserve his undefeated record. The issue continued to creep back up, off and on, for the next few years. Mayweather eventually agreed to a lucrative multi-fight deal with

Showtime, further complicating any Pacquiao fight since Pacquiao remained associated with HBO. Then Pacquiao lost to Timothy Bradley in a controversial split decision in 2012, with a panel of internationally recognized judges later scoring the fight as a decisive Pacquiao victory, a majority by scores of at least nine rounds to three. After Pacquiao was knocked out in his fourth fight with Juan Manuel Marquez later that year, Mayweather may have seen Pacquiao as less of a threat to his undefeated record, and negotiations heated up again over the course of 2014. The match was finally made official in February, with HBO and Showtime jointly producing the pay-per-view.[2]

But the problems didn't end there. Expecting the fight to smash all previous revenue records, HBO and Showtime charged nearly $100 for the high-definition telecast, and charged bars and restaurants so much that some elected not to screen the fight.[3] During the lead-up to the fight, renewed attention was focused on Mayweather's past accusations of domestic abuse, which Mayweather's camp accidentally shined a further spotlight on when two female reporters that had pushed Mayweather on the issue were told their credentials were being revoked the day of the fight. (Both had their credentials restored but refused to attend anyway.)[4] Then there was the fight itself; Mayweather's style of slowly and methodically dismantling his opponent with strong defense consistently won fights but didn't make for exciting television, and that was precisely what he did to Pacquiao.[5] After the fight, Pacquiao revealed that he had suffered an injury to his right shoulder in April and re-injured it in the fourth round, prompting some who had bought the fight to file a class-action lawsuit against Pacquiao, Arum, and others in Arum's Top Rank organization, alleging fraud.[6]

And then there were the issues caused by the fight's very popularity. HBO and Showtime had encouraged people to order the fight well in advance, but the vast majority of people ended up waiting until the day of the fight. Every one of the top ten pay-TV providers found their systems overwhelmed trying to process the rush of orders, resulting in many people being unable to see the pay-per-view and in some cases resulting in issues cropping up on unrelated channels. HBO and Showtime ended up delaying the main event 45 minutes to allow cable operators time to process all the orders, and doubtless the technical issues only heightened the disappointment with the lackluster nature of the fight itself.[7]

As expected, the fight smashed all previous pay-per-view records and even its own lofty expectations, with over 4.6 million buys and $400 million in revenue.[8] But though 4.6 million buys is impressive for pay-per-view, it pales in comparison to what NFL games draw on a regular basis, not to mention America's other major sports championships. No one complains of any issues, except for rare isolated incidents, when watching the Super Bowl or even college football's national championship which, even relegated to ESPN, had more than 24 million viewers each of the last four years of the BCS era.[9] Why were cable operators unable to handle 4.6 million pay-per-view buys yet manage to deliver far larger audiences as a matter of course? The answer to that question is one media companies and others would do well to keep in mind as a new technology stands poised to shake up the sports and television worlds in a way potentially even greater than cable did when HBO first aired the "Thrilla in Manila" over forty years ago.

* * *

Even before ESPN's BCS deal, consumer groups and others were calling for the government to step in and do something about the subsidization of sports networks, and media companies, led by Disney, have resisted those efforts mightily. Disney has spent lavishly for over a decade to schmooze politicians and regulators to keep their business model going, including using some tricks only they have at their disposal, such as getting senators and congressmen to pose with sports legends, bringing them to Walt Disney World in Orlando during Super Bowl Weekend, granting airtime on *Monday Night Football* (still on ABC then) to former FCC commissioner Michael Powell in 2004 when he wanted to push the digital transition. All told, Disney and ESPN have donated more than $400,000 to congressmen's political action committees, most of it since 2000 – chump change when your business model is making you over $7 billion a year, even when you consider their expenses for schmoozing those congressmen.[10]

For a while, the most popular idea was to force cable companies to offer their wares a la carte, allowing you to only pay for the networks you want. In 2006, the FCC released a report suggesting a la carte could reduce costs for 40% of homes with cable. In the aftermath, Senator John McCain introduced an a la carte bill, but Disney's largesse paid off: it failed in the Senate commerce committee on a 20-2 vote.[11] McCain tried again in 2013, this time with the support of none other than Senator Richard Blumenthal, who represents ESPN's own home state,[12] but the bill went nowhere.

A la carte has made more progress north of the border, where cable TV is more tightly regulated. In March 2015, the Canadian Radio-Television and Telecommunications Commission announced that cable companies would be required to offer subscribers a basic package containing local stations and educational channels for no more than CAN$25 a month, a bit over half what cable providers were charging for their most basic packages that offered over a hundred channels. Other channels would be made available on a "pick-and-pay" basis.[13]

Media companies claim that most channels are underpriced compared to what they would receive in an a la carte world, that cable is still a good value for the vast majority of customers who would gladly pay as much as they do now for what they do watch, and that a la carte would actually end up hurting consumers in the long term: because each network would have far fewer customers, it would need to jack up rates considerably. On average, people would end up paying the same or more for their cable than they do now and getting less for it, although sports fans would likely pay more and non-sports fans would pay less. Moreover, as laid out in the last chapter, the same bundle that allows ESPN to break the bank on sports rights also allows other networks to produce the modern boom in quality programming at the heart of the new "golden age of television".[14] Media companies claim the effects of a la carte would be so catastrophic that the vast majority of cable networks would go out of business, especially those targeted towards minorities and underserved communities; the number of networks that would be left might be in the single digits.

You could poke several holes in that logic and point to evidence that the eventual outcome might not be quite so dire, and certainly American media and cable companies will be keeping a close eye on how the Canadian pick-and-pay experiment plays out. But even if things happened exactly as the media companies say, someone with a good grasp of the overall video landscape, and of the forces undermining the deepest assumptions of the cable business, might find reason to say: "So?"

* * *

In the same breath that they stand side by side with media companies in opposition to a la carte, cable companies have also been pushing back against the increased price of sports networks that they're stiffed with and left to pass on to consumers, working to roll back the sports subsidy as much as they can. As early as 1998, when cable operators began chafing under ESPN's rate hikes to pay for the full-season NFL deal, many of them grumbled about trying to curb the high price of sports by moving sports channels to an exclusive tier so only sports fans need to pay for them. Picking a fight with ESPN, which explicitly requires a presence on the most basic level of service in most contracts, wasn't something they were willing to engage in yet, though.[15] Instead, when cable operators started launching sports tiers in the early 2000s, spurred by the increasing popularity of digital cable, it was primarily newer, niche networks that were relegated there, networks cable operators had more leverage against.[16] Placing regional sports networks on a premium tier looked like an option, especially when Cablevision placed YES on a tier with MSG and FSN New York the first year it carried the network,[17] but YES' arbitration victory the following year essentially killed that option.[18]

As a result, sports tiers remained poorly penetrated, with the exception of Cox's, which launched in 1998, contained some non-sports channels, and was one of three "basic" packages all digital cable subscribers had to pick up. With sports tiers failing to grow, networks became more resistant to being placed on them, and with MLB Network launching on basic packages, the most prominent networks on sports tiers, like NBATV and NFL Network, redoubled their efforts to get off them; within six months of MLB Network's launch, Comcast had reached deals to move the other three major sports' networks off their sports tier.[19] The NFL making NFL RedZone available to cable operators, followed by ESPN introducing its similar Goal Line and Buzzer Beater service (which provide similar whiparound coverage to college football and basketball games ESPN holds rights to), represented a more attractive service sports tiers could be marketed around.[20]

Moving the most expensive sports networks to a separate tier may have been off the table, but as the price of sports continued to increase in the aftermath of the BCS deal, cable operators began grumbling again. In 2011, ESPN's nearly $1.9 billion/year agreement for Monday Night Football caused much griping among cable operators, with the New York Post reporting that Dish Network was threatening to drop ESPN if it couldn't offer it on a separate tier. [21] "As contracts come up for renewal, there could be a day when one of the big providers just doesn't have a sports offering, so they can differentiate their programming in a major way. In theory, their cost could be cut by half to the consumer," said Dish Network chairman Charlie Ergen.[22]

No one was quite willing to drop sports entirely – as explained in the last chapter, they couldn't just drop ESPN without dropping other channels like the Disney Channel, which would mean people who might not otherwise have an interest in sports would suddenly have their kids pestering them to get the Disney Channel back. But they were willing to start reducing ESPN's reach. Verizon introduced a "Select HD" package in 2013 completely devoid of sports channels,[23] and multiple companies have since engaged in their own experiments with offering completely sports-free packages to customers. By the start of 2015, those packages had attracted more than 3 million subscribers.[24] That April, Verizon introduced a "Custom TV" package with a base package of 35 channels, with local broadcasters and a few cable networks, plus two additional genre-based packages of 15 or so channels each for $55 per month, plus $10 per month for each additional genre package. Seven genre packages were offered in all, including two sports packages, with ESPN on the more basic one.[25]

Verizon didn't attempt to obtain permission from programmers before announcing "Custom TV", and ESPN was angered enough to sue Verizon, claiming it violated the terms of their carriage agreement forbidding ESPN from being distributed in a sports package (as opposed to simply being excluded from a sports-free package). Verizon, for its part, indicated it believed it had the right to at least test different bundling strategies on a limited basis.[26] Such is typical of the challenges facing companies trying to extract ESPN from the bundle; even when they are allowed to experiment with sports-free packages, the contracts sports networks have with cable companies guarantee them a certain level of penetration, and cable companies can't risk accidentally breaking those contracts. Indeed, a lot of what made the sports-free packages possible was ESPN agreeing to allow several cable companies to reduce their penetration rates for packages containing ESPN from 90% to closer to 80%.[27]

Penetration levels were important to ESPN not just because of subscriber fees, but because its contracts with leagues and conferences guaranteed a certain level of penetration as well. And because of this, even the relatively modest advent of the sports-free package has the potential to completely pop the sports cable bubble. ESPN only has the rights to the new college football playoff because it happens to be in the vast majority of households. How many leagues and conferences would bail on ESPN once people start electing not to pay for it en masse, leaving only sports fans still getting it? How many sports would be willing to risk completely shutting out the casual fan? Considering how few sports went the way of boxing, with all the top-caliber fights on pay-per-view and the remaining fights of any consequence on premium networks like HBO, the answer may not be something any of the programmers of sports networks would like. But it's one ESPN may have to confront sooner rather than later: ESPN went from being in over 100 million homes in July 2011 to 96 million three years later, but lost more than three million more households in just the next year,[28] and a total of seven million households in the past two years. A big part of this trend lies in how the Internet is changing everything about television, much the way it has changed so many fields before.

* * *

It'd be one thing if sports fans were merely passionate enough about their sports that if a cable operator were to drop a sports network they'd leave en masse. But it turns out sports fans are incredibly important to the other half of cable's dual revenue stream, advertising, as well: as said before, they are disproportionately likely to be in the male 18-49 demo, which just so happens to be the most valuable demographic to advertisers, and they're the one type of programming that's DVR-proof, meaning sports fans are a captive audience to actually watch the advertisements. But these two things are connected in a way that casts a long shadow over the future of the entire television industry.

Concerns over time-shifting are nothing new; the television and movie industries attempted to kill the VCR when it came out, and once VCRs caught on, sports rights already became incredibly valuable for their immunity to time-shifting, to the point that many of the same points being made over the sports rights bubble were being made in 1989 in response to CBS' multi-million dollar baseball deal.[29] But these days, DVRs are the least of television programmers' worries, if not so much advertisers'.

The usual reason given for why the 18-49 demographic is so valuable is because they are supposedly more susceptible to advertising, more likely not to have their brand preferences set yet. This research is heavily disputed, but it might not matter. "We don't believe that the focus on adults 18-49 is really so much about the effectiveness of advertising (not to mention there are a bunch of products targeted at people over 50!) as it is about *the availability of viewers*," writes Robert Seidman, co-founder of the TV ratings web site TVbythenumbers.com. "People 50+ watch a lot more TV than people under 50, and people 35-49 watch more TV than people under 35...Advertisers care more about reaching the people who are difficult to reach than they care about reaching the people who are easy to reach. Reaching 18-34 year olds is far more difficult, so advertising to them is expensive relative to reaching viewers 55+ who are much easier to reach. From a supply/demand scarcity point of view, this makes complete sense."[30]

But *why* do those age 18-49 watch so much less television than older people? There are a number of reasons, but perhaps the biggest is because of the rise of the Internet as a source of entertainment. Young people get their entertainment from many more sources than video, and are increasingly impatient to tie what video they do watch down to a linear television schedule. Well aware of the futility of attempting to fight piracy and the rise of YouTube, content providers have increasingly embraced the Internet as an alternative venue for their content, through sites such as Hulu and Netflix. But the Internet challenges some of the deepest assumptions of the television industry in a way it has only slowly come to realize and has resisted at all costs: if non-live programming can be watched any time you want it, why does it need a spot on a linear television schedule at all?

Before the Internet, the only way to consume content was to watch it when someone else told you it was on, unless you rented a video from the video store. You visited the movie theater when they decided the movie was going to start; you watched a program at the time the broadcast station or cable network scheduled it for. Each television station or network, even with the increased capacity of cable and later digital cable, had to be assigned a certain portion of spectrum, a *channel*, that could be used to show one piece of video and one stream of audio at a time, so any program that wanted an audience on television had to find a channel that would show it at a particular time. But once a video is on the Internet, you can pull it up any time you want. You don't need someone else to schedule it for you. The traditional linear television schedule is an artifact of these pre-Internet days.

It's entirely possible the prospect of hundreds of channels falling by the wayside may end up falling on deaf ears, because we may not *need* hundreds of channels anymore. It's very possible that the vast majority of programming that would find itself without a home because of the collapse of so many cable channels would be able to find a home on the Internet without a problem, though admittedly the financial infrastructure that would support that may not be in place yet. It's even tempting to wonder if the Internet could pick up the slack even of live programming, which would render television completely obsolete.

* * *

Today, a la carte and sports-free packages are looking increasingly passe, a reflection of and even an attempt to preserve a system where linear television is the main source of entertainment. Increasingly, many consumers are "cutting the cord" and dropping their television subscriptions entirely. Long feared by media and cable companies, cord-cutting is becoming a growing reality: cable and satellite providers lost 222,000 households over the first three quarters of 2014, more than in all of 2013.[31] The industry regained 101,000 households in the fourth quarter, but record household formation meant a wave of "cord-nevers" – people who never sign up to cable to begin with – propelled 1.4 million American households to either drop cable TV or never sign up for it over the course of the year,[32] and in the second quarter of 2015 alone the industry outright lost over half a million subscribers.[33]

Media companies have tried to put as many roadblocks in the way of the cord-cutting phenomenon as they can. They want the Internet to work for them, not against them, but the way they tend to do so now is to keep people tethered to their cable company – and thus, to the cable bundle and their millions in subscriber fees – as much as possible. ESPN, in many ways, is representative of the shift in thinking. Too tied to cable providers' subscriber fees to embrace online video wholeheartedly even at the start, ESPN's initial foray into the online video space was ESPN360.com, an attempt to apply the cable business model to online video by opening access only to ISPs that paid them a fee, and which eventually renamed ESPN3 to give off the notion of it as an extension of ESPN's linear networks, as it increasingly emphasized live games, including from those same linear networks.[34] But in 2010, ESPN's agreement with Time Warner Cable offered ESPN3 only to those that subscribed to traditional cable as well as broadband.[35] Those that could confirm their subscription to TWC's TV service could also log on to

ESPNNetworks.com, which offered ESPN's complete linear feed (minus events ESPN didn't have the rights to stream yet) and soon ESPN2, ESPNU, and Goal Line/Buzzer Beater.[36] Within a year, with only Verizon FiOS having joined TWC and Bright House, the site had been renamed WatchESPN.com to harmonize with the name of the app for mobile devices, with ESPN3 now being offered through it.[37] A year later, ESPN began blacking out content airing on networks available through WatchESPN on ESPN3, refocusing ESPN3 solely on events not available on ESPN's linear platforms, even though WatchESPN was available in barely half as many homes as ESPN3.[38] And while ESPN3 is still available for free through participating ISPs on desktop, as well as with an Xbox LIVE Gold subscription, viewing ESPN3 content on mobile devices or on streaming boxes like Roku or Chromecast requires logging in to WatchESPN with a TV subscription.[39] ESPN president John Skipper admits that WatchESPN these days is in large part "a significant measure to preserve the current system."[40]

This is the future media and cable companies have been pushing, known as "TV Everywhere", and it allows you to watch the shows you want to watch not just on your TV, but on your computer, tablet, or smartphone – so long as you "authenticate" with a participating cable provider. For many networks, this includes the ability to watch each network's popular shows any time you want to; if you want to watch popular original cable shows like *The Walking Dead* online whenever you want, you need to authenticate with a cable provider that has a TV Everywhere agreement with AMC. With broadcasters' dependence on retransmission consent, the same system applies to them as well: you may be able to watch ABC, NBC, or Fox on a TV with an antenna, but if you want to watch even the live feed on a smartphone or tablet, certainly for sports or primetime shows, you'll almost certainly need a cable subscription. All this means a considerable amount of Internet-delivered video is being restricted to maintain a structure that by all rights should be becoming obsolete. To make matters worse, TV Everywhere agreements usually have to be negotiated piecemeal with each provider, so you may not even have a complete picture of the future yet.

But over the past year or so, there have been some unexpected twists on the road to the future.

* * *

Something fascinating happened in June of 2012: a mass of people took to social media to beg a major media company to take their money, and the company said no. As HBO started another season of its hit show *True Blood*, a web designer named Jake Caputo started a Web site called TakeMyMoneyHBO.com encouraging people to take to Twitter and tell HBO how much they would pay for a standalone version of HBO's TV Everywhere service HBO GO. Like many cord-cutters, Caputo watched shows like *True Blood* and HBO's other hit *Game of Thrones* using piracy and a friend's password, but felt it was ridiculous that he had to.[41]

As a premium service, HBO is effectively already offered a la carte and theoretically isn't dependent on the rest of the cable bundle, so it might seem surprising that it wouldn't be open to selling its wares directly to the consumer. But HBO is owned by Time Warner, and Time Warner is not in the business of letting HBO undermine its other networks that are dependent on the cable bundle – especially TNT, the second-most-expensive national cable network and home to the NBA[42] – certainly not when cord-cutting was a more theoretical than practical possibility, with over a hundred million people remaining tied to cable compared to around two and a half million ditching it in a three-year span.[43] Moreover, a standalone HBO streaming service, unlike a TV Everywhere service, wouldn't be subsidized by the cable companies, meaning any price charged for it would have to support the infrastructure built around it, on top of which HBO would have to spend more on customer service and billing itself. In that light, TakeMyMoneyHBO.com actually provided justification for sticking with the status quo: the average price quoted by those moved to tweet by the site was $12, at *best* on par with the $10-20 range cable customers are charged for HBO.[44] For the moment, HBO was willing to use its shows' status as the most pirated on television as a point of pride.

But less than a year and a half later, HBO reached a deal with Comcast to offer HBO and HBO GO, along with local and other channels, to customers seeking high-speed Internet service under the $50 "Internet Plus" brand. And a year after that, HBO announced that it *would* begin offering HBO standalone over the Internet.[45] The standalone version of HBO, dubbed HBO Now, debuted in April 2015, just before the season premiere of *Game of Thrones*, on Apple's iOS devices and three months later on other platforms, at a price of $14.99 a month.[46] By July, it had already attracted two million subscribers.

What happened to cause such an about-face? Simply put, cord-cutting happened – and more specifically, Netflix happened. The number of households with high-speed Internet but without cable had passed 10 million, and Netflix had passed HBO in number of subscribers.[47] Netflix had made a big push in original content starting in 2013, enhancing the value of their service and insulating it from incumbents withholding content from a potential competitor, and with quality series like *House of Cards* and *Orange is the New Black*, had established itself as every bit as much a player in the new "golden age of television" as cable networks, earning 14 Emmy nominations and winning Outstanding Directing in a Drama Series for the *House of Cards* pilot the first year. Netflix explicitly identified HBO, the 100-pound gorilla in quality TV series, as its rival, with bombastic CEO Reed Hastings routinely tweaking HBO in settings such as earnings calls and dueling parties at the Beverly Hilton following the 2014 Golden Globes, where HBO won two awards to *House of Cards'* one. Chief content officer Ted Sarandos was even more explicit: Netflix's goal was "becom[ing] HBO faster than HBO can become us."[48]

The debut of HBO Now both a point of no return for cord-cutting and a recognition of just how far it had progressed in spite of the obstacles the cable industry put in its way. The cable bundle was such a tightly-knit unit that while techies and the earliest cord-cutters held out hope for tech companies like Apple or Google to swoop in and disrupt the video marketplace in the way they had for music, many thought that, absent Congressional action, the best they could do would be to effectively replicate the cable bundle note for note.[49] But Netflix had produced a service with enough appeal to those with no interest in sports to convince a growing number of people to leave behind whatever appealed to them about cable – which, for seemingly most of them, was limited to HBO – and entrust them with all their entertainment needs. HBO's change of plans was an admission that TV Everywhere had utterly failed at keeping people tied to a traditional cable subscription, something that had seemed ironclad for the foreseeable future just three years before but which Netflix had changed nearly singlehandedly, in the face of all the obstacles the big media companies put in their way. Indeed, within a week of HBO's announcement CBS, the only major broadcast network not part of Hulu, announced CBS All Access, offering a vast back catalog of shows CBS held the rights to as well as back episodes of shows it was currently airing, as well as live streams of certain CBS stations, for $5.99 a month.[50]

Cord-cutting was no longer an abstract, theoretical but seemingly unlikely fear only occasionally entertained by cable executives; it was now such a growing reality that many of them not only were resigned to the Internet replacing television as the core of their business, some actually saw HBO Now as an opportunity to drive broadband subscriptions, and some smaller distributors are considering ditching traditional television services entirely.[51] With the launch of HBO Now, 2015 became the tipping point where it became clear that cord-cutting would – slowly but inevitably – dismantle the entire pay-TV infrastructure and business model at the heart of this book, and while there's still a long way to go before it collapses entirely, it's already making a big impact on the bundle's biggest beneficiaries – namely, a certain four-letter sports outfit in western Connecticut.

* * *

We mentioned in the first chapter that ESPN is the single most powerful driver of the Walt Disney Company's revenue, and that's still true, but Wall Street frowns upon any diminution of a company's profits or even failing to grow them fast enough. From August of 2014 to January of 2015, ESPN launched the SEC Network and aired the first College Football Playoff and its first NFL Wild Card playoff game, all representing considerable increases in expenditures on production and rights fees. As a result, when Disney reported its fiscal second quarter in May, it reported that its cable division's operating earnings fell 9% from the same quarter the previous year, with programming and production costs expected to rise by "low-teen percentage points" for the full fiscal year ending in September, driven by ESPN - all before the company took on the substantial increase in rights fees its new NBA contract is set to entail, and just as its subscriber base has fallen into decline. In June of 2015, one financial analyst looking at Disney's stock price stated that the waning fortunes of ESPN were enough to basically completely offset the massive windfall Disney was expected to rake in from the release of *Star Wars: The Force Awakens* at the end of the year. ESPN may have been the company's driving force, but Wall Street was starting to wonder whether it was also becoming a weight on the company's back.[52]

With ESPN losing 3.2 million subscribers in a year's time and seeing continually rising programming costs, Skipper was reportedly ordered to cut $100 million from the network's budget in 2016 and $250 million in 2017.[53] He elected not to renew Keith Olbermann, the man they'd brought back to neuter the Fox Sports 1 launch, for financial reasons[54] (although Olbermann had also been very critical of Roger Goodell and his handling of the Ray Rice scandal, and as Chapter 5 showed, for ESPN keeping the NFL happy *is* a financial decision). That October, ESPN eliminated 350 positions and laid off 300 employees, including potentially valuable executives and producers.[55] To be sure, ESPN wasn't the only sports outfit cutting costs; Fox elected to stop sending reporters to events it didn't have the rights to, a sign that any ambitions of having Fox Sports 1 truly compete with ESPN wasn't going to be realistic for the foreseeable future.[56] But when ESPN was making these cuts, it was a sign of a phenomenon affecting all of sports media, if not all of media period.

The pressures on ESPN also had the effect of reducing its power when it came to sports rights, and allowing broadcast to score some wins. In May, ESPN announced its NFL Wild Card game in 2016 - only the second under its new contract - would be simulcast on ABC. Skipper said the move was ESPN's idea, not imposed by the NFL, and was intended to increase the audience from the game and did not presage a larger shift in sports back to ABC, but limiting the size of the audience had never been an issue for ESPN before.[57] (ESPN also moved its ESPY award telecast to ABC,[58] although it's easy to wonder how much of that move was related to the non-sports buzz of the Arthur Ashe Courage Award given to Caitlyn Jenner that night.)[59] There was also surely some symbolic value in golf's Open Championship signing a new contract with NBC and Golf Channel; the Open had signed a contract to air live entirely on ESPN shortly before the BCS deal, and now would once again have a live presence on broadcast.

And the situation also had ESPN thinking seriously about its long-term future. On July 27, Disney Chairman Bob Iger told CNBC that it was inevitable that ESPN would eventually divorce itself from the cable bundle and go the same route as HBO, that "eventually ESPN becomes a business that is sold directly to the consumers."[60] The following week during its quarterly earnings call, Disney lowered its expected growth targets for its cable business, citing "modest" subscriber losses at ESPN that Iger attempted to reassure investors was due to an overall drop in cable subscribers – in other words, cord-cutting – rather than people taking ESPN-free packages from cable operators. Iger also claimed that he saw Netflix as "more friend than foe" for all the Disney content it took on and paid for, and reaffirmed that the company would take a longer-term view of the marketplace as it entered new contracts with distributors, including securing its ability to sell ESPN direct to consumers.[61] Wall Street seemed to take it as an admission of the direction the television business was heading. With other media companies reporting their own losses, massive sell-offs of stocks occurred over the next two days, with the S&P 500 media index dropping 8.3 percent over a three-day span, with over half a *trillion* dollars in value evaporating.[62] Disney itself saw its stock price drop 9% the day after the call.[63]

While it certainly was relevant that ESPN intended to position itself to make it worthwhile to offer its wares directly to the consumer when the time came, Iger's comments set off shockwaves in the sports and tech blogospheres in large part because they interpreted it to mean ESPN was already in the planning stages of such a service, with one site declaring the original July 27 interview "the day cable TV as we know it died".[64] But it really shouldn't have. Standalone ESPN was always the logical conclusion of continued cord-cutting and pressure for a la carte for anyone paying attention and who bothered to think about it; Iger was just stating upfront what would happen as cord-cutting continued, without indicating it was already happening. Indeed, he was explicit in the same interview that such a move wouldn't occur within the next five years. If anything, Iger seemed to be more defending the fact ESPN *wasn't* being offered standalone already than announcing that it was going to happen, and analysts' concerns as much as anything had to do with that fact.[65]

ESPN has plenty of reasons not to offer itself directly to consumers in the near future. For one thing, if it were to go that route pay-TV distributors would not only have the right to sell ESPN a la carte, but to do so at lower prices than whatever ESPN charged to sell it directly (although presumably that's part of what Iger hopes to change in future negotiations with distributors).[66] Partly for that reason, ESPN would have to charge $30 a month to make as much money going standalone as it does under the status quo – but again, plenty of would-be sports fans may find that too expensive, and the most prominent sporting events ESPN airs are likely to balk at the reduced subscriber base that would result. ESPN is already maneuvering itself to appeal to cord-cutters and experimenting with over-the-top distribution, but as with ESPN3, they're doing it in a way closer to the model set by the cable bundle – though even here it takes a decidedly different form.

* * *

In 2012, Dish Network introduced its new Hopper DVR service, with a feature called AutoHop that allowed consumers to skip commercials on any primetime show on the four major television networks. All four promptly sued Dish over the AutoHop feature. Two years later, Dish reached a carriage agreement with the Walt Disney Company that included Disney dropping ABC's legal action against Dish, while Dish disabled the AutoHop feature for ABC's programming for three days after the shows air, matching the window when commercial viewing is tracked in the metric used to charge advertisers. But in return, Dish got something arguably more groundbreaking than AutoHop: the right to distribute Disney's networks, including ESPN, on a new service that would be distributed over the Internet.[67]

Ten months later, Dish took the wraps off its new service, called Sling TV, after the Slingbox DVR whose parent company Dish owns a stake in but which otherwise has no relationship with the service. For $20 a month, with no contracts, hardware installation, or hidden fees, customers could sign up for a basic television package including ESPN and other networks from Disney, Turner, and Scripps, with additional content from A&E and Univision added later, plus additional $5 add-on packages of kids, news, sports, and later Spanish-language networks and HBO, with the sports package including all ESPN networks that aren't ESPN or ESPN2.[68] The service doesn't include any content from any other companies, meaning no Discovery, no MTV, no Fox News, USA, or NBC or Fox's sports networks, including regional sports networks. But Sling TV CEO Roger Lynch says he feels content with the 20 or so channels the service already has and is mostly concerned about adding content to the genre packages.[69]

On one level, Sling TV is as much an effort to preserve the existing linear television ecosystem as an attempt to disrupt it. It is still based off of the bundling model: anyone who signs up for Sling TV for Food Network or Cartoon Network is still supporting ESPN even if they never watch a second of it. As such, it's effectively a win-win for ESPN, which gets to appeal to cord-cutters without losing its lucrative business model; if cable operators start thinking they don't need to carry ESPN because sports fans can sign up for Sling TV, ESPN has a provision to pull out if Sling TV attracts too many customers that already have pay-TV subscriptions.[70] But for sports fans, it removes a major obstacle to cutting the cord, at least nominally. To be sure, regional sports networks remain absent (not to mention Fox Sports 1 and NBCSN), but if your only non-NFL sporting interests involve the NBA and you're not particularly attached to your local team, you can sign up for a package that will deliver the nationally televised games on ESPN and TNT for much cheaper than you're likely to get from the cable company, even when you add a separate subscription to the NBA League Pass broadband service.

Perhaps the most noteworthy thing about Sling TV is that – even though it was ABC's objections to AutoHop that landed the Disney networks on the service to begin with – there are no ABC stations on Sling TV. Dish may add broadcast networks to the service at some point down the line, but for an additional fee.[71] Of course, people who can pick up their local ABC station with an antenna have no need to pay an extra fee for broadcast stations through Sling TV. Thus, by taking the precise opposite approach – *not* carrying broadcast stations – Sling TV opens up precisely the possibility that so scared the broadcasters when it came to Aereo: the notion that people might pay for ESPN but pick up broadcast stations without paying for them.[72] Broadcasters may have won the battle over Aereo, but they may still lose the war. That makes the FCC's proposal to treat "online video distributors" under the same rules as cable and satellite providers of considerable interest. Will services such as Sling TV be required to carry broadcast stations on their most basic tiers, and if not how will broadcasters react? The industry does seem open to the notion of allowing services carrying cable networks to opt out of carrying broadcast stations.[73] Stay tuned.

* * *

Cord-cutting may disrupt the business model on which the sports rights boom is built, but that doesn't necessarily mean it'll stop it from growing anytime soon. Because sports has to be watched live, not on the on-demand basis that most over-the-top services focus on, and so much of it is tied up in cable channels that require a subscription to some sort of cable bundle, sports is the single biggest bulwark against widespread cord-cutting. ESPN finished 2014 as the most-watched network across all of cable. That means cable operators will have less appetite to stand up to sports networks that provide much of the reason for people to continue to subscribe to their service. It also could mean even more sports make the move to cable to provide even more reason to sign up for or keep a cable subscription.

That means the Big Ten should still be in for a big payday as it enters negotiations for TV rights that expire after the 2016-17 academic season – especially since it represents the last sports property big enough to move the needle to come up for negotiation for the rest of the decade. Anyone who thinks ESPN's cost-cutting will make them any less likely to pay up for Big Ten rights isn't paying attention; more likely, ESPN is cutting costs hard enough to allow them to afford the rights. As with the Big 12 and Pac-12, it seems likely that ESPN will elect to share rights with Fox, which really needs a property that can move the needle as much as the Big Ten to prop up Fox Sports 1's fortunes, and which is already a co-owner of the Big Ten Network. All that's needed is just the prospect of another competitor with the slightest interest in the rights, or even one of the two going it alone, to force the two to break the bank, and that may not come from Comcast, CBS, Turner, or any other traditional linear outlet.[74]

In the short term, many expect the Internet video boom to only further ratchet up the competition for sports rights as online media companies come into the space. Digital companies have mostly stayed on the sidelines so far, but sports leagues have long been confident it's only a matter of time before they jump in. Many leagues already have relationships with Apple and Google for apps for iOS and Android and a presence on YouTube. Microsoft's Xbox Live platform represents a premium service with access to ESPN3 and various highlights. Netflix and Facebook also offer platforms that intrigue leagues.[75]

In 2015, the NFL took the plunge with experimenting with over-the-top streaming of games by electing to hold back a game between the Buffalo Bills and Jacksonville Jaguars in London to sell to an over-the-top outfit. Yahoo eventually reached an agreement to stream the game live around the world, with CBS, which would have otherwise shown the game as the AFC network, producing the game and using its own announcers to call it.[76] Yahoo and the NFL boasted over 15 million unique viewers and 33 million streams for the game, but those numbers counted anyone that watched as little as three seconds of the game, even if they just happened to visit any of Yahoo's sites where it was autoplaying, as well as international audiences; a measure of average domestic audience, which would allow a more apples-to-apples comparison of Nielsen ratings for linear TV, would come out to closer to 1.6 million viewers, substantially behind other London games in the same time slot airing on traditional networks (even those with similarly unattractive teams) and a figure no NFL game window has sunk as low as even at the nadir of NFL Network distribution.[77] Nonetheless, the NFL has talked with streaming providers about selling separate streaming rights to its Thursday Night Football package.

Audience size is only part of the problem. Ultimately, one of the major purposes of the NFL-Yahoo experiment was simply to determine that the Internet could handle a TV-quality stream of an NFL game delivered to millions of people. The elephant in the room for any live streaming effort is the quality of the stream itself; even as Netflix and its ilk provide high-quality on-demand streams, live streams of high-demand events have remained infamous for buffering, low quality, and being well behind what a linear feed would be showing, whether available for free or through a TV Everywhere system. NBC, infamous for withholding marquee Olympics events for its primetime show, allowed for streaming of every event for the 2012 London games for authenticated subscribers, but the platform promptly choked under the pressure. Things have gotten better in recent years, but not quite out of the woods; in less than a year of existence Sling TV has repeatedly broken down during the NCAA Tournament and other high-demand events, and even the premieres of *Game of Thrones* and *Fear the Walking Dead*, though the company has blamed its issues on planned upgrades that didn't work as intended.[78] Yahoo's NFL game seemed to go off mostly without a hitch, but it also seemed to perform better on streaming devices than accessed directly through the Web.[79]

But even if the technical issues go away, most Internet companies don't seem to be set up very well to make enough money to effectively compete for sports rights, at least without changes that would likely implode the cable sports market anyway. Any free, unrestricted streaming platform would have the same disadvantage broadcast faced when it lost the BCS to ESPN: it would have to make all its money off of advertising, without cable television's dual revenue stream. The sort of paywall model common on the Internet, on the other hand, is most akin to the premium channels and pay-per-view services that have helped kill boxing - recall Netflix explicitly comparing itself to HBO. Many tech companies do run walled gardens within which it could offer games for free or cheap, but those walled gardens tend to be based in hardware the consumer buys himself and tends to form a brand attachment to, limiting any content within those gardens to a fairly arbitrary cross-section of the audience; an event Apple acquires for iTunes isn't likely to be available on Chromecast or Roku, and an event playing on Xbox Live won't be accessible to anyone with a Playstation. It's also not clear why any sports entity would stream content through another entity's site when it could stream it on its own site - most of the potential obstacles to simply putting all your games on your own network don't apply to the Internet. One would think it would take a lot of money to convince a league to sign up with a middleman rather than go it alone.

* * *

Still, does all this add up to the demise of linear television? Should we even mourn its demise given all the advantages of the Internet? Should cable providers be getting ready for a future as solely Internet providers and broadcast stations ready to liquidate their spectrum? What purpose could it possibly serve that couldn't be served by the Internet? Certainly Netflix CEO Reed Hastings thinks there isn't any; he's predicted that sometime in the next 10-20 years, all of television will be delivered over the Internet, with even sports networks adopting an "on-demand" model.[80] Before we're too quick to throw linear television in the dustbin of history, though, let's think about what distinguishes it from the Internet. It all goes back to the fundamental fact at the heart of the sports television boom in the first place: people have to watch sports as it happens.

When you call up a video on Netflix, or any other video service, the device you use to access it sends a message asking for the video and sends it to the ISP or wireless provider, which sends it on its way through the network to Netflix. Netflix receives the message and sends the video on its way back through the network to you. If someone else wants to watch the same video, they go through the same process, even if they're on the same ISP. Streaming a live event works the same way: your device tells the streaming provider it wants to watch the stream, and the streaming provider sends the content of the stream back through the network to you. It does this for each and every person that wants to access the stream, again regardless of whether or not they're on the same ISP, even though they're watching the exact same thing at the same time, with each new person joining the stream joining at the exact same point, yet each of them watching, in effect, on their own individual "channels". It's possible for the source of the stream to send a single stream to a point further down the network, but it requires dedicated architecture, and even then, at some point it still needs to be duplicated for each person trying to access it; as such it's very uncommon.[81]

You can imagine what the effect is when a huge number of people want to watch the same thing at the same time. It's essentially the same problem the Mayweather-Pacquiao fight had, where cable operators collectively had to process every one of the over 4.5 million purchases made across the nation. But just like the problems the Mayweather-Pacquiao fight ran into are unheard of for other big televised events, neither has anyone heard of a television channel regularly freezing while it buffers or fluctuating in picture quality, or even being completely inaccessible, without thinking something was wrong with their signal or connection, yet such is often the norm when it comes to watching things online, at least in the case of a live stream. Broadcast stations send out one signal, and that signal can be received by anyone with an antenna; similarly most cable companies send out their offerings in one burst, and anyone can tune in to the sliver they want while leaving everything else for everyone else. It is infinitely scalable in a way the Internet, at least as described here, can never be.[82]

Video puts a massive strain on the Internet, or any technology used to deliver it; an unmodulated standard-definition signal uses more than a thousand times the bandwidth of a telephone-quality voice signal, and the 6 MHz of an analog broadcast channel, suitable for standard-defintion picture and sound, is 150 times the bandwidth demand of stereo, high-fidelity sound.[83] Netflix alone accounts for over a third of Internet traffic during peak hours, with Netflix and YouTube combined accounting for more than half,[84] and streaming video as a whole making up over 70% of downstream traffic.[85] A disproportionate amount of bandwidth is being used by visitors to a few video sites. The amount of video people consume may well pose the single most serious threat to net neutrality, the backbone of the free and open Internet, and it will only get worse as more and more people discover the selection of video available online and as more and more video currently being consumed on linear television channels moves to the Internet. Interconnection deals, like the one between Comcast and Netflix that was such a point of controversy during the recent debate over the FCC's net neutrality regulations, may help capacity keep pace, but at the expense of allowing ISPs to be gatekeepers by forcing video providers to pay a tax, exactly the antithesis of what has built the Internet – including Netflix itself – into what it is today.

Considering all this, it should be apparent that anything that can take some of the video load off of the Internet as we know it today should not be dismissed out of hand. But considering what advantages the Internet brings to the table to begin with, what sort of content would people be willing to watch at a particular time set by someone else? Certainly people may still want to simply turn on the TV (or whatever would fill that role) and have something on in the background while they do other things or watch a parade of thematically connected programming without having to think too much about actually picking out anything specific, but this question really boils down to, what sort of programming would benefit from the linear television model, in that it inspires a large number of people to tune in to the same thing at the exact same time? Certainly anything, including scripted programming that theoretically can be seen at any time, can inspire people to want to see it as soon as it's available if they wish to avoid being spoiled about it on social media (or conversely if they want to take part in the conversation surrounding it), but what really inspires this sort of behavior is live programming.

And it is here that we come upon the root of the issue, because while live events can encompass a number of things such as awards shows or breaking news, the vast majority of this sort of live programming is sports. Underscoring the point, ESPN research found that 99 of the top 100 telecasts in the 18-49 demographic in 2010 consisted of live events – when it wasn't sports, it was awards shows like the Oscars and other live events like *American Idol*.[86] For all the talk about captive audiences and DVRs and money demos, what ultimately underlies the entire rush to pour so much money into sports, all the skyrocketing contracts and subscriber fees, all the multimillion dollar contracts and abandonment of tradition and principles, all the rush to build new sports networks, is the simple, largely unacknowledged fact that sports is one of the last few things holding people to traditional linear television at all. It is the one thing for which the Internet's advantages regularly fall flat and linear television's advantages have a chance to shine. In turn, the fact that cable networks have been the biggest beneficiary of it is a simple reflection of the fact that cable has so far enjoyed a decided monetary advantage without much in the way of substantial audience loss.

The great irony of this, though, and of the numerous other challenges facing broadcast television, is that a linear television landscape built from scratch would be built on over-the-air broadcasting before any linear channels transmitted over cable. Over-the-air broadcasting can, in theory, reach mobile devices that aren't tethered to any wires in a way that cable can't without using the Internet as an intermediary (thus defeating the point of using linear television as your medium in the first place), and wireless networks will always be more constrained than wired networks, since wireless networks have to compete with one another, with broadcasters, and with numerous other uses for the same spectrum. Moreover, over-the-air broadcasters don't have to be associated with or reach an agreement with any particular Internet provider, making them more true to the spirit of net neutrality. It's the very sports broadcasters are being most deprived of that could best justify their existence. Time will tell if that proves to be cold comfort to the industry.

Notes

Chapter 1: Rags to Riches

[1] Nagle, Dave, "Ribbon-Cutting Today for ESPN's First Building in Southington", *ESPN MediaZone*, 8 Jan 2014, retrieved from http://espnmediazone.com/us/press-releases/2014/01/ribbon-cutting-today-espns-first-building-southington/.

[2] Badenhausen, Kurt, "The Value of ESPN Surpasses $50 Billion", *Forbes*, 29 Apr 2014, retrieved from http://www.forbes.com/sites/kurtbadenhausen/2014/04/29/the-value-of-espn-surpasses-50-billion/.

[3] Nagle, op. cit.; Miller, James Michael, and Tom Shales, *Those Guys Have All the Fun: Inside the World of ESPN*, New York : Back Bay Books, 2011, p13.

[4] Miller and Shales, pp. 5-4, 7-8.

[5] Calabro, Marian, *Zap! A Brief History of Television*, New York : Four Winds Press, 1992, pp. 134, 137-139.

[6] United States Code of Federal Regulations, 47 §73.610; Waldbillig, Larry, "The History of UHF TV", *History's Dumpster*, 15 Mar 2014, retrieved from http://historysdumpster.blogspot.com/2014/03/the-history-of-uhf-tv.html; "Broadcasting Yearbook 1978", Washington : Broadcasting Publications Inc., pp. B1-B79, retrieved from http://www.americanradiohistory.com/Archive-BC-YB/1978/B-Television-Broadcasting-Yearbook-1978-Full.pdf.

[7] Waldbillig, op. cit.; Longley, Lawrence D., "The FCC and the All-Channel Receiver Bill of 1962", *Journal of Broadcasting*, vol. 42, #3, Sum 1969, pp. 293-300, retrieved from https://transition.fcc.gov/Bureaus/OSEC/library/legislative_histories/612.pdf.

[8] "Broadcasting Yearbook 1978", pp. B1-B79, B139.

[9] CFR 47 §73.603 and §73.610; O'Neal, James E., "TV and the Mystique of Channel 6", *TVTechnology*, 14 Apr 2009, retrieved from http://www.tvtechnology.com/news/0002/tv-and-the-mystique-of-channel-6/201146.

[10] "Broadcasting Yearbook 1978", pp. B1-B80. Of the top 50 markets, representing over two-thirds of the country, six had two VHF stations or fewer, 14 had three VHF stations, 16 had four, 11 had five, and three had six or seven. Of the 14 markets with five or more VHF stations, ten were in the top 20 markets.

[11] Waldbillig, op. cit.

[12] Ciciora, Walter S., "The History of Modern Cable Television Technology", 2004 IEEE Conference on the History of Electronics, p4, retrieved from http://ethw.org/images/f/fd/Ciciora.pdf.

[13] "History of Cable", California Cable and Telecommunications Association, retrieved from http://www.calcable.org/learn/history-of-cable/.

[14] Ibid.

[15] Miller and Shales, p5.

[16] Ibid.

[17] Ibid., pp. 6-9.

[18] Parsons, Patrick, "The Evolution of the Cable-Satellite Distribution System", *Journal of Broadcasting and Electronic Media*, Mar 2003, pp. 11-13, retrieved from http://comm.louisville.edu/`al/421/pdfs/parsons.pdf.

[19] Calabro, p139.

[20] Miller and Shales, pp. 5, 146.

[21] Ibid., pp. 19, 24, 58; Bodenheimer, George, with Donald T. Phillips, *Every Town is a Sports Town: Business Leadership at ESPN, from the Mailroom to the Boardroom*", New York : Grand Central Publishing, 2015, p9.

[22] Miller and Shales, pp. 19, 21-23.

[23] Ibid., esp. pp. 17-21, 23-25.

[24] Ibid., pp. 29-31.

[25] Ibid., p60; Sherman, Ed, "ESPN's Chris Berman has seen NFL draft's popularity soar", *Chicago Tribune*, 26 Apr 2015, retrieved from http://www.chicagotribune.com/sports/columnists/ct-nfl-draft-espn-sherman-media-spt-0427-20150426-column.html.

[26] Miller and Shales, pp. 81-85.

[27] Ibid., pp. 60-62, 117.

[28] Ibid., pp. 104-109.

[29] Ibid., pp. 120-122, 173.

[30] Ibid., pp. 126-127, 134; Solomon, Jon, "NCAA Supreme Court ruling felt at O'Bannon trial 30 years later", CBS Sports, 26 Jun 2014, retrieved from http://www.cbssports.com/collegefootball/eye-on-college-football/24598262/ncaa-supreme-court-ruling-felt-at-obannon-trial-30-years-later.

[31] Miller and Shales, pp. 145-151, 211.

[32] Ibid., pp. 189-193, 253.

[33] Ibid., pp. 155-160, 232-239, 260-263, 280-282, 391-401.

[34] Ibid., pp. 312-323.

[35] Ibid., pp. 343-350.

[36] Ibid., p363.

[37] Ibid., pp. 406-411.

[38] "ESPN, ABC And NBA Reach Six-year Agreement", Business Wire, 22 Jan 2002.

[39] Hiestand, Michael, "ABC Sports yields to corporate cousin", USA Today, 11 Aug 2006, C3.

[40] Willow, Molly, "ESPN deal for BCS A victory for viewers", Columbus Dispatch, 19 Nov 2008, retrieved from http://www.dispatch.com/content/stories/life_and_entertainment/2008/11/19/1A_MOLLY1119.ART_ART_11-19-08_E1_2CBSLLM.html.

[41] Weir, Tom, and Michael Hiestand, "BCS officially headed to ESPN starting in 2011", USA Today, 17 Nov 2008, retrieved from http://usatoday30.usatoday.com/sports/college/football/2008-11-17-bcs-fox-espn_n.htm; Dufresne, Chris, "Rose Bowl game moving to ESPN in 2011", Los Angeles Times, 13 Jun 2009, retrieved from http://articles.latimes.com/2009/jun/13/sports/sp-rose-bowl-espn13.

[42] Dufresne, op. cit.

[43] Futterman, Matthew, "ESPN Hauls In Rights to Top College Bowl Games", Wall Street Journal, 18 Nov 2008, B4.

[44] Miller and Shales, pp. 110-114.

[45] Ibid., pp. 408-410.

[46] Travis, Clay, "The 15 Most Valuable Sports Networks", FOX Sports, 7 May 2015, retrieved from http://www.foxsports.com/college-football/outkick-the-coverage/the-15-most-valuable-sports-networks-050715.

[47] Hagey, Keach, "CBS Plays Hardball as Affiliate Fees Pile Up", Wall Street Journal, 20 Aug 2014, retrieved from http://www.wsj.com/articles/cbs-plays-hardball-as-affiliate-fees-pile-up-1408578087.

[48] Ourand, John, and Austin Karp, "We are young", SportsBusiness Journal, 19 Mar 2012, retrieved from http://www.sportsbusinessdaily.com/Journal/Issues/2012/03/19/Media/Sports-demos.aspx.

[49] Badenhausen, op. cit.; Greenfeld, Karl Taro, "ESPN: Everywhere Sports Profit Network", Bloomberg Business, 30 Aug 2012, retrieved from http://www.bloomberg.com/bw/articles/2012-08-30/espn-everywhere-sports-profit-network; Sandomir, Richard, James Andrew Miller, and Steve Eder, "To Protect Its Empire, ESPN Stays on Offense", New York Times, 26 Aug 2013, retrieved from http://www.nytimes.com/2013/08/27/sports/ncaafootball/to-defend-its-empire-espn-stays-on-offensive.html.

[50] Miller and Shales, pp. 209-211.

[51] Thompson, Derek, "Mad About the Cost of TV? Blame Sports", The Atlantic, 2 Apr 2013, retrieved from http://www.theatlantic.com/business/archive/2013/04/mad-about-the-cost-of-tv-blame-sports/274575/.

Chapter 2: Follow the Leader

[1] Lucia, Joe, "Speed fans are angry about Fox Sports 1", Awful Announcing, 22 Aug 2013, retrieved from http://awfulannouncing.com/2013/speed-fans-are-angry-about-fox-sports-1.html.

[2] Lucia, Joe, "Speed fans are angry about Fox Sports 1 – Part II", Awful Announcing, 30 Aug 2013, retrieved from http://awfulannouncing.com/2013/speed-fans-are-angry-about-fox-sports-1-part-ii.html.

[3] Yoder, Matt, "Speed fans are angry about Fox Sports 1 – Part III", Awful Announcing, 19 Sep 2013, retrieved from http://awfulannouncing.com/2013/speed-fans-are-angry-about-fox-sports-1-part-iii.html.

[4] Ourand, John, and Tripp Mickle, "Will Fox launch all-sports network?", Sports Business Daily, 2 Apr 2012, p4, retrieved from http://www.sportsbusinessdaily.com/Journal/Issues/2012/04/02/Media/Fox-channel.aspx; Karp, Austin, "Figures Show Fox Sports 1 Could Launch in Around 85.8 Million U.S. Homes", Sports Business Daily, 8 Aug 2013, retrieved from http://www.sportsbusinessdaily.com/Daily/Issues/2013/08/08/Research-and-Ratings/Distribution.aspx.

[5] Ourand, John, "Distributors hold the line", SportsBusiness Journal, 19 Aug 2013, retrieved from http://www.sportsbusinessdaily.com/Journal/Issues/2013/08/19/Media/Fox-Sports-1.aspx.

[6] Cable Television Consumer Protection and Competition Act of 1992, Public Law 102-385, §4, 5 Oct 1992; Cauley, Leslie, "Ready to Roll: Cable-TV companies have gone digital – with profound implications for both consumers and competitors", Wall Street Journal, 22 Mar 1999, R10.

[7] Miller and Shales, pp. 101-102, 122-123, 146, 159-160, 171, 216-217, 223, 232, 329, 406-407.

[8] Olgeirson, Ian, "Can EchoStar deliver 500-channel capacity?", Denver Business Journal, 6 Dec 1998, retrieved from http://www.bizjournals.com/denver/stories/1998/12/07/newscolumn4.html.

[9] "ARE TV PARTNERS CONCERNED ABOUT NBA CABLE NETWORK LAUNCH?", SportsBusiness Daily, 24 Sep 1999, retrieved from http://www.sportsbusinessdaily.com/Daily/Issues/1999/09/24/Sports-Media/ARE-TV-PARTNERS-CONCERNED-ABOUT-NBA-CABLE-NETWORK-LAUNCH.aspx; "AFTER NBA.COM TV'S LAUNCH, IS WEB SPINOFF NEXT FOR LEAGUE?", SportsBusiness Daily, 8 Nov 1999, retrieved from http://www.sportsbusinessdaily.com/Daily/Issues/1999/11/8/Leagues-Governing-Bodies/AFTER-NBACOM-TVS-LAUNCH-IS-WEB-SPINOFF-NEXT-FOR-LEAGUE.aspx.

[10] Miller and Shales, pp. 497-498; "Lights Out for GE's NBC, As ESPN/ABC Take Over NBA Rights", SportsBusiness Daily, 17 Dec 2001, retrieved from http://www.sportsbusinessdaily.com/Daily/Issues/2001/12/Issue-66/Sports-Media/Lights-Out-For-Ges-NBC-As-ESPNABC-Take-Over-NBA-Rights.aspx; "NBA Finalizes Cable-Heavy TV Deal, Sees 25% Fee Increase", SportsBusiness Daily, 23 Jan 2002, retrieved from http://www.sportsbusinessdaily.com/Daily/Issues/2002/01/Issue-88/Sports-Media/NBA-Finalizes-Cable-Heavy-TV-Deal-Sees-25-Fee-Increase.aspx.

[11] "NBA Finalizes Cable-Heavy TV Deal".

[12] Ibid.; "NBA TV Talks Reportedly Include Creation of New Cable Net", SportsBusiness Daily, 14 Nov 2001, retrieved from http://www.sportsbusinessdaily.com/Daily/Issues/2001/11/Issue-45/Sports-Media/NBA-TV-Talks-Reportedly-Include-Creation-Of-New-Cable-Net.aspx; "Lights Out for GE's NBC"; "Stern Hints League-Backed TV Channel May Be Postponed", SportsBusiness Daily, 12 Apr 2002, retrieved from http://www.sportsbusinessdaily.com/Daily/Issues/2002/04/Issue-142/Sports-Media/Stern-Hints-League-Backed-TV-Channel-May-Be-Postponed.aspx; "Proposed ASN Likely To Be Dumped As NBA TV Will Get Makeover", SportsBusiness Daily, 25 Jun 2002, retrieved from http://www.sportsbusinessdaily.com/Daily/Issues/2002/06/Issue-192/Sports-Media/Proposed-ASN-Likely-To-Be-Dumped-As-NBA-TV-Will-Get-Makeover.aspx.

[13] Miller and Shales, pp. 558-559, 562-564.

[14] Miller and Shales, pp. 563-569.

[15] Katz, Marc, "Ratings climb for prime-time NFL games", Dayton Daily News, 29 Dec 2006, B2; Hiestand, Michael, "Flex concept looking like sweet deal for NBC", USA Today, 25 Oct 2006, C6; Volner, Derek, "ESPN has televised the Top 20 most-viewed programs in cable history", ESPN Front Row, 12 Jan 2015, retrieved from http://www.espnfrontrow.com/2015/01/httpwww-espnfrontrow-com201501espn-has-telecast-the-top-20-most-viewed-programs-in-cable-tv/.

[16] Fang, Ken, "Is ESPN Forcing ABC to Get Out of the Sports Business?", Fang's Bites, 12 Nov 2008, retrieved from http://fangsbites.com/abc-sports/is-espn-forcing-abc-to-get-out-of-the-sports-business.html.

[17] Ourand, John, "NFL Network steps up carriage talks", SportsBusiness Journal, 9 Mar 2009, retrieved from http://www.sportsbusinessdaily.com/Journal/Issues/2009/03/20090309/This-Weeks-News/NFL-Network-Steps-Up-Carriage-Talks.aspx.

[18] Ourand, John, "Touchdown! Time Warner Cable Signs Multiyear Carriage Deal With NFL Network", SportsBusiness Daily, 21 Sep 2012, retrieved from http://www.sportsbusinessdaily.com/Daily/Issues/2012/09/21/Media/NFL-Network.aspx.

[19] Sandomir et al., op. cit.

[20] Ibid.

[21] Ibid.

[22] Ibid.

[23] Travis, op. cit.

[24] James, Meg, "Turmoil at Viacom: In Viacom Split, Moonves Now Looks Better by Half", Los Angeles Times, 6 Sep 2006, C1; "Fortune 500", Fortune, 2015, retrieved from http://fortune.com/fortune500/.

[25] Sandomir, Richard, "CBS Considered Paying ESPN to Take Tourney", New York Times, 5 May 2010, B11.

[26] Ourand, John, "The great cable migration", SportsBusiness Journal, 21 Feb 2011, retrieved from http://www.sportsbusinessdaily.com/Journal/Issues/2011/02/21/In-Depth/Media-story.aspx.

[27] Ourand, John, "NHL annual rights fee to top $200 million", SportsBusiness Journal, 11 Apr 2011, p4, retrieved from http://www.sportsbusinessdaily.com/Journal/Issues/2011/04/11/Media/NHL-TV.aspx.

[28] Fixmer, Andy, and Edmund Lee, "Time Warner, CBS Seen as Candidates for Merger: Real M&A", Bloomberg Businessweek, 22 Apr 2013, retrieved from http://www.bloomberg.com/news/articles/2013-04-21/time-warner-cbs-seen-candidate-for-merger-real-m-a.

[29] Miller and Shales, 357-359.

[30] Ibid., pp. 541-542.

[31] Schechner, Sam, "Comcast-NBC Is a Challenger", Wall Street Journal, 12 Oct 2009, retrieved from http://www.wsj.com/articles/SB20001424052748704882404574463712075917016.

[32] Steel, Emily, and Richard Sandomir, "Fox Challenges ESPN With Pursuit of Time Warner", New York Times, 17 Jul 2014, retrieved from http://www.nytimes.com/2014/07/18/business/media/fox-challenges-espn-with-pursuit-of-time-warner.html.

[33] Miller and Shales, pp. 550-554.

[34] Ourand, John, "Pedigree part of pitch for Fox Sports 1", SportsBusiness Journal, 26 Nov 2012, retrieved from http://www.sportsbusinessdaily.com/Journal/Issues/2012/11/26/Media/FoxSports1.aspx.

[35] Ourand, John, "FS1, ESPN take turns counterprogramming", SportsBusiness Journal, 22 Jul 2013, p5, retrieved from http://www.sportsbusinessdaily.com/Journal/Issues/2012/11/26/Media/FoxSports1.aspx.

[36] E.g., Sandomir et al., op. cit.

[37] Mustich, Emma, "Keith Olbermann: A history of (too much) backbone", Salon, 9 Nov 2010, retrieved from http://www.salon.com/2010/11/09/olbermann_msnbc_statement/.

[38] Cingari, Jennifer, "ESPN Shifts Olbermann to Permanent Afternoon Slot in September", ESPN MediaZone, 26 Aug 2014, retrieved from http://espnmediazone.com/us/press-releases/2014/08/espn-shifts-olbermann-to-permanent-afternoon-slot-in-september-2/.

Chapter 3: Printing Money

[1] James, LeBron, as told to Lee Jenkins, "I'm Coming Home", Sports Illustrated, vol. 121, #2, 21 Jul 2014, p41.

[2] Kerber, Fred, "Bulls snag big man Gasol; LeBron's deal for 2 years", New York Post, 13 Jul 2014, p90.

[3] Ibid.

[4] Ourand, John, "Industry wonders who will challenge ESPN", SportsBusiness Journal, 9 Nov 2009, retrieved from http://www.sportsbusinessdaily.com/Journal/Issues/2009/11/20091109/SBJ-In-Depth/Industry-Wonders-Who-Will-Challenge-ESPN.aspx.

[5] Ourand, John, "Now on deck for next sports rights deal: MLB", SportsBusiness Journal, 4 June 2012, retrieved from http://www.sportsbusinessdaily.com/Journal/Issues/2012/06/04/Leagues-and-Governing-Bodies/MLBTV.aspx.

[6] Ourand, "Now on deck for next sports rights deal".

[7] Ourand, John, "Olympian effort: ESPN talks moved quickly", SportsBusiness Journal, 3 Sep 2012, p37, retrieved from http://www.sportsbusinessdaily.com/Journal/Issues/2012/09/03/Media/MLB-ESPN-side.aspx; Ourand, John, "Bidders angle for more MLB", SportsBusiness Journal, 3 Sep 2012, retrieved from http://www.sportsbusinessdaily.com/Journal/Issues/2012/09/03/Media/MLB-ESPN.aspx.

[8] Ourand, John, "Fox, Turner contribute to $12 billion rights haul for MLB", SportsBusiness Journal, 24 Sep 2012, retrieved from http://www.sportsbusinessdaily.com/Journal/Issues/2012/09/24/Media/MLB-12B.aspx.

[9] Ibid.; Ourand, "Bidders angle for more MLB"; Flint, Joe, "Major League Baseball's next TV deals could reshape landscape", Los Angeles Times, 30 Aug 2012, retrieved from http://articles.latimes.com/2012/aug/30/entertainment/la-et-ct-foxturnerbaseball-20120830.

[10] Mickle, Tripp, and John Ourand, "Fox making strong bid to keep NASCAR", SportsBusiness Journal, 18 Jun 2012, p8, retrieved from http://www.sportsbusinessdaily.com/Journal/Issues/2012/06/18/Media/Fox-NASCAR.aspx.

[11] Mickle, Tripp, and John Ourand, "Fox eyes shift of future Cup races to Speed", SportsBusiness Journal, 20 Jun 2011, retrieved from http://www.sportsbusinessdaily.com/Journal/Issues/2011/06/20/Media/Fox-Cup-Speed.aspx.

[12] Mickle and Ourand, "Fox making strong bid to keep NASCAR".

[13] Ibid.

[14] Mickle, Tripp, and John Ourand, "NASCAR rides hot rights market to increase with Fox", SportsBusiness Journal, 15 Oct 2012, retrieved from http://www.sportsbusinessdaily.com/Journal/Issues/2012/10/15/Media/NASCAR-TV.aspx.

[15] Ourand, John, and Tripp Mickle, "NBC steps up, lands NASCAR", SportsBusiness Journal, 29 Jul 2013, retrieved from http://www.sportsbusinessdaily.com/Journal/Issues/2013/07/29/Media/NASCAR-NBC.aspx.

[16] Mickle, Tripp, and John Ourand, "Fox Sports adds races, years to NASCAR deal", SportsBusiness Journal, 5 Aug 2013, p35, retrieved from http://www.sportsbusinessdaily.com/Journal/Issues/2013/08/05/Media/Fox-NASCAR.aspx.

[17] Ourand and Karp, op. cit.; Ourand, John, and John Lombardo, "NBA ready to discuss rights deal", SportsBusiness Journal, 13 May 2013, retrieved from http://www.sportsbusinessdaily.com/Journal/Issues/2013/05/13/Media/NBA-TV-rights.aspx.

[18] Ibid.

[19] Ourand, John, and John Lombardo, "NBA's talks with ESPN and Turner move forward", SportsBusiness Journal, 2 Jun 2014, retrieved from http://www.sportsbusinessdaily.com/Journal/Issues/2014/06/02/Media/NBA-rights.aspx.

[20] Lombardo, John, and John Ourand, "NBA nearing massive media deals", SportsBusiness Journal, 8 Sep 2014, retrieved from http://www.sportsbusinessdaily.com/Journal/Issues/2014/09/08/Media/NBA-media.aspx.

[21] Lombardo, John, and John Ourand, "ESPN, Turner Will Pay A Combined $24B In New Nine-Year NBA Media Rights Deal", SportsBusiness Daily, 6 Oct 2014, retrieved from http://www.sportsbusinessdaily.com/Daily/Issues/2014/10/06/Media/NBA-media.aspx; Lombardo, John, and John Ourand, "Fast break: NBA media rights", SportsBusiness Journal, 13 Oct 2014, retrieved from http://www.sportsbusinessdaily.com/Journal/Issues/2014/10/13/Media/NBA.aspx.

[22] Ourand, John, "Atlantic 10 Signs Eight-Year Rights Deals With ESPN, CBS Sports Net, NBC Sports Net", SportsBusiness Daily, 2 Oct 2012, retrieved from http://www.sportsbusinessdaily.com/Daily/Issues/2012/10/02/Media/A-10.aspx.

[23] Meltzer, Dave, "White beaming after Fox deal for UFC", Yahoo Sports, 18 Aug 2011, retrieved from http://sports.yahoo.com/mma/news?slug=dm-meltzer_ufc_fox_deal_white_satisfied_081811.

[24] Ibid.

[25] Chiappetta, Mike, "UFC and Fox Officially Announce Details of Landmark 7-Year Broadcast Deal", MMAFighting, 18 Aug 2011, retrieved from http://www.mmafighting.com/2011/08/18/ufc-and-fox-officially-announce-details-of-landmark-7-year-broad.

[26] Mickle, Tripp, and John Ourand, "NBC eyes USA Track & Field to build out Olympic sports roster", SportsBusiness Journal, 28 Apr 2014, retrieved from http://www.sportsbusinessdaily.com/Journal/Issues/2014/04/28/Media/NBC-USATF.aspx.

[27] Ourand, John, "Sports media's next step", SportsBusiness Journal, 11 Nov 2013, retrieved from http://www.sportsbusinessdaily.com/Journal/Issues/2013/11/11/In-Depth/Sports-media-main.aspx.

[28] "THE WORLD IS YOURS: MURDOCH PLANS FOREIGN SPORTS CHANNEL", SportsBusiness Daily, 8 Oct 1997, retrieved from http://www.sportsbusinessdaily.com/Daily/Issues/1997/10/8/Sports-Media/THE-WORLD-IS-YOURS-MURDOCH-PLANS-FOREIGN-SPORTS-CHANNEL.aspx; Trecker, Jamie, "Global games dominate two

Fox channels", SportsBusiness Journal, 13 Mar 2000, retrieved from http://www.sportsbusinessdaily.com/Journal/Issues/2000/03/20000313/No-Topic-Name/Global-Games-Dominate-Two-Fox-Channels.aspx; Harris, Christopher, "History of Premier League on US television", World Soccer Talk, 22 Jul 2009, retrieved from http://worldsoccertalk.com/2009/07/22/history-of-premier-league-on-us-tv/.
[29] "THE WORLD IS YOURS".
[30] Zeigler, Mark, "Fox Sports World is soccer heaven", Daily Breeze (Torrance, CA), 6 Dec 2002, D2.
[31] Trecker, op. cit.
[32] Bernstein, Andy, "NBC, Fox bidding for World Cup", SportsBusiness Journal, 10 Oct 2005, retrieved from http://www.sportsbusinessdaily.com/Journal/Issues/2005/10/20051010/Media/NBC-Fox-Bidding-For-World-Cup.aspx.
[33] Miller and Shales, pp. 417-417 et seq.; Greenfeld, op. cit.
[34] Miller and Shales, pp. 597-598.
[35] Ibid.; Bernstein, Andy, "ABC/ESPN stalks Cup sans SUM", SportsBusiness Journal, 24 Oct 2005, retrieved from http://www.sportsbusinessdaily.com/Journal/Issues/2005/10/20051024/Media/ABCESPN-Stalks-Cup-Sans-SUM.aspx.
[36] Miller and Shales, pp. 597-599; Bernstein, Andy, "FIFA: Slow and steady wins a higher price", SportsBusiness Journal, 7 Nov 2005, retrieved from http://www.sportsbusinessdaily.com/Journal/Issues/2005/11/20051107/Other-News/FIFA-Slow-And-Steady-Wins-A-Higher-Price.aspx; Genzale, John, "Cup TV deal: 'A three-week dash of sleepless nights', SportsBusiness Journal, 5 Jun 2006, retrieved from http://www.sportsbusinessdaily.com/Journal/Issues/2006/06/20060605/This-Weeks-News/Cup-TV-Deal-A-Three-Week-Dash-Of-Sleepless-Nights.aspx.
[37] Miller and Shales, pp. 599, 675, 735, 737, 739-740.
[38] Ibid., pp. 739-740; Mickle, Tripp, "Trip to South Africa? Count 'SportsCenter' in", SportsBusiness Journal, 15 Jun 2009, retrieved from http://www.sportsbusinessdaily.com/Journal/Issues/2009/06/20090615/This-Weeks-News/Trip-To-South-Africa-Count-Sportscenter-In.aspx; Dickson, Glen, "ESPN Formulates World Cup Game Plan", Broadcasting & Cable, vol. 139, #44, 30 Nov 2009, p18; Cohen, Rachel, "ESPN betting U.S. fans will watch World Cup", The Ledger (Lakeland, FL), 9 Jun 2010.
[39] Miller and Shales, pp. 735-736.
[40] Ibid., p599.
[41] Benjamin, Amalie, "Touring European teams could boost US soccer", Boston Globe, 23 Jul 2012, retrieved from https://www.bostonglobe.com/sports/2012/07/22/liverpool-other-european-teams-can-help-soccer-popularity-usa/GaZilYPdal370EHU1php5J/story.html.
[42] Galarcep, Ives, "MLS All-Star Game needs a change as league evolves and draws more stars", Goal.com, 29 Jul 2015, retrieved from http://www.goal.com/en-us/news/1110/major-league-soccer/2015/07/29/13987252/mls-all-star-game-needs-a-change-as-league-evolves-and-draws.
[43] Botta, Christopher, and John Ourand, "The sky's the limit?", SportsBusiness Journal, 30 Jul 2012, p15, retrieved from http://www.sportsbusinessdaily.com/Journal/Issues/2012/07/30/In-Depth/English-Premier-League.aspx.
[44] Hiestand, Michael, "Fox to test Saturday soccer with Champions League final", USA Today, 20 May 2010, retrieved from http://usatoday30.usatoday.com/SPORTS/usaedition/2010-05-21-fox21_ST_U.htm.
[45] "ESPN Gets Record Cable Soccer Audience For ManU-Man City EPL Match", SportsBusiness Daily, 2 May 2012, retrieved from http://www.sportsbusinessdaily.com/Daily/Issues/2012/05/02/Media/Soccer-TV.aspx; Botta and Ourand, op. cit.
[46] Baxter, Kevin, "Foreign owners invade English Premier League", Los Angeles Times, 29 Mar 2014, retrieved from http://articles.latimes.com/2014/mar/29/sports/la-sp-soccer-baxter-20140330.
[47] Dreier, Fred, "Teams shift focus as soccer fans mature", SportsBusiness Journal, 15 Nov 2010, retrieved from http://www.sportsbusinessdaily.com/Journal/Issues/2010/11/20101115/This-Weeks-Issue/Teams-Shift-Focus-As-Soccer-Fans-Mature.aspx.
[48] Crupi, Anthony, "FIFA Deals Blow to TV Sports Powers", Adweek, 24 Oct 2011, retrieved from http://www.adweek.com/news/television/fifa-deals-blow-tv-sports-powers-136024.
[49] Yoder, Matt, "Fox Beats ESPN And NBC For 2018 And 2022 World Cup Rights", Awful Announcing, 21 Oct 2011, retrieved from http://awfulannouncing.com/2011-articles/fox-beats-espn-and-nbc-for-2018-and-2022-world-cup-rights.html.
[50] Reynolds, Mike, "GolTV Renews Key German League Rights", Multichannel News, 31 Oct 2011, retrieved from http://www.multichannel.com/news/content/goltv-renews-key-german-league-rights/361324.
[51] Vivarelli, Nick, "Al Jazeera's (R)Evolution", Variety, vol. 430, #1, 11 Feb 2013, pp. 14-15; Miles, Hugh, Al Jazeera: The Inside Story of the Arab News Channel that is Challenging the West, Grove Press : New York, 2005, pp. 28-29, 47-60.
[52] Miles, pp. 405-406, 420-421.
[53] Belson, Ken, "Al Jazeera, Seeking U.S. Viewers, Bets on Soccer", New York Times, 31 Aug 2012, A1.
[54] Vivarelli, op. cit.

[55] Ourand, John, "NBC Signs Three-Year Deal With MLS For Fox Soccer's Television Package", SportsBusiness Daily, 10 Aug 2011, retrieved from http://www.sportsbusinessdaily.com/Daily/Issues/2011/08/10/Media/MLS-NBC.aspx.

[56] Ourand, John, and Christopher Botta, "Several Networks Submit Bids For U.S. Rights To EPL Ahead Of Today's Deadline", SportsBusiness Daily, 18 Oct 2012, retrieved from http://www.sportsbusinessdaily.com/Daily/Issues/2012/10/18/Media/EPL-Rights.aspx.

[57] Deitsch, Richard, "NBC outlines vast Premier League coverage with new TV deal", Sports Illustrated, 16 Apr 2013, retrieved from http://www.si.com/soccer/2013/04/16/english-premier-league-nbc-tv-coverage.

[58] Ibid.; Goff, Steven, "English Premier League gets a big American stage on NBC", Washington Post, 16 Aug 2013, retrieved from https://www.washingtonpost.com/sports/dcunited/english-premier-league-gets-a-big-american-stage-on-nbc/2013/08/16/54b7e2da-06b9-11e3-bfc5-406b928603b2_story.html.

[59] Ourand, Matt, "NBC and the English Premier League will continue the best marriage in sports media", Awful Announcing, 11 Aug 2015, retrieved from http://awfulannouncing.com/2015/nbc-and-the-english-premier-league-will-continue-the-best-marriage-in-sports-media.html.

[60] Cardillo, Mike, "EPL Games Garnering More Viewers Than NHL Games on NBCSN, Rights Fees for Next TV Deal Should Only Increase", The Big Lead, 19 Dec 2014, retrieved from http://thebiglead.com/2014/12/19/epl-games-garnering-more-viewers-than-nhl-games-on-nbcsn-rights-fees-for-next-tv-deal-should-only-increase/.

[61] Yoder, "NBC and the English Premier League"; Cohen, Rachel, "NBC renews deal with Premier League for 6 years", Yahoo Sports, 10 Aug 2015, retrieved from http://sports.yahoo.com/news/nbc-renews-deal-english-premier-league-6-years-171957294-sow.html.

[62] Ourand, "NBC Signs Three-Year Deal With MLS".

[63] Ourand, John, and Christopher Botta, "MLS's big play", SportsBusiness Journal, 12 May 2014, retrieved from http://www.sportsbusinessdaily.com/Journal/Issues/2014/05/12/Media/MLS.aspx; Botta, Christopher, "Univision shows MLS the love with new deal", SportsBusiness Journal, 12 May 2014, p29, retrieved from http://www.sportsbusinessdaily.com/Journal/Issues/2014/05/12/Media/Univision-MLS.aspx.

[64] Mickle, Tripp, "Rough Water", SportsBusiness Journal, 17 Sep 2012, p16, retrieved from http://www.sportsbusinessdaily.com/Journal/Issues/2012/09/17/In-Depth/Americas-Cup.aspx.

[65] "Sports Comment: Due to mismanagement, America's Cup has become a joke", Capital (Annapolis), 18 Jul 2013, B5.

[66] Ourand, John, "Sailing Takes Me Away: NBC To Air America's Cup From S.F. In September '13", SportsBusiness Daily, 1 Mar 2012, retrieved from http://www.sportsbusinessdaily.com/Daily/Issues/2012/03/01/Media/Americas-Cup.aspx.

[67] Ibid.; Mickle, "Rough Water".

[68] Ourand, "Sailing Takes Me Away".

[69] Knecht, G. Bruce, "Larry Ellison's Dangerous America's Cup", Wall Street Journal, 18 May 2013, A13.

[70] Mickle, "Rough Water".

[71] "Sports Comment".

[72] Ibid.; Knecht, op. cit.

[73] Ibid.

[74] "Sports Comment"; Matier and Ross, "America's Cup could cost S.F. millions", San Francisco Chronicle, 10 Feb 2013, retrieved from http://www.sfgate.com/bayarea/matier-ross/article/America-s-Cup-could-cost-S-F-millions-4265828.php.

[75] Knecht, op. cit.; Stevenson, Seth, "Fast, Expensive, and Out of Control", Slate, 9 May 2013, retrieved from http://www.slate.com/articles/sports/sports_nut/2013/05/andrew_simpson_dead_did_the_british_sailor_drown_because_the_america_s_cup.html.

[76] "Sports Comment".

[77] Randewich, Noel, "Mechanical snafu again mars America's Cup racing", Reuters, 19 Aug 2013, retrieved from http://www.reuters.com/article/2013/08/19/us-sailing-americascup-breakdowns-idUSBRE97I11220130819.

[78] Levin, Josh, "The Miracle on San Francisco Bay", Slate, 25 Sep 2013, retrieved from http://www.slate.com/articles/sports/sports_nut/2013/09/america_s_cup_2013_oracle_team_usa_s_billionaire_funded_cheat_tastic_comeback.html.

Chapter 4: Big Man on Campus

[1] Watson, Graham, "Texas A&M freshman QB arrested then poses for shirtless mugshot", Yahoo! Sports, 29 Jun 2012, retrieved from http://sports.yahoo.com/blogs/dr-saturday/texas-m-freshman-qb-arrested-then-poses-shirtless-162345159--ncaaf.html.

[2] Thompson, Wright, "The trouble with Johnny", ESPN, 6 Aug 2013, retrieved from http://espn.go.com/espn/otl/story/_/id/9521439/heisman-winner-johnny-manziel-celebrity-derail-texas-aggies-season-espn-magazine.

[3] Krider, Dave, "Johnny Manziel is already a Texas legend", MaxPreps, 2 Dec 2010, retrieved from http://www.maxpreps.com/news/ruZ4kv5AEd-XkQAcxJSkrA/johnny-manziel-is-already-a-texas-legend.htm; Auping,

Jonny, "Johnny Kerrville", Slate, 5 Dec 2014, retrieved from
http://www.slate.com/articles/sports/sports_nut/2014/12/johnny_manziel_kerrville_even_in_the_town_where_he_
learned_to_play_the_game.single.html; Rauch, Isaac, "Who The Hell Is Johnny Manziel, And Why Wasn't He
Wearing A Shirt In His Mug Shot/ A Guide", Deadspin, 11 Nov 2012, retrieved from
http://deadspin.com/5959588/who-the-hell-is-johnny-manziel; Gregorian, Vahe, "A&M's Manziel is adjusting to
celebrity", St. Louis Post-Dispatch, 7 Jan 2013, B4.
⁴ Thompson, Wright, op. cit.
⁵ Rauch, op. cit.
⁶ Rauch, op. cit.; Auping, op. cit.
⁷ Sharp, Andrew, "The Night of Johnny Football", Grantland, 9 May 2014, retrieved from http://grantland.com/the-
triangle/the-night-of-johnny-football/.
⁸ Cabot, Mary Kay, "Johnny Manziel officially signs his four-year, $8.25 million contract with the Cleveland Browns",
Cleveland.com, 18 Jun 2014, retrieved from
http://www.cleveland.com/browns/index.ssf/2014/06/johnny_manziel_officially_sign.html.
⁹ Reed, Allen, "Texas A&M breaks fundraising record with $740 million in donations", The Eagle (Bryan-College
Station, TX), 17 Sep 2013, retrieved from http://www.theeagle.com/news/local/article_82266d1a-11c0-543b-b75a-
4c3613357abe.html.
¹⁰ Schroeder, George, "At Texas A&M, life after Johnny Manziel just as bright", USA Today, 11 Mar 2014, retrieved
from http://www.usatoday.com/story/sports/ncaaf/sec/2014/03/11/college-football-texas-am-aggies-johnny-manziel-
kevin-sumlin/6262023/; Murschel, Matt, "Johnny Manziel left Texas A&M, but his impact still lingers", Orlando
Sentinel, 15 Jul 2014, retrieved from http://articles.orlandosentinel.com/2014-07-15/sports/os-aggies-johnny-manziel-
0716-20140715_1_johnny-manziel-johnny-football-kyle-field.
¹¹ Miller, James Andrew, Steve Eder, and Richard Sandomir, "College Football's Most Dominant Player? It's ESPN",
New York Times, 25 Aug 2013, retrieved from http://www.nytimes.com/2013/08/25/sports/ncaafootball/college-
footballs-most-dominant-player-its-espn.html
¹² Staples, Andy, "How television changed college football - and how it will again", Sports Illustrated, 6 Aug 2012,
retrieved from http://www.si.com/college-football/2012/08/06/tv-college-football.
¹³Miller et al., op. cit.; Gunther, Ed, "'There is what is, and there is what we would like it to be'", The National
Championship Issue, 3 Jan 2009, retrieved from http://thenationalchampionshipissue.blogspot.com/2009/01/there-
is-what-is-and-there-is-what-we.html.
¹⁴ "Nebraska and other 5-7 teams are bowl-eligible this year, based on academic scores", SB Nation, 30 Nov 2015,
retrieved from http://www.sbnation.com/college-football/2015/11/19/9757930/bowl-game-eligibility-rules-ncaa-five-
wins-nebraska.
¹⁵ Smith, Michael, and John Ourand, "ESPN pays $2.25B for SEC rights", SportsBusiness Journal, 25 Aug 2008,
retrieved from http://www.sportsbusinessdaily.com/Journal/Issues/2008/08/20080825/This-Weeks-News/ESPN-
Pays-$225B-For-SEC-Rights.aspx.
¹⁶ Greenstein, Teddy, "Big Ten could see TV money skyrocket with expansion", Chicago Tribune, 13 May 2010,
retrieved from http://articles.chicagotribune.com/2010-05-13/sports/chi-100514-big-ten-expansion-greenstein_1_btn-
big-ten-network-tv-executive.
¹⁷ Frank the Tank, "The Big Ten Expansion Index: A Different Shade of Orange", FRANK THE TANK'S SLANT, 27
Dec 2009, retrieved from http://frankthetank.me/2009/12/27/the-big-ten-expansion-index-a-different-shade-of-
orange/.
¹⁸ Greenfeld, Karl Taro, "Head of the Pac", Bloomberg Businessweek, 15 Dec 2011, retrieved from
http://www.bloomberg.com/bw/magazine/head-of-the-pac-12152011.html.
¹⁹ Ibid.; Staples, op. cit.
²⁰ Staples, op. cit.; Ourand, John, and Michael Smith, "Pac-10 seeks college's richest TV contract", SportsBusiness
Journal, 21 Mar 2011, p3, retrieved from
http://www.sportsbusinessdaily.com/Journal/Issues/2011/03/21/Media/Pac-10.aspx.
²¹ Ourand, John, "Bidding war over the Pac-10's TV rights is already developing", SportsBusiness Journal, 28 Jun
2010, retrieved from http://www.sportsbusinessdaily.com/Journal/Issues/2010/06/20100628/Media/Bidding-War-
Over-The-Pac-10S-TV-Rights-Is-Already-Developing.aspx.
²² Ourand, John, and Michael Smith, "For rivals, it was unite or lose", SportsBusiness Journal, 9 May 2011, retrieved
from http://www.sportsbusinessdaily.com/Journal/Issues/2011/05/09/Media/Pac-10.aspx.
²³ Staples, op. cit.; Greenfeld, "Head of the Pac".
²⁴ Smith, Michael, and John Ourand, "Pac-12 keeping networks' ownership to itself", SportsBusiness Journal, 16 Sep
2013, p8, retrieved from http://www.sportsbusinessdaily.com/Journal/Issues/2013/09/16/Colleges/Pac-12-
ownership.aspx.
²⁵ Smith, Michael, and John Ourand, "The complicated case of the Pac-12 Networks", SportsBusiness Journal, 30 Nov
2015, retrieved from http://www.sportsbusinessdaily.com/Journal/Issues/2015/11/30/In-Depth/Pac12.aspx.

[26] Berkowitz, Steve, "Pac-12 leads leagues in revenues; Larry Scott top-paid college commissioner", USA Today, 21 May 2015, retrieved from http://www.usatoday.com/story/sports/college/2015/05/21/pac-12-revenues-larry-scott/27717251/.

[27] Ourand, John, "Fox and ESPN: What's behind unlikely alliance?", SportsBusiness Journal, 4 Mar 2013, retrieved from http://www.sportsbusinessdaily.com/Journal/Issues/2013/03/04/Media/ESPN-Fox.aspx.

[28] Ibid.

[29] Frank the Tank, "No One Goes to Hooters For Wings: Crazy Like a Fox Part 2, BlogPoll Ballot, Football Parlay and Classic Music Video of the Week", FRANK THE TANK'S SLANT, 23 Oct 2012, retrieved from http://frankthetank.me/2012/10/23/no-one-goes-to-hooters-for-wings-crazy-like-a-fox-part-2-blogpoll-ballot-football-parlay-and-classic-music-video-of-the-week/.

[30] Smith, Michael, and John Ourand, "Network for SEC back in play", SportsBusiness Journal, 24 Oct 2011, retrieved from http://www.sportsbusinessdaily.com/Journal/Issues/2011/10/24/Media/SEC.aspx.

[31] Staples, op. cit.

[32] Smith, Michael, and John Ourand, "SEC, ESPN progress on net", SportsBusiness Journal, 17 Sep 2012, retrieved from http://www.sportsbusinessdaily.com/Journal/Issues/2012/09/17/Media/SEC.aspx; Smith, Michael, and John Ourand, "Up next: SEC network", SportsBusiness Journal, 15 Apr 2013, retrieved from http://www.sportsbusinessdaily.com/Journal/Issues/2013/04/15/Media/SEC.aspx.

[33] Sandomir, Richard, "SEC Will Start TV Network in 2014", New York Times, 3 May 2013, B16.

[34] Ourand, John, and Michael Smith, "ACC faced with tepid TV response", SportsBusiness Journal, 8 Mar 2010, retrieved from http://www.sportsbusinessdaily.com/Journal/Issues/2010/03/20100308/This-Weeks-News/ACC-Faced-With-Tepid-TV-Response.aspx.

[35] Ourand, John, and Michael Smith, "ESPN fends off Fox for ACC rights", SportsBusiness Journal, 17 May 2010, retrieved from http://www.sportsbusinessdaily.com/Journal/Issues/2010/05/20100517/This-Weeks-News/ESPN-Fends-Off-Fox-For-ACC-Rights.aspx.

[36] Ibid.; Smith, Michael, and John Ourand, "ACC network may stall over rights issues", SportsBusiness Journal, 20 May 2013, retrieved from http://www.sportsbusinessdaily.com/Journal/Issues/2013/05/20/Media/ACC-net.aspx.

[37] Berman, Mark, "ESPN prepared to get more bang for its ACC buck", The Roanoke Times, 30 Aug 2011, C1.

[38] Smith, Michael, and John Ourand, "ACC's Renegotiated Deal With ESPN Will Pay $3.6B Over 15 Years", SportsBusiness Daily, 9 May 2012, retrieved from http://www.sportsbusinessdaily.com/Daily/Closing-Bell/2012/05/09/ACC.aspx.

[39] Smith, Michael, and John Ourand, "ACC panel will study whether to launch net", SportsBusiness Journal, 14 Jan 2013, retrieved from http://www.sportsbusinessdaily.com/Journal/Issues/2013/01/14/Colleges/ACC.aspx.

[40] Smith and Ourand, "ACC network may stall over rights issues".

[41] Ourand, John, "How high can rights fees go?", SportsBusiness Journal, 6 Jun 2011, retrieved from http://www.sportsbusinessdaily.com/Journal/Issues/2011/06/06/In-Depth/Rights-Fees.aspx.

[42] Petchesky, Barry, "Did ESPN Bone The Big East Because They Wouldn't Sign A TV Deal?", Deadspin, 10 Oct 2011, retrieved from http://deadspin.com/5848348/did-espn-bone-the-big-east-because-they-wouldnt-sign-a-tv-deal; Wieberg, Steve, and Steve Berkowitz, "Is ESPN the force behind realignment?", USA Today, 1 Nov 2011, A1.

[43] Thamel, Pete, "Potential television windfall driving Big Ten's latest expansion efforts", Sports Illustrated, 18 Nov 2012, retrieved from http://www.si.com/more-sports/2012/11/18/big-ten-expansion-tv-money.

[44] Miller et al., "College Football's Most Dominant Player".

[45] Ibid.

[46] Glier, Ray, "Week 1 Mismatches Yield to Can't-Miss Matches", New York Times, 3 Sep 2015, B13, retrieved from http://www.nytimes.com/2015/09/03/sports/ncaafootball/marquee-matchups-aim-to-grab-college-football-fans-right-from-week-1.html.

[47] Miller et al., "College Football's Most Dominant Player".

[48] Ibid.

[49] Ibid.

[50] Eder, Steve, Richard Sandomir, and James Andrew Miller, "At Louisville, Athletic Boom Is Rooted in ESPN Partnership", New York Times, 25 Aug 2013, retrieved from http://www.nytimes.com/2013/08/26/sports/at-louisville-an-athletic-boom-made-for-and-by-tv.html.

[51] Ibid.

[52] Miller et al., "College Football's Most Dominant Player".

[53] Briggs, David, "Bowl games a win-lose situation for college football teams", The Blade (Toledo, OH), 22 Dec 2013, retrieved from http://www.toledoblade.com/sports/2013/12/22/Bowl-games-a-win-lose-situation.html.

[54] Schwarz, Andy, "Teams In The Orange Bowl Don't Make Any Money, And Other Lies", Deadspin, 4 Jan 2014, retrieved from http://regressing.deadspin.com/teams-in-the-orange-bowl-dont-make-any-money-and-othe-1494130032.

[55] "Revenues & Expenses - NCAA Division I Intercollegiate Athletics Programs Report, 2004-2014", National Collegiate Athletic Association, Sep 2015, retrieved from http://www.ncaa.org/sites/default/files/2015%20Division%20I%20RE%20report.pdf.

[56] Brady, Erik, Steve Berkowitz and Christopher Schnaars, "College athletics finance report: Non-Power 5 schools face huge money pressure", USA Today, 26 May 2015, retrieved from http://www.usatoday.com/story/sports/college/2015/05/26/ncaa-athletic-finances-revenue-expense-division-i/27971457/.

[57] Branch, Taylor, "The Shame of College Sports", Atlantic, Oct 2011, retrieved from http://www.theatlantic.com/magazine/archive/2011/10/the-shame-of-college-sports/308643/.

[58] Ibid.; Lewis, Jason, "The NCAA from top to bottom is dirty", Los Angeles Sentinel, 9 Jun 2011, B1; Collins, Donnie, "NCAA Lacks Institutional Control", Times-Tribune [Scranton], 21 Feb 2013; Whitlock, Jason, "NCAA rules breed a culture of corruption", Deseret News, 27 May 2010, retrieved from http://www.deseretnews.com/article/700035637/NCAA-rules-breed-a-culture-of-corruption.html?pg=all.

[59] McCann, Michael, "What the appeals court ruling means for O'Bannon's ongoing NCAA lawsuit", Sports Illustrated, 30 Sep 2015, retrieved from http://www.si.com/college-basketball/2015/09/30/ed-obannon-ncaa-lawsuit-appeals-court-ruling.

[60] Strauss, Ben, "Labor Board Rejects Northwestern Players' Union Bid", New York Times, 18 Aug 2015, B13.

[61] Warner, Dave, "Why College Sports Prevail Over Minor Leagues: Brands Matter", What You Pay For Sports, 29 Jan 2014, retrieved from http://www.whatyoupayforsports.com/2014/01/why-college-sports-prevail-over-minor-leagues-brands-matter/.

[62] Frank the Tank, "The Hypocrisy of College Sports Leaders and Pay-for-Play: Why Minor Leagues Aren't a Substitute", FRANK THE TANK'S SLANT, 26 Sep 2013, retrieved from http://frankthetank.me/2013/09/26/the-hypocrisy-of-college-sports-leaders-and-pay-for-play-why-minor-leagues-arent-a-substitute/.

[63] Warner, "Why College Sports Prevail".

[64] Sheridan, Phil, "NCAA is root of corruption", Philadelphia Inquirer, 27 Aug 2003, F1.

[65] Warner, "Why College Sports Prevail".

Chapter 5: King of Sports

[1] Miller and Shales, pp. 427-428, 472-474, 483-484, 495-496.

[2] Miller and Shales, pp. 510-511.

[3] Miller and Shales, pp. 513-516.

[4] Miller and Shales, pp. 516-517.

[5] Lipsyte, Robert, "Winning ugly: ESPN journalism prevails", ESPN, 15 Oct 2013, retrieved from http://espn.go.com/blog/ombudsman/post/_/id/176/winning-ugly-espn-journalism-prevails.

[6] Hayden, Ryan, "TCA Flashback: When ESPN and Frontline Touted Concussion Doc (Transcript)", Hollywood Reporter, 23 Aug 2013, retrieved from http://www.hollywoodreporter.com/live-feed/tca-flashback-espn-frontline-touted-613579.

[7] "Author Jim Miller Discusses ESPN Backing Off Of 'Frontline' Film", SportsBusiness Daily, 23 Aug 2013, retrieved from http://www.sportsbusinessdaily.com/Daily/Closing-Bell/2013/08/23/ESPN-Frontline.aspx; Boren, Cindy, "ESPN pulls out of 'Frontline' investigation, denies pressure from NFL", Washington Post, 23 Aug 2013, retrieved from http://www.washingtonpost.com/blogs/early-lead/wp/2013/08/23/nfl-concussions-espn-pull-out-of-frontline-investigation/; Lipsyte, op. cit.

[8] Yoder, Matt, "ESPN pulls out of PBS documentary on NFL concussions", Awful Announcing, 22 Aug 2013, retrieved from http://awfulannouncing.com/2013/espn-pulls-out-of-pbs-documentary-on-nfl-concussions.html.

[9] Lipsyte, op. cit.

[10] Miller, James Andrew, and Ken Belson, "N.F.L. Pressure Said to Lead ESPN to Quit Film Project", New York Times, 23 Aug 2013, retrieved from http://www.nytimes.com/2013/08/24/sports/football/nfl-pressure-said-to-prompt-espn-to-quit-film-project.html.

[11] Ibid.; "Author Jim Miller Discusses ESPN Backing Off Of 'Frontline' Film".

[12] "A Note from FRONTLINE: ESPN and 'League of Denial'", Frontline, 22 Aug 2013, retrieved from http://www.pbs.org/wgbh/pages/frontline/sports/league-of-denial/a-note-from-frontline-espn-and-league-of-denial/; King, Peter, "Letdowns, New Leases and Late-Night Football", Sports Illustrated, 7 Oct 2013, retrieved from http://mmqb.si.com/2013/10/07/tony-romo-monday-morning-quarterback/2/; Lipsyte, op. cit.

[13] Florio, Mike, "ESPN's crisis of concussion conscience goes deeper than NFL pressure", ProFootballTalk, 26 Aug 2013, retrieved from http://profootballtalk.nbcsports.com/2013/08/26/espns-crisis-of-concussion-conscience-goes-deeper-than-nfl-pressure/.

[14] Thompson, Derek, op. cit.

[15] Bien, Louis, "A complete timeline on the Ray Rice assault case", SB Nation, 28 Nov 2014, retrieved from http://www.sbnation.com/nfl/2014/5/23/5744964/ray-rice-arrest-assault-statement-apology-ravens.

[16] Ibid.

[17] Ibid.

[18] Fatsis, Stefan, "Giving Up on Goodell", Slate, 15 Sep 2014, retrieved from http://www.slate.com/articles/sports/sports_nut/2014/09/roger_goodell_and_the_nfl_thought_they_had_the_press_under_control_not_any.single.html.

[19] Ourand, John, "Lobbying begins: CBS, Fox tout strength of late Sunday windows", SportsBusiness Journal, 9 Feb 2015, retrieved from http://www.sportsbusinessdaily.com/Journal/Issues/2015/02/09/Media/Sports-Media.aspx; Ourand, John, "Prime-time power", SportsBusiness Journal, 17 Sep 2012, retrieved from http://www.sportsbusinessdaily.com/Journal/Issues/2012/09/17/Leagues-and-Governing-Bodies/Katz-NFL.aspx.

[20] Ourand, John, "How networks make their play for games", SportsBusiness Journal, 17 Sep 2012, p27, retrieved from http://www.sportsbusinessdaily.com/Journal/Issues/2012/09/17/Leagues-and-Governing-Bodies/NFL-networks-lobbying.aspx.

[21] Ibid.; Ourand, "Prime-time power".

[22] Ourand, "Lobbying begins" and "Prime-time power".

[23] Ourand, John, "NFL schedule navigated World Series, other conflicts", SportsBusiness Journal, 26 Apr 2010, retrieved from http://www.sportsbusinessdaily.com/Journal/Issues/2010/04/20100426/This-Weeks-News/NFL-Schedule-Navigated-World-Series-Other-Conflicts.aspx; Ourand, "Prime-time power".

[24] Ourand, "Prime-time power".

[25] Miller and Shales, pp. 259, 441, 443-445.

[26] Ourand, John, "Meet the NFL's scheduling guru", SportsBusiness Journal, 17 Jan 2011, retrieved from http://www.sportsbusinessdaily.com/Journal/Issues/2011/01/20110117/Media/NFL-ratings.aspx; Ourand, "Prime-time power".

[27] Ourand, "Prime-time power"; Sandomir, Richard, "CBS and Fox Play Favorites as N.F.L. Flexes Its Schedule", New York Times, 17 Oct 2006, D6.

[28] Rosenthal, Gregg, "2014 NFL Schedule: Flex games can now start in Week 5", NFL.com, 23 Apr 2014, retrieved from http://www.nfl.com/news/story/0ap2000000343369/article/2014-nfl-schedule-flex-games-can-now-start-in-week-5.

[29] Ourand, John, and John Lombardo, "NBA's TV partners want flex scheduling", SportsBusiness Journal, 28 Apr 2014, retrieved from http://www.sportsbusinessdaily.com/Journal/Issues/2014/04/28/Media/NBA-flex.aspx.

[30] Ourand, "Meet the NFL's scheduling guru".

[31] Ourand, John, and Daniel Kaplan, "NFL shops new 8-game package", SportsBusiness Journal, 27 Jun 2011, retrieved from http://www.sportsbusinessdaily.com/Journal/Issues/2011/06/27/Media/NFL-TV.aspx; Ourand, John, "Thursday night TV package, equity in NFL Network in play", SportsBusiness Journal, 1 Aug 2011, retrieved from http://www.sportsbusinessdaily.com/Journal/Issues/2011/08/01/NFL-Special-Report/NFL-TV.aspx.

[32] Ourand, John, "NFL's pause on package of games surprises networks", SportsBusiness Journal, 19 Sep 2011, retrieved from http://www.sportsbusinessdaily.com/Journal/Issues/2011/09/19/Media/NFL-package.aspx.

[33] Ourand, John, "No new NFL TV package on the horizon", SportsBusiness Journal, 13 Feb 2012, retrieved from http://www.sportsbusinessdaily.com/Journal/Issues/2012/02/13/Media/NFL-net.aspx.

[34] Ourand, John, "Sources: NFL Wants Thursday Games Simulcast On NFL Network", SportsBusiness Daily, 15 Jan 2014, retrieved from http://www.sportsbusinessdaily.com/Daily/Closing-Bell/2014/01/15/thursdays.aspx.

[35] Sandomir, Richard, "N.F.L. Explores New TV Deal", New York Times, 12 Jan 2014, retrieved from http://www.nytimes.com/2014/01/13/sports/football/nfl-may-sell-tv-rights-to-some-thursday-games.html?_r=1; Ourand, John, "How CBS won Thursday night", SportsBusiness Journal, 10 Feb 2014, retrieved from http://www.sportsbusinessdaily.com/Journal/Issues/2014/02/10/Media/NFL-CBS.aspx.

[36] Ourand, "How CBS won Thursday night"; Flint, Joe, "NFL's Thursday TV plans raises questions about its own network", Los Angeles Times, 21 Jan 2014, retrieved from http://www.latimes.com/entertainment/envelope/cotown/la-et-ct-nfl-thursday-tv-20140121-story.html; Sandomir, Richard, "CBS Will Broadcast Thursday Night Games", New York Times, 5 Feb 2014, retrieved from http://www.nytimes.com/2014/02/06/sports/football/cbs-to-carry-8-thursday-night-nfl-games-next-season.html; Ourand, John, "NFL: No quick call on Thursday option expected", SportsBusiness Journal, 25 Aug 2014, p27, retrieved from http://www.sportsbusinessdaily.com/Journal/Issues/2014/08/25/Media/CBS-Thursday-night.aspx.

[37] Sandomir, "CBS Will Broadcast Thursday Night Games"; Cherner, Reid, "CBS-NFL marriage extended to Thursday nights in 2014", USA Today, 5 Feb 2014, retrieved from http://www.usatoday.com/story/sports/nfl/2014/02/05/cbs-thursday-tv-games-nfl-network/5227869/.

[38] Ourand, "How CBS won Thursday night"; Florio, Mike, "NFLN exits the game production business", ProFootballTalk, 5 Feb 2014, retrieved from http://profootballtalk.nbcsports.com/2014/02/05/nfln-exits-the-game-production-business/; Crupi, Anthony, "Insiders Say NBC Has the Best Chance at Getting the NFL's Thursday Night Package", Adweek, 26 Jan 2014, retrieved from http://www.adweek.com/news/television/insiders-say-nbc-has-best-chance-getting-nfl-s-thursday-night-package-155206.

[39] Ourand, John, "With CBS's games done for year, NFL still evaluating Thursday", SportsBusiness Journal, 3 Nov 2014, p11, retrieved from http://www.sportsbusinessdaily.com/Journal/Issues/2014/11/03/Media/Sports-Media.aspx.

[40] Ourand, John, "NFL stands to make a lot more money from Thursday package", SportsBusiness Journal, 17 Nov 2014, p12, retrieved from http://www.sportsbusinessdaily.com/Journal/Issues/2014/11/17/Media/Sports-Media.aspx.

[41] Ourand, John, "NFL Exercises Option To Keep "TNF" Games On CBS For '15 Season", SportsBusiness Daily, 18 Jan 2015, retrieved from http://www.sportsbusinessdaily.com/Daily/Weekend-Rap/2015/01/18/CBS.aspx.

[42] Paulsen, "NFL Week 2 Finals: Slight Increase Gives TNF Record Start", Sports Media Watch, 18 Sep 2015, retrieved from http://www.sportsmediawatch.com/2015/09/nfl-ratings-thursday-night-football-record-audience-broncos-chiefs-cbs/.

[43] "'Thursday Night Football' Moves Exclusively to NFL Network With Undefeated Cincinnati Bengals Hosting Cleveland Browns", NFL Communications, 4 Nov 2015, retrieved from https://nflcommunications.com/Pages/Thursday-Night-Football'-Moves-Exclusively-to-NFL-Network-With-Undefeated-Cincinnati-Bengals-Hosting-Cleveland-Browns.aspx.

[44] Guthrie, Marisa, "NFL Targets Massive Payday in Thursday Night TV Deal", Hollywood Reporter, 23 Nov 2015, retrieved from http://www.hollywoodreporter.com/news/nfl-targets-massive-payday-thursday-842646.

Chapter 6: All Sports are Local

[1] Beck, Howard, "From Ivy Halls to the Garden, Surprise Star Jolts the N.B.A.", New York Times, 8 Feb 2012, A1; Viera, Mark, "Colleges Passed on Lin Before the N.B.A. Did", New York Times, 13 Feb 2012, D1; House, LaChel, "The phenomenon known as Jeremy Lin", Charleston Gazette, 1 Mar 2012, E8.

[2] Viera, op. cit.

[3] House, op. cit.

[4] Ibid.; Beck, op. cit.; Benbow, Julian, "Harvard saw something like this coming: Former Ivy star Lin suddenly NBA's global sensation", Boston Globe, 17 Feb 2012, A1; Torre, Pablo S., "From Couch to Clutch", Sports Illustrated, 20 Feb 2012, retrieved from http://www.si.com/vault/2012/02/20/106161469/from-couch-to-clutch.

[5] Beck, op. cit.; Lupica, Mike, "It's All Unrave-Lin'", New York Daily News, 11 Mar 2012, p52.

[6] Torre, op. cit.; Berman, Marc, "Knicks Run Into No-Lin Situation; Winning streak ends vs. lowly Hornets at Garden", New York Post, 18 Feb 2012, p61.

[7] Isola, Frank, "Nets Leave Lin At Loss; Knicks flop as Melo return fizzles", New York Daily News, 21 Feb 2012, p43.

[8] Isola, Frank, "Time for Melo to be Trave-Lin: One Garden Honcho Gives Moneyball Nod to Jeremy", New York Daily News, 14 Mar 2012, p58.

[9] Berman, Marc, "Knicks turning to star power: Woodson ready to bury Lin, ride Melo and Amar'e", New York Post, 16 Mar 2012, p113.

[10] Beck, Howard, "Knicks' Push For Playoffs Will Go On Without Lin", New York Times, 1 Apr 2012, SP1.

[11] Leitsch, Will, "Linsanity: The Sequel", GQ, 16 Oct 2012, retrieved from http://www.gq.com/story/jeremy-lin-gq-november-2012-cover-story.

[12] Barron, David, "Jeremy Lin: From face of Rockets to trade to Lakers in two years", Houston Chronicle, 11 Jan 2014, retrieved from http://blog.chron.com/ultimaterockets/2014/07/jeremy-lin-from-face-of-rockets-to-trade-to-lakers-in-two-years/.

[13] Bondy, Stefan, "Lin: Knicks said no to Linsanity II", New York Daily News, 18 Oct 2015, p68.

[14] Reynolds, Mike, "MSG, Time Warner Cable Moving Toward License Fee Disconnect", Multichannel News, 30 Dec 2011, retrieved from http://www.multichannel.com/news/marketing/msg-time-warner-cable-moving-toward-license-fee-disconnect/289966.

[15] Berman, Marc, and Claire Atkinson, "MSG gets kick from Rangers, Knicks", New York Post, 25 Aug 2012, p27.

[16] Brown, Maury, "Through July, MLB Telecasts On Regional Sports Networks Dominate Prime Time TV [UPDATED]", Forbes, 5 Aug 2014, retrieved from http://www.forbes.com/sites/maurybrown/2014/08/05/mlb-telecasts-on-regional-sports-networks-dominate-prime-time-television/.

[17] Brown, Maury, "Prime Time TV Ratings For All 29 U.S. MLB Teams Show Baseball Ruling Summer Programming", Forbes, 17 Jul 2015, retrieved from http://www.forbes.com/sites/maurybrown/2015/07/17/prime-time-tv-ratings-for-all-29-u-s-mlb-teams-shows-baseball-ruling-summer-programming/.

[18] Sherman, Alex, "For Sports Networks, You Gotta Pay to Play", Bloomberg Businessweek, 5 Apr 2012, retrieved from http://www.bloomberg.com/bw/articles/2012-04-05/for-sports-networks-you-gotta-pay-to-play.

[19] Wolfley, Bob, "ESPN continues to lead cable by a mile in terms of subscriber fees", Journal Sentinel (Milwaukee, WI), 1 Mar 2012, retrieved from http://www.jsonline.com/blogs/sports/141097593.html.

[20] Miller and Shales, pp. 252-253.

[21] "FOX AND LIBERTY OUTLINE PLANS FOR NEW CABLE VENTURE", SportsBusiness Daily, 1 Nov 1995, retrieved from http://www.sportsbusinessdaily.com/Daily/Issues/1995/11/1/Sports-Media/FOX-AND-LIBERTY-OUTLINE-PLANS-FOR-NEW-CABLE-VENTURE.aspx; "CHISOX, MARINERS AND A'S LEAD THE WAY FOR FX/FOX SPORTS NET", SportsBusiness Daily, 7 Mar 1997, retrieved from http://www.sportsbusinessdaily.com/Daily/Issues/1997/03/7/Sports-Media/CHISOX-MARINERS-AND-AS-LEAD-THE-WAY-FOR-FXFOX-SPORTS-NET.aspx; "SPORTS LANDSCAPE ALTERED WITH FOX/LIBERTY-

CABLEVISION DEAL", SportsBusiness Daily, 23 Jun 1997, retrieved from
http://www.sportsbusinessdaily.com/Daily/Issues/1997/06/23/Sports-Media/SPORTS-LANDSCAPE-ALTERED-WITH-FOXLIBERTY-CABLEVISION-DEAL.aspx.

[22] Finley, Patrick, "Behind the screens: Pac-10 prefers working with Fox, even if ESPN provides more exposure",
Arizona Daily Star, 11 Jan 2007, retrieved from http://tucson.com/sports/basketball/college/wildcats/behind-the-screens/article_2e49ccbc-a7b2-5b06-8739-d05e0a1b45a2.html; Powers, Craig, "PAC-10 TV CONTRACT: FSN/FCS
Scheduling Provides Unintentional Humor/Frustration", CougCenter, 30 Aug 2010, retrieved from
http://www.cougcenter.com/2010/8/30/1658326/pac-10-tv-contract-fsn-fcs.

[23] Schlosser, Joe, "ESPN West goes south", Broadcasting and Cable, 20 Jul 1998, pp. 52-54.

[24] Lefton, Terry, "Getting to YES: Channel was born in a battle", SportsBusiness Journal, 30 Apr 2012, p8, retrieved
from http://www.sportsbusinessdaily.com/Journal/Issues/2012/04/30/Media/YES-launch.aspx.

[25] "CABLEVISION STEPS UP TO NAB MSG; ITT FIRES BACK AT HILTON", SportsBusiness Daily, 7 Mar 1997,
retrieved from http://www.sportsbusinessdaily.com/Daily/Issues/1997/03/7/Franchises/CABLEVISION-STEPS-UP-TO-NAB-MSG-ITT-FIRES-BACK-AT-HILTON.aspx; Bernstein, Andy, "Yanks get no-lose TV deal with IMG unit",
SportsBusiness Journal, 24 Jul 2000, retrieved from
http://www.sportsbusinessdaily.com/Journal/Issues/2000/07/20000724/No-Topic-Name/Yanks-Get-No-Lose-TV-Deal-With-IMG-Unit.aspx.

[26] Sandomir, Richard, "Yanks and Nets Form Team, Merging Business Operations", New York Times, 25 Feb 1999,
retrieved from http://www.nytimes.com/1999/02/25/sports/yanks-and-nets-form-team-merging-business-operations.html.

[27] "BOSS TO SELL YANKS? NEWSDAY SAYS CABLEVISION DEAL POSSIBLE", SportsBusiness Daily, 19 Mar
1998, retrieved from http://www.sportsbusinessdaily.com/Daily/Issues/1998/03/19/Franchises/BOSS-TO-SELL-YANKS-NEWSDAY-SAYS-CABLEVISION-DEAL-POSSIBLE.aspx.

[28] Ibid.; "THE DAY AFTER: BOTH SIDES DOWNPLAY YANKS/CABLEVISION TALKS", SportsBusiness Daily,
20 Mar 1998, retrieved from http://www.sportsbusinessdaily.com/Daily/Issues/1998/03/20/Franchises/THE-DAY-AFTER-BOTH-SIDES-DOWNPLAY-YANKS-CABLEVISION-TALKS.aspx; "N.Y. POST HAS CABLEVISION
TALKS ON YANKS 'HEATING UP'", SportsBusiness Daily, 16 Sep 1998, retrieved from
http://www.sportsbusinessdaily.com/Daily/Issues/1998/09/16/Franchises/NY-POST-HAS-CABLEVISION-TALKS-ON-YANKS-HEATING-UP.aspx; Bagli, Charles V., "Sale Might Let Steinbrenner Run 3 Teams, Officials Say", New
York Times, 17 Sep 1998, retrieved from http://www.nytimes.com/1998/09/17/nyregion/sale-might-let-steinbrenner-run-3-teams-officials-say.html; "STEINBRENNER DENIES REPORTS OF A DONE DEAL WITH CABLEVISION",
SportsBusiness Daily, 23 Nov 1998, retrieved from
http://www.sportsbusinessdaily.com/Daily/Issues/1998/11/23/Franchises/STEINBRENNER-DENIES-REPORTS-OF-A-DONE-DEAL-WITH-CABLEVISION.aspx; "SWING AND A MISS! CABLEVISION DEAL FOR YANKEES
IS CALLED OFF", SportsBusiness Daily, 25 Nov 1998, retrieved from
http://www.sportsbusinessdaily.com/Daily/Issues/1998/11/25/Franchises/SWING-AND-A-MISS-CABLEVISION-DEAL-FOR-YANKEES-IS-CALLED-OFF.aspx; "THE LATEST DISH ON YANKS/CABLEVISION; DOLAN EYES
SKINS?", SportsBusiness Daily, 4 Dec 1998, retrieved from
http://www.sportsbusinessdaily.com/Daily/Issues/1998/12/4/Franchises/THE-LATEST-DISH-ON-YANKSCABLEVISION-DOLAN-EYES-SKINS.aspx.

[29] Sandomir, "Yanks and Nets Form Team"; Sandomir, Richard, "They're the YankeeNets: A Marriage Made for the
Tube", New York Times, 26 Feb 1999, retrieved from http://www.nytimes.com/1999/02/26/sports/they-re-the-yankeenets-a-marriage-made-for-the-tube.html.

[30] "CONFLICTING REPORTS OUT OF N.Y. SPECULATE ON YANKEES TV DEAL", SportsBusiness Daily, 2
May 2000, retrieved from http://www.sportsbusinessdaily.com/Daily/Issues/2000/05/2/Sports-Media/CONFLICTING-REPORTS-OUT-OF-NY-SPECULATE-ON-YANKEES-TV-DEAL.aspx.

[31] Bernstein, Andy, "Yanks get no-lose TV deal with IMG unit", SportsBusiness Journal, 24 Jul 2000, retrieved from
http://www.sportsbusinessdaily.com/Journal/Issues/2000/07/20000724/No-Topic-Name/Yanks-Get-No-Lose-TV-Deal-With-IMG-Unit.aspx.

[32] "YANKEES STYMIED IN INITIAL EFFORT TO CREATE RSN", SportsBusiness Daily, 1 Aug 2000, retrieved
from http://www.sportsbusinessdaily.com/Daily/Issues/2000/08/1/Sports-Media/YANKEES-STYMIED-IN-INITIAL-EFFORT-TO-CREATE-RSN.aspx.

[33] Kaplan, Daniel, "TWI reportedly gets $50M, one-year cable deal", SportsBusiness Journal, 13 Nov 2000, retrieved
from http://www.sportsbusinessdaily.com/Journal/Issues/2000/11/20001113/No-Topic-Name/TWI-Reportedly-Gets-$50M-One-Year-Cable-Deal.aspx.

[34] Raissman, Bob, "YANKS, MSG OK 1-YEAR, $52M DEAL", New York Daily News, 17 Nov 2000, retrieved from
http://www.nydailynews.com/archives/sports/yanks-msg-1-year-52m-deal-article-1.892753.

[35] Sandomir, Richard, "Yankees Could Start Own Network After Agreeing to Deal With MSG", New York Times, 25
Apr 2001, retrieved from http://www.nytimes.com/2001/04/25/sports/baseball-yankees-could-start-own-network-after-agreeing-to-deal-with-msg.html.

[36] "No Surprise In YankeeNets Move To End MSG Net Partnership", SportsBusiness Daily, 21 Jun 2001, retrieved from http://www.sportsbusinessdaily.com/Daily/Issues/2001/06/Issue-181/Sports-Media/No-Surprise-In-Yankeenets-Move-To-End-MSG-Net-Partnership.aspx.

[37] Ourand, John, "Not all imitators succeeded, but idea took root", SportsBusiness Journal, 30 Apr 2012, p9, retrieved from http://www.sportsbusinessdaily.com/Journal/Issues/2012/04/30/Media/YES-team.aspx; Van Riper, Tom, "TV Money Is A Game Changer For Baseball And The Dodgers", Forbes, 21 Mar 2012, retrieved from http://www.forbes.com/sites/tomvanriper/2012/03/21/the-new-moneyball/.

[38] "Main Challenges For YankeeNets RSN: Channel Space, Economy", SportsBusiness Daily, 11 Sep 2001, retrieved from http://www.sportsbusinessdaily.com/Daily/Issues/2001/09/Issue-236/Sports-Media/Main-Challenges-For-Yankeenets-RSN-Channel-Space-Economy.aspx.

[39] Ourand, "Not all imitators succeeded".

[40] "Congressman Implores Selig To Get Involved In YES Dispute", SportsBusiness Daily, 5 Apr 2002, retrieved from http://www.sportsbusinessdaily.com/Daily/Issues/2002/04/Issue-137/Sports-Media/Congressman-Implores-Selig-To-Get-Involved-In-YES-Dispute.aspx.

[41] Lefton, op. cit.

[42] Moore, Aaron, "Coming soon to the ballpark: Rollerball", SportsBusiness Journal, 9 Jul 2011, retrieved from http://www.sportsbusinessdaily.com/Journal/Issues/2001/07/20010709/This-Weeks-Issue/Coming-Soon-To-The-Ballpark-Rollerball.aspx.

[43] "YES Debuts Today; CEO Says Net Not A 'House Organ' For Yanks", SportsBusiness Daily, 19 Mar 2002, retrieved from http://www.sportsbusinessdaily.com/Daily/Issues/2002/03/Issue-126/Sports-Media/YES-Debuts-Today-CEO-Says-Net-Not-A-147House-Organ148-For-Yanks.aspx.

[44] "YES Network's Senior Management; Net Now Must Get On Systems", SportsBusiness Daily, 25 Sep 2001, retrieved from http://www.sportsbusinessdaily.com/Daily/Issues/2001/09/Issue-10/Sports-Media/YES-Networks-Senior-Management-Net-Now-Must-Get-On-Systems.aspx.

[45] Ourand, John, "Original YES executives help shape sports media landscape", SportsBusiness Journal, 30 Apr 2012, p11, retrieved from http://www.sportsbusinessdaily.com/Journal/Issues/2012/04/30/Media/Sports-Media.aspx.

[46] Bernstein, Alex, "Time Warner balks at cost of adding Yankees' network", SportsBusiness Journal, 3 Dec 2001, retrieved from http://www.sportsbusinessdaily.com/Journal/Issues/2001/12/20011203/This-Weeks-Issue/Time-Warner-Balks-At-Cost-Of-Adding-Yankees146-Network.aspx; "It's A YES Or No Question: Will Yanks Net Be Basic Or Pay?", SportsBusiness Daily, 22 Jan 2002, retrieved from http://www.sportsbusinessdaily.com/Daily/Issues/2002/01/Issue-87/Sports-Media/Its-A-YES-Or-No-Question-Will-Yanks-Net-Be-Basic-Or-Pay.aspx.

[47] Lefton, op. cit.

[48] Bernstein, Andy, "Teams say 'YES!' to cable settlement", SportsBusiness Journal, 29 Mar 2004, retrieved from http://www.sportsbusinessdaily.com/Journal/Issues/2004/03/20040329/Media/Teams-Say-YES-To-Cable-Settlement.aspx; Bernstein, Andy, "Deal could move sports nets to tiers", SportsBusiness Journal, 24 Mar 2003, retrieved from http://www.sportsbusinessdaily.com/Journal/Issues/2003/03/20030324/This-Weeks-Issue/Deal-Could-Move-Sports-Nets-To-Tiers.aspx.

[49] Ourand, "Not all imitators succeeded".

[50] Bernstein, "Time Warner balks at cost of adding Yankees' network".

[51] Ourand, "Not all imitators succeeded".

[52] Bruton, Mike, "Comcast Scores Big With Sports Network", Philadelphia Inquirer, 22 Jul 1997, retrieved from http://articles.philly.com/1997-07-22/news/25549267_1_sportschannel-philadelphia-comcast-sportsnet-cable-systems.

[53] "HTS now Comcast SportsNet, adding sports news coverage", Baltimore Sun, 4 Apr 2001, retrieved from http://articles.baltimoresun.com/2001-04-04/sports/0104040237_1_comcast-sportsnet-orioles-home-team-sports.

[54] Brown, Kathi, Wired to Win: Entrepreneurs of the American Cable Industry, 2003, pp. 146, 274, retrieved from http://cablecenter.org/education/exhibits/wiredtowin/Chapter9.htm and http://cablecenter.org/education/exhibits/wiredtowin/Chapter17.htm; Stern, Christopher, "FCC Clears Comcast's AT&T Deal: Acquisition Creates Cable-Internet Giant", Washington Post, 14 Nov 2002, E1.

[55] Amdur, Meredith, and John Dempsey, "Cabler Comcast eyes local Fox sports nets", Variety, 22 May 2003, retrieved from http://variety.com/2003/scene/news/cabler-comcast-eyes-local-fox-sports-nets-1117886772/.

[56] Sherman, Ed, "Cubs-Sox TV net possible", Chicago Tribune, 28 Feb 2003, retrieved from http://articles.chicagotribune.com/2003-02-28/sports/0302280200_1_new-cable-provider-sports-network-comcast; Kirk, Jim, "Teams to sideline Fox", Chicago Tribune, 30 Sep 2003, retrieved from http://articles.chicagotribune.com/2003-09-30/business/0309300226_1_comcast-sports-cable-channel-scott-reifert.

[57] Sherman, Ed, "Fox Sports Net forced to adjust", Chicago Tribune, 1 Oct 2003, retrieved from http://articles.chicagotribune.com/2003-10-01/sports/0310010064_1_cable-venture-cable-channel-fox.

[58] Kirk, Jim, "Comcast may buy Chicago channel", Chicago Tribune, 11 Sep 2003, retrieved from http://articles.chicagotribune.com/2003-09-11/business/0309110287_1_regional-channels-team-related-programming-cubs-games.

[59] Kirk, "Teams to sideline Fox"; Sherman, "Fox Sports Net forced to adjust".

[60] Bernstein, Andy, "Chicago clubs look for homes after dropping FSN deals", SportsBusiness Journal, 6 Oct 2003, retrieved from http://www.sportsbusinessdaily.com/Journal/Issues/2003/10/20031006/Media/Chicago-Clubs-Look-For-Homes-After-Dropping-FSN-Deals.aspx.

[61] Umstead, R. Thomas, "Comcast Takes Chicago, Eyes Other Regionals", Multichannel News, 7 Dec 2003, retrieved from http://www.multichannel.com/news/orphan-articles/comcast-takes-chicago-eyes-other-regionals/152920.

[62] "Kings Not Getting The Royal Treatment With Broadcast Deals", SportsBusiness Daily, 29 Apr 2003, retrieved from http://www.sportsbusinessdaily.com/Daily/Issues/2003/04/Issue-149/Sports-Media/Kings-Not-Getting-The-Royal-Treatment-With-Broadcast-Deals.aspx.

[63] Swett, Clint, "Sacramento Kings seek cable TV contract", Sacramento Bee, 2 Jul 2004.

[64] "NBA Kings Games To Anchor New Comcast RSN In California", SportsBusiness Daily, 9 Sep 2004, retrieved from http://www.sportsbusinessdaily.com/Daily/Issues/2004/09/Issue-241/Sports-Media/NBA-Kings-Games-To-Anchor-New-Comcast-RSN-In-California.aspx.

[65] "Time Warner, Comcast To Join Mets In New Team-Branded RSN", SportsBusiness Daily, 13 Oct 2004, retrieved from http://www.sportsbusinessdaily.com/Daily/Issues/2004/10/Issue-22/Sports-Media/Time-Warner-Comcast-To-Join-Mets-In-New-Team-Branded-RSN.aspx.

[66] Ourand, John, "After 10 years of growth, Comcast looking for more RSNs", SportsBusiness Journal, 1 Oct 2007, retrieved from http://www.sportsbusinessdaily.com/Journal/Issues/2007/10/20071001/This-Weeks-News/After-10-Years-Of-Growth-Comcast-Looking-For-More-Rsns.aspx.

[67] Ourand, John, "In Houston, a shootout over Astros rights", SportsBusiness Journal, 22 Feb 2010, retrieved from http://www.sportsbusinessdaily.com/Journal/Issues/2010/02/20100222/This-Weeks-News/In-Houston-A-Shootout-Over-Astros-Rights.aspx.

[68] Settimi, Christina, "Baseball's Biggest Cable Deals", Forbes, 21 Mar 2012, retrieved from http://www.forbes.com/sites/christinasettimi/2012/03/21/baseballs-biggest-cable-deals/; Ourand, John, "Tune in Tomorrow?", SportsBusiness Journal, 16 Aug 2010, retrieved from http://www.sportsbusinessdaily.com/Journal/Issues/2010/08/20100816/SBJ-In-Depth/Tune-In-Tomorrow.aspx.

[69] Settimi, op. cit.

[70] "McCourt Has Only Held Preliminary Discussions About New FSN Deal", SportsBusiness Daily, 29 Sep 2010, retrieved from http://www.sportsbusinessdaily.com/Daily/Issues/2010/09/0929/Media/Dodgers-FSN.aspx.

[71] Lombardo, John, and John Ourand, "Lakers, Time Warner Cable run fast break", SportsBusiness Journal, 21 Feb 2011, retrieved from http://www.sportsbusinessdaily.com/Journal/Issues/2011/02/21/Media/LakersTWC.aspx.

[72] Shaikin, Bill, and David Wharton, "Bud Selig rejects Dodgers TV contract, nullifying McCourt divorce deal", Los Angeles Times, 21 Jun 2011, retrieved from http://articles.latimes.com/2011/jun/21/sports/la-sp-mccourt-fox-selig-20110621.

[73] Weisman, Jon, "MLB laid out numerous reasons for denying Fox-Dodgers TV deal", Variety, 22 Jul 2011, retrieved from http://variety.com/2011/tv/news/selig-10107/.

[74] Kaplan, Daniel, "Sources: MLB Ready To Provide Dodgers With Bankruptcy Financing", SportsBusiness Daily, 28 Jun 2011, retrieved from http://www.sportsbusinessdaily.com/Daily/Morning-Buzz/2011/06/28/Dodgers.aspx; "FS West Files Lawsuit Against Dodgers To Halt Sale Of TV Rights", SportsBusiness Daily, 28 Sep 2011, retrieved from http://www.sportsbusinessdaily.com/Daily/Issues/2011/09/28/Franchises/Dodgers.aspx; "MLB Files Motion To Force Sale Of Dodgers, Indicates It Will Reject Any Deal For TV Rights", SportsBusiness Daily, 26 Sep 2011, retrieved from http://www.sportsbusinessdaily.com/Daily/Issues/2011/09/26/Franchises/Dodgers.aspx.

[75] "McCourt, MLB Reach Agreement To Put Dodgers Up For Auction", SportsBusiness Daily, 2 Nov 2011, retrieved from http://www.sportsbusinessdaily.com/Daily/Issues/2011/11/02/Franchises/Dodgers.aspx; Sandomir, Richard, "Agreeing to Sell, McCourt Gives Dodgers Fans Hope", New York Times, 2 Nov 2011, retrieved from http://www.nytimes.com/2011/11/03/sports/baseball/mccourt-agrees-to-sell-los-angeles-dodgers.html?_r=0.

[76] "Magic Johnson, Stan Kasten, Guggenheim Partners Purchase Dodgers For Record $2B", SportsBusiness Daily, 28 Mar 2012, retrieved from http://www.sportsbusinessdaily.com/Daily/Issues/2012/03/28/Franchises/Dodgers.aspx.

[77] Shaikin, Bill, "Dodgers, Fox Sports talking $6-billion TV deal", Los Angeles Times, 25 Nov 2012, retrieved from http://articles.latimes.com/2012/nov/25/sports/la-sp-dn-dodgers-fox-sports-6-billion-tv-deal-20121125.

[78] Block, Alex Ben, "Fox's Dodgers TV Deal on Hold as MLB Talks Continue Over Splitting $6.1 Billion", Hollywood Reporter, 18 Dec 2012, retrieved from http://www.hollywoodreporter.com/news/foxs-los-angeles-dodgers-tv-404181.

[79] Ourand, John, and Eric Fisher, "Dodgers Officially Agree To Nearly $8B Deal With TWC That Includes Own Channel", SportsBusiness Daily, 28 Jan 2013, retrieved from http://www.sportsbusinessdaily.com/Daily/Issues/2013/01/28/Media/Dodgers-TWC.aspx; "Sources: Fox May Have Matching Rights for TWC's Dodgers Deal", SportsBusiness Daily, 22 Jan 2013, retrieved from http://www.sportsbusinessdaily.com/Daily/Closing-Bell/2013/01/22/dodgers.aspx.

[80] Hoffarth, Tom, "Dodgers' SportsNet launch reinforces lack of MLB TV access in L.A.", Los Angeles Daily News, 6 Mar 2014, retrieved from http://www.dailynews.com/sports/20140306/dodgers-sportsnet-launch-reinforces-lack-of-mlb-tv-access-in-la.

[81] Barron, op. cit.; Hoffarth, Tom, "LAKERS: DirecTV strikes a deal with Time Warner Cable", Los Angeles Daily News, 15 Nov 2012, retrieved from http://www.dailynews.com/sports/20121115/lakers-directv-strikes-a-deal-with-time-warner-cable.

[82] Barron, David, "CSNH distribution of Rockets games stuck at 40 percent", Houston Chronicle, 30 Nov 2012, retrieved from http://blog.chron.com/ultimaterockets/2012/11/defense-tv-distribution-top-rockets-priorities/.

[83] Barron, David, "Astros owner Crane worries about CSNH's financial pinch", Houston Chronicle, retrieved from http://www.houstonchronicle.com/sports/astros/article/Astros-owner-Crane-worries-about-CSNH-s-financial-4527113.php?cmpid=hcec.

[84] Ourand, John, "Houston numbers could hurt sports in carriage battles", SportsBusiness Journal, 10 Jun 2013, retrieved from http://www.sportsbusinessdaily.com/Journal/Issues/2013/06/10/Media/CSN-Houston.aspx.

[85] Barron, David, "CSN Houston faces 'total gridlock,' Comcast/NBC wants bankruptcy trustee to oversee troubled network", Houston Chronicle, 28 Sep 2013, retrieved from http://blog.chron.com/sportsupdate/2013/09/csn-houston-faces-total-gridlock-comcastnbc-wants-bankruptcy-trustee-to-oversee-troubled-network/

[86] Barron, David, "UPDATE: Crane says Astros will fight bankruptcy case against CSN Houston, hearing set for Oct. 28", Houston Chronicle, 30 Sep 2013, retrieved from http://blog.chron.com/sportsupdate/2013/09/jim-crane-astros-will-fight-bankruptcy-case-against-comcastsportsnet-houston/; Barron, David, "Federal judge must rule on Astros' request to dismiss bankruptcy case in CSN flap", Houston Chronicle, 7 Oct 2013, retrieved from http://blog.chron.com/ultimateastros/2013/10/07/astros-seek-dismissal-of-csn-houstons-bankruptcy-filing/; Barron, David, "CSN Houston 'will not' survive without bankruptcy, Comcast says", Houston Chronicle, 15 Oct 2013, retrieved from http://blog.chron.com/ultimateastros/2013/10/15/astros-threaten-to-take-game-broadcasts-away-from-csn-houston/; Barron, David, "Astros say they and Rockets have different needs in CSN Houston bankruptcy case", Houston Chronicle, 24 Oct 2013, retrieved from http://blog.chron.com/sportsupdate/2013/10/astros-rockets-have-different-needs-in-comcast-bankruptcy-ruling/; Barron, David, "Rockets' position on Comcast dispute differs from Astros", Houston Chronicle, 22 Oct 2013, retrieved from http://blog.chron.com/ultimaterockets/2013/10/rockets-take-different-stance-than-astros-on-csn-houston-bankruptcy/.

[87] Barron, David, "Judge allows Astros to seek new TV partner", Houston Chronicle, 29 Oct 2013, retrieved from http://blog.chron.com/sportsupdate/2013/10/judge-gives-astros-negotiating-power-in-csn-houston-dispute/.

[88] Barron, David, "Rockets take charge in CSN Houston negotiations", Houston Chronicle, 12 Dec 2013, retrieved from http://blog.chron.com/ultimaterockets/2013/12/rockets-take-charge-in-csn-houston-negotiations/.

[89] Barron, David, "Rockets may continue negotiating for CSN Houston, judge rules", Houston Chronicle, 7 Jan 2014, retrieved from http://blog.chron.com/ultimaterockets/2014/01/rockets-may-continue-negotiating-for-csn-houston-judge-rules/.

[90] Barron, David, "Bankruptcy ruling keeps CSN Houston afloat amid carriage dispute", Houston Chronicle, 4 Feb 2014, retrieved from http://www.chron.com/sports/article/Bankruptcy-ruling-keeps-CSN-Houston-afloat-amid-5205441.php.

[91] Kosman, Josh, and Claire Atkinson, "Pay-TV providers playing hardball on TWC sports channel", New York Post, 28 Nov 2013, retrieved from http://nypost.com/2013/11/28/pay-tv-providers-playing-hardball-on-twc-sports-channel/; Farrell, Mike, "White: DirecTV Subs in L.A. Could See RSN Surcharge Increases", Multichannel News, 20 Feb 2014, retrieved from http://www.multichannel.com/news/content/white-directv-subs-la-could-see-rsn-surcharge-increases/356128.

[92] Flint, Joe, "Dodger channel debuts Tuesday but much of region will be shut out", Los Angeles Times, 24 Feb 2014, retrieved from http://www.latimes.com/entertainment/envelope/cotown/la-et-ct-dodgers-channel-launch-20140224-story.html; Flint, Joe, "Fans may strike out in battle over Dodgers' new TV home", Los Angeles Times, 18 Feb 2014, retrieved from http://www.latimes.com/entertainment/envelope/cotown/la-et-ct-dodger-tv-20140218-story.html.

[93] Simers, T.J., "Simers: Dodgers' turn to play everyone for a fool", Orange County Register, 3 Mar 2014, retrieved from http://www.ocregister.com/articles/dodgers-604079-cable-time.html; Plaschke, Bill, "A new outlet for fan anger", Los Angeles Times, 5 Mar 2014, C1; Shaikin, Bill, "Tune in later to get your Dodgers", Los Angeles Times, 12 Mar 2014, C1; "Dodgers' Kasten Hopeful Carriers Will Pick Up TWC SportsNet L.A. Closer To Opening Day", SportsBusiness Daily, 13 Mar 2014, retrieved from http://www.sportsbusinessdaily.com/Daily/Issues/2014/03/13/Media/Dodgers.aspx; Carlisle, Jim, "Carlisle: TWC, Dodgers leave many fans in the dark", Ventura County Star, 19 Mar 2014, quoted in "SportsNet LA Still Only On Time Warner Cable As MLB Regular Season Approaches", SportsBusiness Daily, 21 Mar 2014, retrieved from http://www.sportsbusinessdaily.com/Daily/Issues/2014/03/21/Media/Dodgers-TV.aspx; Hewitt, Michael, "Watcher: Dodgers fans left waiting for cable deals", Orange County Register, 25 Mar 2014, retrieved from http://www.ocregister.com/articles/time-606864-warner-cable.html.

[94] Flint, Joe, "DirecTV balks at price to carry Dodgers", Los Angeles Times, 4 Apr 2014, B1.

[95] Shaikin, Bill, "INSIDE BASEBALL: ON BASEBALL: Maybe Dodgers TV issue can be settled with Magic", Los Angeles Times, 20 Apr 2014, C6.

[96] Atkinson, Claire, "You can't watch a Dodgers game in LA on DirecTV", New York Post, 14 May 2014, retrieved from http://nypost.com/2014/05/14/you-cant-watch-a-dodgers-game-in-la-on-directv/.

[97] Flint, Joe, "Dish Network unlikely to carry Dodger channel", Los Angeles Times, 4 Mar 2014, retrieved from http://www.latimes.com/entertainment/envelope/cotown/la-et-ct-dish-network-dodgers-20140304-story.html.

[98] Ourand, John, "Distributors' new leverage may hold implications for Clippers", SportsBusiness Journal, 9 Jun 2014, p13, retrieved from http://www.sportsbusinessdaily.com/Journal/Issues/2014/06/09/Media/Sports-Media.aspx.

[99] Atkinson, "You can't watch a Dodgers game in LA on DirecTV".

[100] Flint, Joe, and Mike Hiserman, "TWC wants arbitration for SportsNet LA", Los Angeles Times, 29 Jul 2014, C4.

[101] Ozanian, Mike, "The Most Expensive Regional Sports Networks To Watch", Forbes, 15 May 2014, retrieved from http://www.forbes.com/sites/mikeozanian/2014/05/15/the-most-expensive-regional-sports-networks/; Lucia, Joe, "Sportsnet LA may help kill a potential Comcast-Time Warner merger", Awful Announcing, 25 Aug 2014, retrieved from http://awfulannouncing.com/2014/sportsnet-la-may-help-kill-a-potential-comcast-time-warner-merger.html.

[102] Flint, Joe, "Dodger brass not worried about distribution for new cable channel", Los Angeles Times, 15 Jan 2014, retrieved from http://www.latimes.com/entertainment/envelope/cotown/la-et-ct-dodgers-time-warner-cable-channel-20140115-story.html; Shaikin, Bill, "All Dodgers, all the time! MLB approves new TV deal", Los Angeles Times, 16 Jan 2014, retrieved from http://www.latimes.com/sports/dodgers/dodgersnow/la-sp-dn-dodgers-time-warner-cable-mlb-tv-deal-20140115-story.html.

[103] Flint, Joe, "Dodgers fans remain shut out: Season is half over and little progress made in TV dispute", Los Angeles Times, 18 Jul 2014, A1.

[104] Flint, "Fans may strike out".

[105] Plunkett, Bill, "KDOC to air final 6 games", Orange County Register, 16 Sep 2014.

[106] Flint, Joe, "Dodgers TV Fiasco, a Game Changer", Wall Street Journal, 30 Sep 2014, B1.

[107] Ourand, John, "Three show interest in Houston rights", SportsBusiness Journal, 26 May 2014, p3, retrieved from http://www.sportsbusinessdaily.com/Journal/Issues/2014/05/26/Media/Houston-rights.aspx.

[108] Barron, David, "UPDATED: Bankruptcy court plan calls for AT&T, DirecTV to take over Comcast SportsNet Houston", Houston Chronicle, 6 Aug 2014, retrieved from http://blog.chron.com/ultimateastros/2014/08/06/att-directv-to-take-over-comcast-sportsnet-houston/.

[109] Barron, David, "Root Sports Houston gets clearance to launch", Houston Chronicle, 6 Nov 2014, retrieved from http://blog.chron.com/sportsupdate/2014/11/root-sports-houston-gets-clearance-to-launch/.

[110] Barron, David, "Root Sports Southwest channel debuts Monday", Houston Chronicle, 16 Nov 2014, retrieved from http://blog.chron.com/sportsupdate/2014/11/root-sports-southwest-channel-debuts-monday/.

[111] Lev, Michael, "Charter plans to carry SportsNet LA for Dodgers games", Orange County Register, 26 May 2015, retrieved from http://www.ocregister.com/articles/charter-663044-sportsnet-expanding.html.

[112] "Vin Scully: 2016 will be final season in booth for Dodgers", USA Today, 29 Aug 2015, retrieved from http://www.usatoday.com/story/sports/mlb/2015/08/29/vin-scully-2016--final-season-booth-dodgers/71395736/.

Chapter 7: Fighting for Scraps

[1] Healey, Jon, "Bamboom takes over-the-air TV over the top", Los Angeles Times, 14 Apr 2011, retrieved from http://latimesblogs.latimes.com/technology/2011/04/bamboom-takes-over-the-air-tv-over-the-top.html; Torikka, Mikko, "Bamboom Labs raises $4.5M for live TV over the Web", VentureBeat, 15 Apr 2011, retrieved from http://venturebeat.com/2011/04/15/bamboom-labs-raises-4-5m-for-live-tv-over-the-web/.

[2] Ibid.; O'Neill, Jim, "Bamboom raises the stakes on online television", FierceCable, 29 May 2011, retrieved from http://www.fiercecable.com/story/bamboom-raises-stakes-online-television/2011-05-29.

[3] "Aereo Announces $20.5M Series A Financing Led by IAC; New Technology Platform Allows Consumers Access to Live TV Over the Internet", Market Wired, 14 Feb 2012, retrieved from http://www.marketwired.com/press-release/aereo-announces-205m-series-a-financing-led-iac-new-technology-platform-allows-consumers-nasdaq-iaci-1619629.htm; Stelter, Brian, "New Service Will Stream Local TV Stations in New York", New York Times, 14 Feb 2012, retrieved from http://mediadecoder.blogs.nytimes.com/2012/02/14/new-service-will-stream-local-tv-stations-in-new-york/?smid=tw-nytimestv&seid=auto&_r=0.

[4] Winslow, George, "Broadcasters File Suits Against Aereo", Multichannel News, 1 Mar 2012, retrieved from http://www.multichannel.com/news/orphan-articles/broadcasters-file-suits-against-aereo/126438.

[5] Winslow, George, "Judge Denies Request to Shut Down Aereo", Broadcasting and Cable, 11 Jul 2012, retrieved from http://www.broadcastingcable.com/news/news-articles/judge-denies-request-shut-down-aereo/113359.

[6] Eggerton, John, "Cablevision Backs Broadcasters in Aereo Challenge", Multichannel News, 24 Sep 2012, retrieved from http://www.multichannel.com/news/orphan-articles/cablevision-backs-broadcasters-aereo-challenge/126024.

[7] Eggerton, John, "Appeals Court Sides With Aereo", Multichannel News, 1 Apr 2013, retrieved from http://www.multichannel.com/news/tv-everywhere/appeals-court-sides-aereo/307175.

[8] Eggerton, John, "Bring It On: Aereo Supports Broadcaster Petition to Supreme Court", Multichannel News, 12 Dec 2013, retrieved from http://www.multichannel.com/news/content/bring-it-aereo-supports-broadcaster-petition-supreme-court/356728.

[9] Eggerton, John, "Broadcasters to Supremes: Aereo is Stealing On Massive Scale", Broadcasting & Cable, 24 Feb 2014, retrieved from http://www.broadcastingcable.com/news/washington/broadcasters-supremes-aereo-stealing-massive-scale/129392.

[10] Eggerton, John, "ACA: Aereo is Nothing Like a Cable System", Multichannel News, 3 Apr 2014, retrieved from http://www.multichannel.com/aca-aereo-nothing-cable-system/373612.

[11] Eggerton, John, "Aereo to Supremes: We're Heirs to Rabbit Ears & Betamax", Multichannel News, 26 Mar 2014, retrieved from http://www.multichannel.com/news/policy/aereo-supremes-were-heirs-rabbit-ears-betamax/338176.

[12] Eggerton, John, "Diller: Online Video Should Be Subject to Same Obligations as Traditional Distributors", Multichannel News, 24 Apr 2012, retrieved from http://www.multichannel.com/news/policy/diller-online-video-should-be-subject-same-obligations-traditional-distributors/263958.

[13] "A Battle Over Broadcast", Wall Street Journal, 2 Jun 2013, retrieved from http://www.wsj.com/articles/SB10001424127887323728204578515441298859264.

[14] Eggerton, John, "Kanojia Calls Broadcasters' 'Rube Goldberg' Knock On Aereo 'Insane'", Multichannel News, 17 Apr 2014, retrieved from http://www.multichannel.com/news/content/kanojia-calls-broadcasters-rube-goldberg-knock-aereo-insane/373934.

[15] Eggerton, John, "Supremes Rule Against Aereo", Multichannel News, 25 Jun 2014, retrieved from http://www.multichannel.com/news/technology/supremes-rule-against-aereo/375377.

[16] Eggerton, John, "Aereo Shuts Down, Considers Options", Multichannel News, 29 Jun 2014, retrieved from http://www.multichannel.com/news/policy/aereo-shuts-down-considers-options/375459.

[17] Lafayette, Jon, "Aereo Urges Subscribers To Contact Lawmakers", Multichannel News, 1 Jul 2014, retrieved from http://www.multichannel.com/aereo-urges-subscribers-contact-lawmakers/375656.

[18] Eggerton, John, "Aereo: A Cable System, Subject to Statutory Licence", Multichannel News, 9 Jul 2014, retrieved from http://www.multichannel.com/news/distribution/aereo-were-cable-system-subject-statutory-license/375819.

[19] Eggerton, John, "Diller: If Aereo Loses In Court, 'We're Finished'", Multichannel News, 2 Apr 2014, retrieved from http://www.multichannel.com/news/finance/diller-if-aereo-loses-court-were-finished/373578.

[20] Eggerton, John, "Copyright Office: Aereo Isn't Cable", Multichannel News, 17 Jul 2014, retrieved from http://www.multichannel.com/news/policy/copyright-office-aereo-isnt-cable/382572.

[21] Baumgartner, Jeff, "Aereo Files For Bankruptcy", Multichannel News, 21 Nov 2014, retrieved from http://www.multichannel.com/news/technology/aereo-files-bankruptcy/385771.

[22] Baumgartner, Jeff, "Aereo Auction Raises Less Than $2 Million", Multichannel News, 26 Feb 2015, retrieved from http://www.multichannel.com/news/technology/aereo-auction-raises-less-2-million/388423; Randazzo, Sara, "Judge Signs Off on Aereo Sales to TiVo, RPX", Wall Street Journal, 11 Mar 2015, retrieved from http://www.wsj.com/articles/judge-signs-off-on-aereo-sales-to-tivo-rpx-1426105845.

[23] Baumgartner, Jeff, "Aereo, Broadcasters Reach Settlement", Multichannel News, 22 Apr 2015, retrieved from http://www.multichannel.com/news/technology/aereo-broadcasters-reach-settlement/389976.

[24] Brill, Matthew A., and Matthew T. Murchison, "How the FCC Can Protect Consumers in the Battle Over Retransmission Consent", Bloomberg BNA, 11 Sep 2013, retrieved from http://www.bna.com/how-the-fcc-can-protect-consumers-in-the-battle-over-retransmission-consent/.

[25] McAvoy, Kim, "New year should be busy one in Washington", Broadcasting, 31 Dec 1990, p38; Stump, Matt, "Retransmission consent: rocky House reception", Broadcasting, 1 Jul 1991, p21.

[26] McAvoy, op. cit.; Jessell, Harry A., "Can cable win for losing?", Broadcasting, 24 Sep 1990, p23.

[27] Jessell, op. cit.; McAvoy, Kim, "Inouye and Hollings vow to move cable bill", Broadcasting, 18 Mar 1991, p25.

[28] Lyons, Daniel, "Telecom law primer: Retransmission consent and must carry rules", TechPolicyDaily, 5 Mar 2014, retrieved from http://www.techpolicydaily.com/communications/telecom-law-primer-retransmission-consent-must-carry-rules/.

[29] Brill, Matthew A., and Matthew T. Murchison, "How the FCC Can Protect Consumers in the Battle Over Retransmission Consent", Bloomberg BNA, 11 Sep 2013, retrieved from http://www.bna.com/how-the-fcc-can-protect-consumers-in-the-battle-over-retransmission-consent/; Lafayette, Jon, "Cable's Billion-Dollar Question Needs An Answer", Broadcasting & Cable, 13 Sep 2010, retrieved from http://www.broadcastingcable.com/news/news-articles/cables-billion-dollar-question-needs-answer/111186.

[30] Grego, Melissa, "Retrans...The Bloody Battle to Save Broadcast Television", Broadcasting & Cable, 12 Dec 2009, retrieved from http://www.broadcastingcable.com/news/news-articles/cover-story-retransthe-bloody-battle-save-broadcast-television/110623.

[31] Ourand, John, "Big deals, bigger questions", SportsBusiness Journal, 9 Nov 2009, retrieved from http://www.sportsbusinessdaily.com/Journal/Issues/2009/11/20091109/SBJ-In-Depth/Big-Deals-Bigger-Questions.aspx; Lauria, Peter, "Ranting on ratings", New York Post, 13 Dec 2009, retrieved from http://nypost.com/2009/12/13/ranting-on-ratings/.

[32] Grego, op. cit.; Brill and Murchison, op. cit.

[33] Schechner, Sam, "TV Networks, Local Stations Do Battle Over Cable Fees", Wall Street Journal, 14 Dec 2009, B4.

³⁴ Grego, op. cit.; Malone, Michael, "Fox, Affiliates Up Retrans Rhetoric With Twin Missives", Broadcasting & Cable, 9 Feb 2011, retrieved from http://www.broadcastingcable.com/blog/station-station/fox-affiliates-retrans-rhetoric-twin-missives/66823.

³⁵ Malone, Michael, "Sook: Networks in For Fight If They Want Our Retrans Cash", Broadcasting & Cable, 11 Nov 2009, retrieved from http://www.broadcastingcable.com/news/local-tv/sook-networks-fight-if-they-want-our-retrans-cash/42023.

³⁶ Grego, op. cit.

³⁷ Malone, Michael, "Network-Affiliate Frenemies Go Nose To Nose", Broadcasting & Cable, 21 Mar 2011, retrieved from http://www.broadcastingcable.com/news/local-tv/network-affiliate-frenemies-go-nose-nose/42786.

³⁸ Atkinson, Claire, "CBS Retrans Fees Expected to Double in 2010", Broadcasting & Cable, 5 Nov 2009, retrieved from http://www.broadcastingcable.com/news/programming/cbs-retrans-fees-expected-double-2010/35716.

³⁹ Malone, Michael, "What's in the Cards for Stations", Broadcasting & Cable, 18 Jul 2011, retrieved from http://www.broadcastingcable.com/news/local-tv/whats-cards-stations/42979.

⁴⁰ Hagey, Keach, "CBS Plays Hardball as Affiliate Fees Pile Up", Wall Street Journal, 20 Aug 2014, retrieved from http://www.wsj.com/articles/cbs-plays-hardball-as-affiliate-fees-pile-up-1408578087.

⁴¹ Whitmer, Melinda, Testimony before the United States Senate Committee on Commerce, Science and Transportation Hearing on "The Cable Act at 20", 24 Jul 2012, retrieved from http://www.commerce.senate.gov/public/_cache/files/bd33c7c9-bd4d-43c0-93d5-091e1fd3328b/398DC98E4A665C0C9D224098FCD701F1.witmer-testimony.pdf; Eggerton, John, "Mediacom's Commisso Says Broadcasters Engaging in 'Economic Blackmail'", Broadcasting and Cable, 7 Jan 2010, retrieved from http://www.broadcastingcable.com/news/washington/mediacoms-commisso-says-broadcasters-engaging-economic-blackmail/56968.

⁴² Whitmer, op. cit., pp. 13-14.

⁴³ Fixmer, Andy, "News Corp. to Take Fox Off Air If Courts Back Aereo", Bloomberg Business, 9 Apr 2013, retrieved from http://www.bloomberg.com/news/articles/2013-04-08/news-corp-says-it-will-take-fox-off-air-if-courts-ok-aereo-1-.

⁴⁴ Patten, Dominic, "Les Moonves Says CBS Could Go To Cable In 'A Few Days' If It Loses Aereo Suit", Deadline, 30 Apr 2013, retrieved from http://deadline.com/2013/04/les-moonves-cbs-cable-threat-aereo-lawsuit-487262/.

⁴⁵ Malone, "Network-Affiliate Frenemies".

⁴⁶ Grego, op. cit.

⁴⁷ Lafayette, "Cable's Billion-Dollar Question Needs an Answer".

⁴⁸ Baine, Derek, Scott Robson, John Fletcher, and Adam Gajo, "Rising sports costs top of mind with both programmers, multi-channel operators", SNL Kagan, Jan 2015, p2, retrieved from http://go.snl.com/rs/snlfinancialllc/images/Kagan_RisingSports_WP_FINAL.pdf.

⁴⁹ "83% of U.S. Households Subscribe to a Pay-TV Service", Leichtman Research Group, 3 Sep 2015, retrieved from http://www.leichtmanresearch.com/press/090315release.html.

⁵⁰ Lafayette, "Cable's Billion-Dollar Question Needs an Answer".

⁵¹ Lafayette, Jon, "The 'Mad Men' Lesson: Buzz Lights Up a Network", Broadcasting and Cable, 19 Jul 2010, pp. 18-20; Lafayette, Jon, "Original Programming Costs Raise Concern", Broadcasting and Cable, 20 Jan 2014, pp. 8-10.

⁵² Lowry, Brian, "Blackouts' black eye", Variety, 30 Jul-5 Aug 2012, pp. 2, 9.

⁵³ Davidson, Adam, "How cable created its golden age", International Herald Tribune, 8 Dec 2012, p15; Lafayette, "The 'Mad Men' Lesson"; James, Meg, "Cost of Cable TV Content Soars: Spending on sports and original shows has shot up in the last 5 years", Los Angeles Times, 8 Dec 2011, B1.

⁵⁴ Koblin, John, "Beyond Brain Candy", New York Times, 26 Oct 2015, B1.

⁵⁵ Seidman, Robert, "List of how many homes each cable network is in as of July 2015", TVbytheNumbers, 21 Jul 2015, retrieved from http://tvbythenumbers.zap2it.com/2015/07/21/list-of-how-many-homes-each-cable-network-is-in-as-of-july-2015/434373/; Scripps Networks Interactive, "Our Brands", retrieved from http://www.scrippsnetworksinteractive.com/our-brands/; Discovery Communications, Inc., "Businesses & Brands", retrieved from http://corporate.discovery.com/businesses-and-brands/; "NBCUniversal", retrieved from http://www.nbcuniversal.com; Time Warner Inc., "Turner Broadcasting System", retrieved from http://www.timewarner.com/company/operating-divisions/turner-broadcasting-system; "Disney | ABC Television Group", retrieved from http://www.disneyabcpress.com/disneyabctv/; Tarmey, Kerri, "A+E NETWORKS NAMED 2015 COMPANY OF DISTINCTION AT BANFF WORLD MEDIA FESTIVAL", A+E Networks, 15 Oct 2014, retrieved from http://www.aenetworks.com/article/ae-networks-named-2015-company-distinction-banff-world-media-festival; 21ˢᵗ Century Fox, "Business Units", retrieved from http://www.21cf.com/Business_Segments/Business_Units/; Viacom, "Viacom Brands", retrieved from http://www.viacom.com/brands/pages/default.aspx.

⁵⁶ Seidman, "List of how many homes each cable network is in"; CBS Corporation, "Our Portfolio", retrieved from http://www.cbscorporation.com/portfolio.php.

⁵⁷ Thompson, Derek, "Prisoners of Cable", Atlantic, Nov 2012, retrieved from http://www.theatlantic.com/magazine/archive/2012/11/prisoners-of-cable/309109/

[58] Ourand, John, "Cablevision takes on carriage deals", SportsBusiness Journal, 6 May 2013, p19, retrieved from http://www.sportsbusinessdaily.com/Journal/Issues/2013/05/06/In-Depth/Cablevision.aspx.

[59] Ramachandran, Shalini, "Cablevision Alleges Coercion – Firm Says Viacom 'Strong-Armed' It, Threatening $1 Billion Penalty on Package", Wall Street Journal, 8 Mar 2013, B2.

[60] Farrell, Mike, "Cablevision, Viacom Resolve Litigation", Multichannel News, 16 Oct 2015, retrieved from http://www.multichannel.com/news/cable-operators/cablevision-viacom-resolve-litigation/394624.

[61] Flint, Joe, "Viacom is sued over TV 'bundles'", Los Angeles Times, 27 Feb 2013, B1.

[62] Schechner, Sam, and Christopher S. Stewart, "Fuse Is a Flash Point in Cable Fight", Wall Street Journal, 27 Dec 2011, B4.

[63] Ourand, John, "Thaw took months of talks", SportsBusiness Journal, 25 May 2009, retrieved from http://www.sportsbusinessdaily.com/Journal/Issues/2009/05/20090525/This-Weeks-News/Thaw-Took-Months-Of-Talks.aspx.

[64] James, Meg, "FCC rules for Tennis Channel", Los Angeles Times, 25 Jul 2012, B4

[65] Atkinson, Claire, "Comcast served: Tennis Channel bid for basic tier nixed", New York Post, 29 May 2013, p30.

[66] Stelter, Brian, "Comcast Ordered to Place Bloomberg With TV Peers", New York Times, 28 Sep 2013, B5.

[67] Lafayette, "Cable's Billion-Dollar Question Needs an Answer".

[68] Ourand, John, "Turning away from sports tiers", SportsBusiness Journal, 12 Nov 2007, retrieved from http://www.sportsbusinessdaily.com/Journal/Issues/2007/11/20071112/This-Weeks-News/Turning-Away-From-Sports-Tiers.aspx

[69] Bernstein, Andy, "NBA TV revamping; live telecasts delayed", SportsBusiness Journal, 26 Aug 2002, retrieved from http://www.sportsbusinessdaily.com/Journal/Issues/2002/08/20020826/This-Weeks-Issue/NBA-TV-Revamping-Live-Telecasts-Delayed.aspx.

[70] Weprin, Alex, "Niche networks get a shot, thanks to Comcast deal", Politico, 27 Feb 2014, retrieved from http://www.capitalnewyork.com/article/media/2014/02/8540967/niche-networks-get-shot-thanks-comcast-deal.

[71] Moss, Linda, "Networks Feel Pressure Points", Multichannel News, 28 Jul 2014, retrieved from http://www.multichannel.com/news/carriage-deals/networks-feel-pressure-points/382755

[72] Belson, op. cit.

[73] Mickle, Tripp, and John Ourand, "Concerns about distribution end talk of Fuel deal", SportsBusiness Journal, 19 Apr 2010, retrieved from http://www.sportsbusinessdaily.com/Journal/Issues/2010/04/20100419/This-Weeks-News/Concerns-About-Distribution-End-Talk-Of-Fuel-Deal.aspx.

[74] Mickle and Ourand, "Concerns about distribution end talk of Fuel deal".

[75] Fernandez, Bob, "Fight continues over retransmission fees", Philadelphia Inquirer, 5 Jan 2014, C1.

[76] Spangler, Todd, "Time Warner Cable Gives Tips For Getting Fox Shows Online, Over The Air", Multichannel News, 30 Dec 2009, retrieved from http://www.multichannel.com/news/policy/time-warner-cable-gives-tips-getting-fox-shows-online-over-air/266695.

[77] Ramachandran, Shalini, "TWC Lost Subscribers During Fight With CBS", Wall Street Journal, 12 Sep 2013, B8.

[78] Baumgartner, Jeff, "TWC To NYC Subs: Give Aereo a Try", Multichannel News, 5 Aug 2013, retrieved from http://www.multichannel.com/blog/bauminator/twc-nyc-subs-give-aereo-try/373155.

[79] Stelter, Brian, and Brooks Barnes, "At the Last Minute, a Disney-Cablevision Truce", New York Times, 8 Mar 2010, B1.

[80] Farrell, Mike, "CBS, Time Warner Cable Finally Sign Carriage Agreement", Multichannel News, 2 Sep 2013, retrieved from http://www.multichannel.com/news/content/cbs-time-warner-cable-finally-sign-carriage-agreement/357668.

[81] Farrell, Mike, "Dish, Turner Agree to Extension", Multichannel News, 21 Nov 2014, retrieved from http://www.multichannel.com/dish-turner-agree-extension/385780.

[82] Farrell, Mike, "Dish, Turner Sign Carriage Deal", Multichannel News, 1 Apr 2015, retrieved from http://www.multichannel.com/news/satellite/dish-turner-sign-carriage-deal/389367.

[83] Lowry, op. cit.

[84] Ramachandran, "TWC Lost Subscribers During Fight With CBS".

[85] Trefis, "DirecTV To Raise Its Subscription Prices Amid A Continued Growth In Programming Costs", Forbes, 5 Jan 2015, retrieved from http://www.forbes.com/sites/greatspeculations/2015/01/05/directv-to-raise-its-subscription-prices-amid-a-continued-growth-in-programming-costs/.

[86] Ourand, John, "Comcast's Burke takes on critics of company's dual strategies", SportsBusiness Journal, 13 Apr 2009, retrieved from http://www.sportsbusinessdaily.com/Journal/Issues/2009/04/20090413/Media/Comcasts-Burke-Takes-On-Critics-Of-Companys-Dual-Strategies.aspx.

[87] Ourand, "Carriage talks have industry's attention".

[88] Ourand, "Comcast's Burke takes on critics of company's dual strategies".

[89] Krause, Reinhardt, "Comcast, Fox Forge Digital Age Programming Deal", Investor's Business Daily, 12 Feb 2013, retrieved from http://news.investors.com/technology/021213-644091-comcast-fox-network-reach-programming-agreement.htm.

[90] Farrell, Mike, "Kent: Viacom Return Unlikely", Multichannel News, 24 Feb 2015, retrieved from http://www.multichannel.com/news/cable-operators/kent-viacom-return-unlikely/388321.

[91] Ramachandran, Shalini, and Joe Flint, "Pugnacious Dish Boss Racks Up TV Brawls", Wall Street Journal, 23 Dec 2014, B1.

[92] Ourand, "Tune in Tomorrow!"; Ourand, John, "Despite successes, launching a sports channel is no slam dunk", SportsBusiness Journal, 23 Aug 2010, retrieved from http://www.sportsbusinessdaily.com/Journal/Issues/2010/08/20100823/Media/Despite-Successes-Launching-A-Sports-Channel-Is-No-Slam-Dunk.aspx.

[93] Ourand, John, "DirecTV's competitors see an opening", SportsBusiness Journal, 21 Jan 2013, p17, retrieved from http://www.sportsbusinessdaily.com/Journal/Issues/2013/01/21/In-Depth/Competitors.aspx.

[94] Ourand, John, "DirecTV's tough tack on Versus a strategy shift?", SportsBusiness Journal, 7 Sep 2009, retrieved from http://www.sportsbusinessdaily.com/Journal/Issues/2009/09/20090907/This-Weeks-News/Directvs-Tough-Tack-On-Versus-A-Strategy-Shift.aspx.

[95] Ourand, John, "A different game for DirecTV", SportsBusiness Journal, 21 Jan 2013, retrieved from http://www.sportsbusinessdaily.com/Journal/Issues/2013/01/21/In-Depth/DirecTV.aspx.

[96] Ibid.

[97] Ramachandran, Shalini, and Kevin Clark, "DirecTV Reaches NFL Pact, Clearing Way for AT&T Deal", Wall Street Journal, 2 Oct 2014, B9.

[98] Ibid.

[99] Ourand, John, "Disney, Comcast Announce Comprehensive 10-Year Carriage Deal", SportsBusiness Journal, 4 Jan 2012, retrieved from http://www.sportsbusinessdaily.com/Daily/Closing-Bell/2012/01/04/Disney-Comcast.aspx.

[100] Lafayette, Jon, "DirecTV Signs Broad Carriage Deal With Disney", Broadcasting and Cable, 23 Dec 2014, retrieved from http://www.broadcastingcable.com/news/currency/directv-signs-broad-carriage-deal-disney/136628.

[101] Yu, Roger, "Dish, Disney reach carriage deal with streaming options", USA Today, 4 Mar 2014, retrieved from http://www.usatoday.com/story/money/business/2014/03/03/dish-network-walt-disney-internet-tv/5984663/.

[102] Ourand, John, "ESPN to offer Classic-for-ESPNU swap", SportsBusiness Journal, 30 Mar 2009, retrieved from http://www.sportsbusinessdaily.com/Journal/Issues/2009/03/20090330/This-Weeks-News/ESPN-To-Offer-Classic-For-ESPNU-Swap.aspx.

[103] Applications of AT&T Inc. and DIRECTV for Consent to Assign or Transfer Licenses and Authorizations, Description of Transaction, Public Interest Showing, and Related Demonstrations, 11 Jun 2014, pp. 34-37, retrieved from http://apps.fcc.gov/ecfs/document/view?id=7521303307.

[104] Applications of Comcast Corporation and Time Warner Cable, Inc., for Consent To Transfer Control of Licenses and Authorizations, Applications and Public Interest Statement, 8 Apr 2014, pp. 68-75, retrieved from http://apps.fcc.gov/ecfs/document/view?id=7521097357; Applications of Charter Communications, Inc., Time Warner Cable Inc., and Advance/Newhouse Partnership for Consent to the Transfer of Control of Licenses and Authorizations, Public Interest Statement, 25 Jun 2015, pp. 54-57, retrieved from http://apps.fcc.gov/ecfs/document/view?id=60001097273.

[105] Federal Communications Commission, Implementation of Section 19 of the 1992 Cable Act (Annual Assessment of the Status of Competition in the Market for the Delivery of Video Programming), 2004 Report, 4 Feb 2005, p119, retrieved from https://apps.fcc.gov/edocs_public/attachmatch/FCC-05-13A1.pdf.

[106] Federal Communications Commission, Implementation of Section 19 of the 1992 Cable Act (Annual Assessment of the Status of Competition in the Market for the Delivery of Video Programming), 14th Report, 20 Jul 2012, pp. 60-61, retrieved from https://apps.fcc.gov/edocs_public/attachmatch/FCC-12-81A1.pdf.

[107] "Major Pay-TV Providers Lost About 190,000 Subscribers in 3Q 2015", Leichtman Research Group, 16 Nov 2015, retrieved from http://www.leichtmanresearch.com/press/111615release.html. Count of top six includes Comcast, AT&T-DirecTV, Charter-Time Warner-Bright House, Dish, Verizon FiOS, and Cablevision-Suddenlink; uses estimate of 2.5 million Bright House subscribers from Bright House Networks, "About Bright House Networks", retrieved from http://brighthouse.com/about/about-us/about-us.html.

[108] Hagey, Keach, and Amol Sharma, "Riches and Risks for Fox In Time Warner Takeover", Wall Street Journal, 18 Jul 2014, B1.

[109] Turner, S. Derek, "Cease to Resist: How the FCC's Failure to Enforce Its Rules Created a New Wave of Media Consolidation", Free Press, 2013, p14, retrieved from http://www.freepress.net/sites/default/files/resources/Cease_to_Resist_Oct_2013_0.pdf.

[110] Albiniak, Paige, "B&C's Top 25 Station Groups 2010", Broadcasting and Cable, 12 Apr 2010, p14.

[111] Ibid.; Albiniak, Paige, "Who's a Buyer, Who's a Seller?", Broadcasting and Cable, 13 Apr 2015, pp. 6-8, 10.

[112] Flint, Joe, "FCC proposes eliminating UHF discount from TV ownership rules", Los Angeles Times, 26 Sep 2013, retrieved from http://articles.latimes.com/2013/sep/26/entertainment/la-et-ct-fcc-uhf-discount-20130926.

[113] Albiniak, "B&C's Top 25 Station Groups 2010" (CBS, Fox, NBC, Tribune, ABC, Sinclair, Gannett, Hearst, Belo, Raycom); Albiniak, "Who's a Buyer, Who's a Seller?" (Tribune, CBS, Sinclair, Fox, NBCUniversal, Gannett, Media General, ABC, Hearst, E.W. Scripps).

[114] Turner, op. cit., pp. 1-44.

[115] "ACA Documents Decreasing Competition Among Local Broadcasters", American Cable Association, 6 Mar 2012, retrieved from http://americancable.org/node/3440.

[116] Wood, Matt, Written Testimony before the House of Representatives Committee on Energy and Commerce Subcommittee on Communications and Technology regarding "Reauthorization of the Satellite Television Extension and Localism Act", 12 Mar 2014, retrieved from http://www.freepress.net/sites/default/files/resources/Free_Press_Written_Testimony_3-12-14_STELA_Hearing.pdf.

[117] Jessell, Harry A., "Sinclair Giving Up 3 Stations To Appease FCC", TVNewsCheck, 29 May 2014, retrieved from http://www.tvnewscheck.com/article/76663/sinclair-giving-up-3-stations-to-appease-fcc.

[118] 2014 Quadrennial Regulatory Review – Review of the Commission's Broadcast Ownership Rules and Other Rules Adopted Pursuant to Section 202 of the Telecommunications Act of 1996, Comments of the National Association of Broadcasters, 6 Aug 2014, pp. 38-59, retrieved from http://apps.fcc.gov/ecfs/document/view?id=7521751016.

Chapter 8: Breaking Free

[1] Diaz, George, "Fighting for Survival: Boxing Hits Canvas as Mainstream Sport", Orlando Sentinel, 10 Aug 2003, C1; Christ, Scott, "Mayweather vs. Pacquiao: The Complete Timeline for the Fight of the Century", SBNation, 29 Apr 2015, retrieved from http://www.sbnation.com/2015/4/29/8504023/pacquiao-vs-mayweather-2015-fight-timeline.

[2] Christ, op. cit.; Iole, Kevin, "WBO concludes Manny Pacquiao topped Timothy Bradley, but Bob Arum still wants investigation", Yahoo! Sports, 21 Jun 2012, retrieved from http://www.sbnation.com/2015/4/29/8504023/pacquiao-vs-mayweather-2015-fight-timeline.

[3] McQuade, Dan, "How Mayweather-Pacquiao gives PPV cops a chance to make big money", The Guardian, 28 Apr 2015, retrieved from http://www.theguardian.com/sport/2015/apr/28/floyd-mayweather-manny-pacquiao-fight-pay-per-view-cops.

[4] Pugmire, Lance, "Mayweather-Pacquiao: Nichols, Beadle credential situations cause stir", Los Angeles Times, 2 May 2015, retrieved from http://www.latimes.com/sports/boxing/la-sp-sn-mayweather-pacquiao-credential-nichols-beadle-20150502-htmlstory.html; Beadle, Michelle, "Thoughts on a weekend...", TwitLonger, 5 May 2015, retrieved from http://www.twitlonger.com/show/n_1sm2oaj.

[5] Goff, Brian, "Floyd Mayweather Is a Boring Boxer But May Be The Best Businessman In Sports", Forbes, 4 May 2015, retrieved from http://www.forbes.com/sites/briangoff/2015/05/04/floyd-mayweather-is-a-boring-boxer-but-maybe-the-best-business-man-in-sports/.

[6] Pugmire, Lance, "Pacquiao sued by fans alleging fraud", Los Angeles Times, 6 May 2015, D2; Rovell, Darren, "Fans file class-action lawsuit against Manny Pacquiao over injury", ESPN, 5 May 2015, retrieved from http://espn.go.com/boxing/story/_/id/12827249/two-fans-file-class-action-lawsuit-manny-pacquiao-undisclosed-injury.

[7] Rovell, Darren, "Pay-per-view problems pop up prior to Mayweather-Pacquiao fight", ABC News, 2 May 2015, retrieved from http://abcnews.go.com/Sports/pay-view-problems-pop-prior-mayweather-pacquiao-fight/story?id=30763560; Lowe, Kinsey, "Mayweather-Pacquiao Fight Delayed By Widespread Cable & Satellite Outages – Update", Deadline, 2 May 2015, retrieved from http://deadline.com/2015/05/cable-satellite-providers-reporting-outages-ahead-of-mayweather-pacquiao-fight-1201419774/; Rosenthal, Seth, "Mayweather vs. Pacquiao is breaking Pay-Per-View and everyone's freaking out", SBNation, 2 May 2015, retrieved from http://www.sbnation.com/lookit/2015/5/2/8538211/mayweather-vs-pacquiao-is-breaking-pay-per-view-freak-out-comcast-time-warner.

[8] Patten, Dominic, "Mayweather Vs. Pacquiao Fight KOs PPV Revenue & Viewership Record", Deadline, 12 May 2015, retrieved from http://deadline.com/2015/05/mayweather-pacquiao-pay-per-view-record-ppv-viewership-1201425241/.

[9] Paulsen, "BCS TV Ratings: Fewer Viewers For Final BCS Title Game, Despite 'Megacast'", Sports Media Watch, 8 Jan 2014, retrieved from http://www.sportsmediawatch.com/2014/01/bcs-tv-ratings-fewer-viewers-for-final-bcs-title-game-despite-megacast/.

[10] Sandomir et al., op. cit.

[11] Ibid.

[12] Ibid.

[13] Kwong, Matt, "Pick-and-pay TV: Consumer choice, but at what cost?", CBC News, 20 Mar 2015, retrieved from http://www.cbc.ca/news/business/pick-and-pay-tv-consumer-choice-but-at-what-cost-1.3002418.

[14] Thompson, "Prisoners of Cable".

[15] Cauley, Leslie, "Cable Firms Consider Removing ESPN From Basic Tier, Passing Costs to Fans", Wall Street Journal, 4 May 1998, B6.

[16] Bernstein, Andy, "Time Warner to move some sports to pay tier", SportsBusiness Journal, 1 Apr 2002, retrieved from http://www.sportsbusinessdaily.com/Journal/Issues/2002/04/20020401/This-Weeks-Issue/Time-Warner-To-Move-Some-Sports-To-Pay-Tier.aspx.

[17] Bernstein, "Deal could move sports nets to tiers".

[18] Bernstein, "Teams say 'YES!' to cable settlement".

[19]Ourand, "Turning away from sports tiers"; Bernstein, Andy, "NFL Network accepts spot on Cox sports tier", SportsBusiness Journal, 11 Apr 2005, retrieved from http://www.sportsbusinessdaily.com/Journal/Issues/2005/04/20050411/Media/NFL-Network-Accepts-Spot-On-Cox-Sports-Tier.aspx; Ourand, John, and John Lombardo, "Comcast Moves NBA TV To Digital Classic Tier, Adds 8.8 Million Subs", SportsBusiness Daily, 4 Jun 2009, retrieved from http://www.sportsbusinessdaily.com/Daily/Issues/2009/06/Issue-178/Sports-Media/Comcast-Moves-NBA-TV-To-Digital-Classic-Tier-Adds-88-Million-Subs.aspx.

[20] Ourand, John, "Four things we've learned from Disney-Time Warner Cable deal", SportsBusiness Journal, 13 Sep 2010, retrieved from http://www.sportsbusinessdaily.com/Journal/Issues/2010/09/20100913/Media/Four-things-weve-learned-from-Disney-Time-Warner-Cable-deal.aspx.

[21] Atkinson, Claire, "Dish Network may boot ESPN over higher rights fees", New York Post, 9 Sep 2011, retrieved from http://nypost.com/2011/09/09/dish-network-may-boot-espn-over-higher-rights-fees/.

[22] Ourand, John, "Dish shows there's life without every RSN, but at what cost?", SportsBusiness Journal, 14 Nov 2011, p12, retrieved from http://www.sportsbusinessdaily.com/Journal/Issues/2011/11/14/Media/Sports-Media.aspx.

[23] Mullins, Richard, "Verizon offers no-sports cable TV package", Tampa Tribune, 21 Jan 2013, retrieved from http://www.tbo.com/news/business/verizon-offers-no-sports-cable-tv-package-612937.

[24] Ourand, John, "Will Dish's offering kill cable bundle?", SportsBusiness Journal, 12 Jan 2015, p3, retrieved from http://www.sportsbusinessdaily.com/Journal/Issues/2015/01/12/Media/ESPN-Sling-TV.aspx.

[25] Ward-Bailey, Jeff, "Bucking cable tradition, Verizon offers custom TV bundles (+video)", Christian Science Monitor, 17 Apr 2015, retrieved from http://www.csmonitor.com/Technology/2015/0417/Bucking-cable-tradition-Verizon-offers-custom-TV-bundles-video.

[26] Kafka, Peter, "Disney Says Verizon's Bundle-Breaking Pay TV Plan Breaks Its Rules", Re/code, 17 Apr 2015, retrieved from http://recode.net/2015/04/17/disney-says-verizons-bundle-breaking-pay-tv-plan-breaks-their-rules/; Flint, Joe, "ESPN Sues Verizon Over New TV Bundles", Wall Street Journal, 28 Apr 2015, B1.

[27] Ourand, John, "The moves that forced ESPN's cuts", SportsBusiness Journal, 26 Oct 2015, retrieved from http://www.sportsbusinessdaily.com/Journal/Issues/2015/10/26/Media/ESPN.aspx.

[28] Warner, Dave, "The Numbers Behind ESPN's Grim Meathook Future", What You Pay For Sports, 17 Jul 2015, retrieved from http://www.whatyoupayforsports.com/2015/07/the-numbers-behind-espns-grim-meathook-future/.

[29] Eifling, Sam, "Expensive Cable Sports are Always Expensiver Than Ever", Deadspin, 26 Jan 2013, retrieved from http://deadspin.com/5979252/expensive-cable-sports-are-always-expensiver-than-ever.

[30] Seidman, Robert, "FAQ: Do Total Viewers Matter?", TVbytheNumbers, 12 Dec 2009, retrieved from http://tvbythenumbers.zap2it.com/2009/12/12/faq-do-total-viewers-matter/36064/.

[31] Ramachandran, Shalini, "Pay-TV 'Cord-Cutting' Accelerates", Wall Street Journal, 6 Nov 2014, retrieved from http://www.wsj.com/articles/pay-tv-cord-cutting-accelerates-1415321442.

[32] Spangler, Todd, "Cord-Cutting Picks Up: 1.4 Million U.S. Households Tuned Out Pay TV in 2014", Variety, 25 Feb 2015, retrieved from http://variety.com/2015/digital/news/cord-cutting-picks-up-1-4-million-u-s-households-tuned-out-pay-tv-last-year-1201441530/.

[33] Spangler, Todd, "Cord-Cutting Gets Ugly: U.S. Pay-TV Sector Drops 566,000 Customers in Q2", Variety, 8 Aug 2015, retrieved from http://variety.com/2015/digital/news/cord-cutting-gets-ugly-u-s-pay-tv-sector-drops-566000-customers-in-q2-1201559878/.

[34] Ourand, John, "Can World Cup boost ESPN3?", SportsBusiness Journal, 31 May 2010, retrieved from http://www.sportsbusinessdaily.com/Journal/Issues/2010/05/20100531/This-Weeks-News/Can-World-Cup-Boost-ESPN3.aspx.

[35] Ourand, John, "Disney, TWC Deal Includes Creation Of New ESPN-Branded Services", SportsBusiness Daily, 3 Sep 2010, retrieved from http://www.sportsbusinessdaily.com/Daily/Issues/2010/09/Issue-245/Sports-Media/Disney-TWC-Deal-Includes-Creation-Of-New-ESPN-Branded-Services.aspx.

[36] Ourand, John, "Four things we've learned from Disney-Time Warner Cable deal", SportsBusiness Journal, 13 Sep 2010, retrieved from http://www.sportsbusinessdaily.com/Journal/Issues/2010/09/20100913/Media/Four-things-weve-learned-from-Disney-Time-Warner-Cable-deal.aspx; Lawler, Richard, "ESPN2, ESPNU and ESPN Buzzer Beater now available online for Time Warner & Brighthouse", Engadget, 25 Jan 2011, retrieved from http://www.engadget.com/2011/01/25/espn2-espnu-and-espn-buzzer-beater-now-available-online-for-tim/.

[37] Spangler, Todd, "ESPN Changes 'TV Everywhere' Login Site To WatchESPN.com", Multichannel News, 31 Aug 2011, retrieved from http://www.multichannel.com/news/cable-operators/espn-changes-tv-everywhere-login-site-watchespncom/327371.

[38] Burke, Timothy, "ESPN Prepping Its Talent For A Twitter Shitstorm After Deciding To No Longer Air Must-Watch Games On ESPN3", Deadspin, 29 Aug 2012, retrieved from http://deadspin.com/5938857/espn-prepping-its-talent-for-a-twitter-shitstorm-after-deciding-to-no-longer-air-must-watch-games-on-espn3.

[39] "Frequently Asked Questions about WatchESPN", ESPN, retrieved from http://espn.go.com/watchespn/faq on 25 Nov 2015.

[40] Sandomir et al., op. cit.

[41] Thompson, "Prisoners of Cable"; Riesz, Megan, "The battle for standalone HBO GO", Christian Science Monitor, 20 Jun 2012, p18.

[42] Warner, Dave, "How The NBA On TNT Keeps HBO Tied To Cable", What You Pay For Sports, 8 Oct 2013, retrieved from http://www.whatyoupayforsports.com/2013/10/how-the-nba-on-tnt-keeps-hbo-tied-to-cable/.

[43] Thompson, "Prisoners of Cable".

[44] Ibid.; Riesz, op. cit.

[45] James, Meg, and Ryan Faughnder, "HBO to offer its programs online", Los Angeles Times, 16 Oct 2014, A1.

[46] Lawler, Richard, "HBO Now is cutting the cord, but there are still a few strings", Engadget, 9 Mar 2015, retrieved from http://www.engadget.com/2015/03/09/hbo-now-strings/.

[47] James and Faughnder, op. cit.

[48] "Upstart Netflix is giving HBO a run for its money", Buffalo News, 18 Feb 2014, B14.

[49] Thompson, "Prisoners of Cable".

[50] Snider, Mike, "CBS launches 'All Access' streaming service", USA Today, 17 Oct 2014, B4.

[51] Hagey, Keach, "Cablevision to Offer HBO Streaming", Wall Street Journal, 17 Mar 2015, B6; Farrell, Mike, "Another Form of Cord-Cutting", Multichannel News, 10 Sep 2015, retrieved from http://www.multichannel.com/blog/money/another-form-cord-cutting/393642.

[52] Crum, Rex, "Why Cash-Cow ESPN Is Becoming a Drag on Disney", TheStreet, 29 Jun 2015, retrieved from http://www.thestreet.com/story/13199865/1/why-cash-cow-espn-is-becoming-a-drag-on-disney.html.

[53] Guthrie, Marisa, "Keith Olbermann, ESPN to Part Ways Once Again", Hollywood Reporter, 8 Jul 2015, retrieved from http://www.hollywoodreporter.com/news/keith-olbermann-espn-part-ways-807458; Ramachandran, Shalini, and Joe Flint, "ESPN Is Tightening Belt As Pressure On It Mounts", Wall Street Journal, 10 Jul 2015, B1.

[54] Ramachandran and Flint, "ESPN Is Tightening Belt As Pressure On It Mounts".

[55] Ourand, "The moves that forced ESPN's cuts"; Soshnick, Scott, and Christopher Palmeri, "Disney's ESPN Said Planning to Eliminate as Many as 350 Jobs", Bloomberg Business, 20 Oct 2015, retrieved from http://www.bloomberg.com/news/articles/2015-10-20/disneys-espn-said-planning-to-eliminate-as-many-as-350-jobs.

[56] Yoder, Matt, "Exploding rights fees putting the squeeze on sports networks", Awful Announcing, 6 Jul 2015, retrieved from http://awfulannouncing.com/2015/exploding-rights-fees-putting-the-squeeze-on-sports-networks.html.

[57] Sandomir, Richard, "A Departure Looms Large at ESPN's Advertiser Event", New York Times, 13 May 2015, B5; Flint, Joe, "ESPN to Simulcast NFL Wild Card Game on ABC", Wall Street Journal, 12 May 2015, retrieved from http://blogs.wsj.com/cmo/2015/05/12/espn-to-simulcast-nfl-wild-card-game-on-abc/.

[58] Ibid.

[59] Bitner, Adam, "ESPN Got It Right in Honoring Caitlyn Jenner", Pittsburgh Post-Gazette, 4 Jun 2015, A6.

[60] Ramachandran, Shalini, "Disney's Bob Iger: Inevitable that ESPN Goes Direct-to-Consumer", Wall Street Journal, 27 Jul 2015, retrieved from http://blogs.wsj.com/cmo/2015/07/27/disneys-bob-iger-inevitable-that-espn-goes-direct-to-consumer/.

[61] Lieberman, David, "Disney Lowers Forecast Citing ESPN Sub Drop, But Says It's Still A 'Must Have'", Deadline, 4 Aug 2015, retrieved from http://deadline.com/2015/08/disney-lower-financial-forecast-espn-subscriber-loss-1201491732/.

[62] Atkinson, Claire, "Bundle busters Netflix kiss, ESPN dis wreak $536B media havoc", New York Post, 7 Aug 2015, p27.

[63] Lafayette, Jon, "Media Stocks Hit With A Bundle of Trouble", Broadcasting and Cable, 6 Aug 2015, retrieved from http://www.broadcastingcable.com/news/currency/media-stocks-hit-bundle-trouble/143127.

[64] "July 27, 2015: The Day Cable TV As We Know It Died... ESPN Plans Standalone Service...", CordCutters News, 28 Jul 2015, retrieved from http://cordcuttersnews.com/july-27-2015-the-day-cable-tv-as-we-know-it-died-espn-plans-standalone-service/.

[65] O'Reilly, Lara, "Lots of people aren't convinced by Disney CEO Bob Iger's argument that ESPN will continue to dominate for years to come", Business Insider, 5 Aug 2015, retrieved from http://www.businessinsider.com/people-arent-convinced-by-disney-ceo-bob-igers-defense-of-espn-2015-8.

[66] Ramachandran and Flint, "ESPN Is Tightening Belt As Pressure On It Mounts".

[67] James, Meg, and Joe Flint, "Disney-Dish deal may boost Web TV", Los Angeles Times, 5 Mar 2014, B1.

[68] "Sling TV to Launch Live, Over-the-Top Service for $20 Per Month; Watch on TVs, Tablets, Computers, Smartphones, Game Consoles", Dish Network Corporation, 5 Jan 2015, retrieved from http://about.dish.com/press-release/products-and-services/sling-tv-launch-live-over-top-service-20-month-watch-tvs-tablets; "Sling TV - Watch Live TV Programming Any Time and Anywhere", retrieved from https://www.sling.com/package on 4 Dec 2015.

[69] Farrell, Mike, "Sling TV: 20 Channels May Be Enough", Multichannel News, 11 May 2015, retrieved from http://www.multichannel.com/news/satellite/sling-tv-20-channels-may-be-enough/390534.

[70] Ourand, "Will Dish's offering kill cable bundle?"

[71] Roettgers, Janko, "Dish's new Sling TV service liberates ESPN from the cable bundle", GigaOm, 5 Jan 2015, retrieved from https://gigaom.com/2015/01/05/dishs-new-sling-tv-service-liberates-espn-from-the-cable-bundle/.

[72] Kafka, Peter, "Would You Pay $30 a Month to Watch These Channels on the Web?", Re/code, 6 Jun 2014, retrieved from http://recode.net/2014/06/06/would-you-pay-30-a-month-to-watch-these-channels-on-the-web/.

[73] Promoting Innovation and Competition in the Provision of Multichannel Video Programming Distribution Services, Comments of the National Association of Broadcasters, 3 Mar 2015, pp. 6-10, retrieved from http://apps.fcc.gov/ecfs/document/view?id=60001039050.

[74] Sherman, Ed, "Big Ten's next pact will be a big deal", Chicago Tribune, 13 Mar 2015, p4; Gaines, Cork, "Why ESPN is laying off hundreds of people", Business Insider, 21 Oct 2015, retrieved from http://www.businessinsider.com/espn-layoffs-2015-10; Ourand, John, "Projecting how Big Ten rights race will play out", SportsBusiness Journal, 23 Nov 2015, p11, retrieved from http://www.sportsbusinessdaily.com/Journal/Issues/2015/11/23/Media/Sports-Media.aspx.

[75] Ourand, John, "Digital players on the radar", SportsBusiness Journal, 14 May 2012, p20, retrieved from http://www.sportsbusinessdaily.com/Journal/Issues/2012/05/14/In-Depth/Digital-media-companies.aspx.

[76] Ourand, John, "NFL Picks Yahoo For Live Stream Of Bills-Jaguars Game, With CBS To Handle Production", SportsBusiness Daily, 3 Jun 2015, retrieved from http://www.sportsbusinessdaily.com/Daily/Issues/2015/06/03/Media/Yahoo-NFL.aspx.

[77] Ourand, John, "Yahoo Earns Nearly 34 Million Streams For Bills-Jaguars, Receives Mostly Positive Reviews", SportsBusiness Daily, 26 Oct 2015, retrieved from http://www.sportsbusinessdaily.com/Daily/Issues/2015/10/26/Media/Yahoo.aspx.

[78] Baumgartner, Jeff, "Sling TV Pinpoints Streaming Issue", Multichannel News, 31 Aug 2013, retrieved from http://www.multichannel.com/news/next-tv/sling-tv-pinpoints-streaming-issue/393356.

[79] Bode, Karl, "Yahoo NFL Stream Was Success, Failure, Depending Who You Ask", DSLReports, 26 Oct 2015, retrieved from http://www.dslreports.com/shownews/Yahoo-NFL-Stream-Was-Success-Failure-Depending-Who-You-Ask-135479.

[80] Stevenson, Abigail, "Netflix CEO: All TV will be Internet in 10-20 yrs", CNBC, 20 Sep 2015, retrieved from http://www.cnbc.com/2015/09/18/netflix-ceo-all-tv-will-be-internet-in-10-20-yrs.html.

[81] Keath, Chris, "What is the exact technological difference between broadcasting and streaming?", Quora, 6 Jun 2011, retrieved from https://www.quora.com/What-is-the-exact-technological-difference-between-broadcasting-and-streaming; Wilson, Tracy V., "How Streaming Video and Audio Work", HowStuffWorks, 12 Oct 2007, http://computer.howstuffworks.com/internet/basics/streaming-video-and-audio.htm; "How internet video streaming works", Techradar, 16 Sep 2012, retrieved from http://www.techradar.com/us/news/internet/how-internet-video-streaming-works-1095211.

[82] Keath, op. cit.; "Gordon Smith Speech at ATSC Broadcast TV Conference", National Association of Broadcasters, 8 May 2014, retrieved from https://www.quora.com/What-is-the-exact-technological-difference-between-broadcasting-and-streaming.

[83] Ciciora, p3.

[84] Spangler, Todd, "Netflix Bandwidth Usage Climbs to Nearly 37% of Internet Traffic at Peak Hours", Variety, 28 May 2015, retrieved from http://variety.com/2015/digital/news/netflix-bandwidth-usage-internet-traffic-1201507187/.

[85] Kafka, Peter, "Streaming Video Now Accounts for 70 Percent of Broadband Usage", Re/code, 7 Dec 2015, retrieved from http://recode.net/2015/12/07/streaming-video-now-accounts-for-70-percent-of-broadband-usage/.

[86] Ourand, "How high can rights fees go?"

Index

www.ingramcontent.com/pod-product-compliance
Lightning Source LLC
Chambersburg PA
CBHW021827020426
42334CB00014B/524